THE
GLIMMER TRAIN

Guide to
Writing Fiction

INSPIRATION
AND DISCIPLINE

Edited by Susan Burmeister-Brown
and Linda B. Swanson-Davies

WRITER'S DIGEST BOOKS
Cincinnati, Ohio
www.writersdigest.com

The Glimmer Train Guide to Writing Fiction: Inspiration and Discipline

 Published by Writer's Digest Books, an imprint of F+W Publications, Inc., 4700 East Galbraith Road, Cincinnati, OH 45236. (800) 289-0963. First edition.

Distributed in Canada by Fraser Direct, 100 Armstrong Avenue, Georgetown, ON, Canada L7G 5S4, Tel: (905) 877-4411. Distributed in the U.K. and Europe by David & Charles, Brunel House, Newton Abbot, Devon, TQ12 4PU, England, Tel: (+44) 1626 323200, Fax: (+44) 1626 323319, E-mail: postmaster@davidandcharles.co.uk. Distributed in Australia by Capricorn Link, P.O. Box 704, Windsor, NSW 2756 Australia, Tel: (02) 4577-3555.

Visit our Web site at www.writersdigest.com for information on more resources for writers. To receive a free weekly e-mail newsletter delivering tips and updates about writing and about Writer's Digest products, register directly at our Web site at http://newsletters.fwpublications.com.

11 10 09 08 07   5 4 3 2 1

Library of Congress Cataloging-in-Publication Data

The Glimmer Train guide to writing fiction. Inspiration and discipline / edited by Susan Burmeister-Brown and Linda B. Swanson-Davies.
    p. cm.
  Includes index.
  ISBN-13: 978-1-58297-447-7 (hbk. : alk. paper)
  ISBN-10: 1-58297-447-0 (hbk. : alk. paper)
 1. Fiction--Authorship. 2. Authors--Interviews. I. Burmeister-Brown, Susan. II. Swanson-Davies, Linda B. III. Title: Inspiration and discipline.
  PN3355.G56 2007
  808.3--dc22   2007004239

Edited by Lauren Mosko
Designed by Grace Ring
Production coordinated by Mark Griffin

ABOUT THE EDITORS

⟫◆⟪

Susan Burmeister-Brown and Linda B. Swanson-Davies are sisters and the co-editors of the literary short story quarterly *Glimmer Train Stories*, founded in 1990, and *Writers Ask*—the quarterly from which *The Glimmer Train Guide to Writing Fiction* evolved—founded in 1998. They live in Portland, Oregon.

ACKNOWLEDGMENTS

⟫◆⟪

We took great personal pleasure in poring over hundreds of dense and varied interviews conducted over a 17-year period to find the hunks of inspired perspective in these pages. The authors interviewed, and the interviewers who engaged them, are the people who made this volume possible and necessary. We are grateful to each of them for sharing their words here.

Without the intelligence and diligence of Scott Allie and Paul Morris, we could not have managed to transform this material into an actual book. As in all things *Glimmer Train*, we are indebted to them both. Lauren Mosko constantly kept us moving forward by her obvious love of the material. How grateful we are to have a truly literary, warmly human, and effective editor. We thank our friend and advocate Sheila Levine for helping us meet our legal and ethical responsibilities to our contributors.

And, as always, the unswaying love and support of our families, especially our husbands and children, give us the courage to joyfully pursue our passions.

TABLE OF CONTENTS

FOREWORD

Sometimes a man hits upon a place to which he mysteriously feels that he belongs. Here is the home he sought, and he will settle amid scenes that he has never seen before, among men he has never known, as though they were familiar to him from his birth. Here at last he finds rest.

—*The Moon and Sixpence* by W. Somerset Maugham, 1919

Writers belong to a largely invisible community of people who are driven to capture and convey some significant bit of humanity to readers they may never know.

But why are some people driven to write?

I couldn't get free of my mind.

My goal is to write that chapter of history …

I tend to get obsessed with what I don't understand.

You can travel the whole world for an experience like that …

I want to pursue it, to explore what about it bothers me.

I didn't grow up among writers … I just knew I wanted to do this.

I'm trying to survive the story.

I am transported and never want it to end.

And how does a particular piece of writing come to exist?

You have to live your characters' lives with them.

Working is shaking the black ball and seeing what surfaces.

There are no bare facts. A fact has all kinds of reasons to be.

I finally decided that it was now or never.

This is something you have to work at.

You'll find scores of different answers from the accomplished writers represented in these pages. Some you'll recognize as your own, others will offer you completely different views, but you will find two essential threads throughout: inspiration and discipline.

Welcome to Book 2 in our series of writing guidebooks. We hope you enjoy the wisdom and community of the writers represented in these pages as they discuss how they came to be writers, how they bring a particular piece of writing into existence, and why the writing life means so much to them.

—*Linda & Susan*

CHAPTER

1

WRITING AWAY
FROM HOME

Arizona, 1938

A.J. Verdelle: I admit to a feeling of desperation. I felt like: "I'm not getting any younger." Age is supposed to affect your ability to write—writing has to do with knowing what you want to say. At the same time, I felt like: "I've got to start this now!" So I took all the savings that I had and moved to New Mexico. I thought, "I'm going to isolate myself for a while. I have enough money to live for a year."

as interviewed by Nancy Middleton

VIKRAM CHANDRA

interviewed by Jennifer Levasseur and Kevin Rabalais

What is your relationship with India now?

I spend five, maybe five and a half, months in India every year. Bombay and India are home to me. I think of myself as an expatriate Indian writer, although the United States is like a second home for me. I've spent many of my growing-up years here, and I'm deeply connected to it. I intend to keep going back and forth. I think, also, that going away from India remains useful for me. The disengagement allows all of those elements I absorb from Indian landscapes to settle, so I can start to see them imaginatively and shape them. The distance helps. I suppose writers, artists of every sort, from all over the world, have done this. You go away from where your material is to get some distance on it. The book I'm working on now stays within India, but I'm sure I will write about America and the West again.

THE WIDE WORLD OUT THERE

Patricia Henley, interviewed by Andrew Scott

⟹⟸

You've traveled the world for your novels. What is it about another place that inspires you to write?

You know, until I was sixteen I had never been farther away from home than Indianapolis. But I knew from reading voraciously that there was a wide world out there. As soon as I was able, I started traveling. If I stay at home too long, I fall victim to what I think of as a Midwestern complacency, but it might just be the complacency of the stay-at-home. I have to get out. I have to shake myself up. Have you heard about the novelty-seeking gene? I'm sure I have it.

But about the particulars. The western United States—its people and climate and landscape—moved me to write my first two collections of stories. I went to Guatemala for the mountains and the indigenous cultures, never dreaming that that first trip would be the beginning of a ten-year journey that culminated in the publication of *Hummingbird House*. And I went to Vietnam after I'd developed the storyline for *In the River Sweet*. I just knew I couldn't write about it without spending a little time there. I had to do that down-on-the-street research.

I'm not sure I'm really answering your question. Another way to answer is this: I've always been fascinated with cultures rubbing up against each other. Something about the life lived by the writer-explorer is exciting, too. As unfashionable as it might seem, I have a framed photo of Ernest Hemingway over my desk in my office on campus. And me—a vegetarian.

TAKE IT, HAVE IT, ENJOY IT

Philip Levine, interviewed by Jim Schumock

⇒◆⇐

Spain seemed to be a real turning point for you. What is it that you found in Spain that changed your perception of what was going on in the world?

Well, I think one of the most important things that happened to me in Spain didn't have a lot to do with Spain. It had to do with the fact that I wasn't teaching. I suddenly had all this time to write. My teaching job was a tough one. I taught either four or five courses a semester, and I taught a lot of freshman English and things like that. I was also suddenly very close to my family in a way that I hadn't been. I was with my kids a lot more. I began reliving my own childhood as I lived their childhoods.

It was so extraordinary. I remember in 1972, I think it was, my wife and I and our youngest son, who was then fifteen, drove from Paris to Barcelona. We drove into the Pyrenees to cross them. We were going to cross at a place called Andorra, that little principality. It was perfect weather. It was perhaps April, and it was a beautiful day. We got out of the car and we began just walking in this field, and the farmer came over to us. He spoke Spanish even though he was French, and he asked us what we wanted, and we said, "We just wanted to walk in this field if you don't mind." He said, "No." He looked at us with total understanding. He knew exactly why we were there. My son told him in Spanish, "It's so sweet here." The guy just smiled and gave us this welcoming gesture like, "Take it, have it, enjoy it." A warm wind was coming through this field of tall grass. I felt like my wife and son and I, we were like one being, in a sense. And we were not separate from this man. This farmer was welcoming us to the field. You can travel a whole world looking for an experience like that and never forget it.

JULIA ALVAREZ

interviewed by Mike Chasar and Constance Pierce

The García Girls ends, "wailing over some violation that lies at the center of my art." People always ask me, what does it mean? I'm not one-hundred percent sure, but the more I think about it, the violation is already extant in being a writer, a woman, in English, going against the grain of what she was taught, violating her tradition. But see, I'm no longer a "Dominican writer." I'm a … hybrid person. I'm a combination person, which is what multicultural means, this combination of different influences making me up. Especially since I'm first generation, I'm aware of it because none of it has yet been made into a weave that somehow seems whole. It seems to clash. I'm so aware that I am that hybrid. I'm a woman who has to wear her azabache pinned on her bra, but at the same time, she's writing novels. But all these things make sense to me, the ways that I am a mix of this and that.

If anything, writing in English gave me a certain amount of protection, because a lot of people didn't know what I was saying. It's like Sandra Cisneros talks about, that her father can't read her books because he doesn't read English. And that gives her a kind of space in which to say things that maybe, if she felt that he were right there listening to that language, she might not say. So that helped—until they were all translated into Spanish!

THOMAS E. KENNEDY

interviewed by Linda B. Swanson-Davies

How has being an expatriate affected your writing? Being always to some degree an outsider?

That's very aptly put, because it's true—I'm both an outsider in the U.S. now, and I'm also an outsider in Denmark. But anyway, all writers are outsiders, I think, no matter where they are. I mean, Joyce left Dublin, yet he never left Dublin in his heart, etc. I think one of the good things that getting away from the U.S. gave me was an opportunity to look back on my home culture through the lens of another culture, and that was very instructive. I think that helped my writing, helped me to get a little more understanding of myself.

. . . .

Lynn Freed: During my thirty-odd years in America, things have changed. At first, I was so homesick for South Africa that I could not possibly have written about the place. Even after some years, when I was over the worst of it and had begun to write stories placed in South Africa, those stories were sunk by longing and nostalgia. Sentiment and nostalgia are fatal for fiction. One must go into the territory of the imagination with sure feet, not fainting with glorious misery.

as interviewed by Sarah Anne Johnson

THE WRITER WITHOUT A COUNTRY

Askold Melnyczuk, interviewed by William Pierce

Was there a time when you, like Nick in Ambassador of the Dead, tried to ignore or reject your Ukrainian heritage?

When I went away to college, I broke away from a near-total immersion in a conservative Ukrainian Catholic culture and family. At first, the rupture was emotionally violent. I rejected Catholicism vigorously. I never denied my family's Ukrainian origins, but I was too interested in exploring American and English and world literature to keep up with developments in "the old country," which were about all that mattered to my parents at the time. This was a very painful period, and it lasted nearly fifteen years. On the other hand, the "rejection" was hardly monolithic. I translated poems from Ukrainian, wrote reviews about matters Ukrainian. There is much that I still reject about a certain kind of émigré response to exile—for myself, anyway. On the other hand, it is very brave and a sign of great love when people forced to leave their place of origin attempt to preserve as much of its integrity as they can.

The guilt I feel for "abandoning" the community in which I grew up is thickly mixed with a sadness that recognizes the inevitability of it all. To stay inside the Ukrainian émigré community would mean negotiating the truly tough life of the writer without a country. I applaud the courage of all those who dare to do it, so long as they don't wind up narrow and angry at the larger community when it ignores them, as it more or less will and even has to. Consider how many hundreds of émigré subcultures we have here.

Besides, I remind myself, I'm not an émigré. I was born in New Jersey.

PETER CAREY

interviewed by Kevin Bacon and Bill Davis

Australians wishing to excuse my betrayal, the betrayal that I acted out by leaving, my exile, would say, "Well, it must be really useful for you to be away; you can see Australia better."

And for two years or so I said, "Well, no, I don't think so." But I think, finally, yes; I think so. I've become very obsessed once again with ideas about Australia and what makes Australia so weird, and I'm enjoying seeing its total weirdness.

So ... are you in exile?

I think maybe if I was broke I could use the word "exile." I'm not broke. I could get on an airplane tomorrow; I can talk to people over my telephone. I don't feel in exile.

....

THE PERPETUAL FOREIGNER

Lynn Freed, interviewed by Sarah Anne Johnson

I had spent my childhood in South Africa both loving the place and, concomitantly, dreaming of getting out. These are not as mutually exclusive as one might imagine. South Africa is an outpost. When I was growing up, it was a quasi-colonial outpost. Anyone who grows up in such a place understands the tremendous need to get out, at least temporarily—to go north to the source, to what is fondly known as the "real world." I have had people from Australia, from Indonesia, from Hawaii, from the Caribbean, even from the vastness of Alaska—oh, from so many, many places—tell me how they spent their childhoods longing to leave. And then how, in leaving, they put themselves into the bind, so familiar to the expatriate, of belonging nowhere. Of living the life of someone always longing for home and yet not belonging there anymore. It is a bind for which there is no solution. Not only this, it is a bind for which the victim wants no solution. The shuttle itself becomes a form of life. If one is such a person, one needs to leave the place in order to be able to return there. Does this make any sense? One needs to put one's self at a distance. To be perpetually the foreigner. This, it seems to me, is the life of the writer.

WHAT YOU CAN'T LEAVE BEHIND
David Malouf, interviewed by Kevin Rabalais

The South African novelist Lynn Freed said that estrangement is a necessary ingredient to her work because it gives her the perspective of another world from which to examine her own. Do you agree?

Yes. Being away makes me more rational and objective, because I have a different reference frame now. I can write with my brain and not just my emotions.

Did you know you would return to Australia when you went away as a young man?

Not necessarily. But everything that mattered to me, I'd never left. Almost all of my work is written out of strong memories that had already been laid down by then. If I hadn't come back to Australia in 1968, it may well be that my writing would be no different.

VALERIE MARTIN
interviewed by Janet Benton

Not long after the movie rights sold for *Mary Reilly*, you left your teaching position at the University of Massachusetts at Amherst and lived in Rome for several years. How did that influence your writing?

After I went to Italy in '93, I didn't write very well, and I wrote very little—in the almost three years I was there, I wrote a short story and part of a novel. And it really stunned me. I was very alienated. But it gave me new subject matter. I got two books out of our time there, the St. Francis book and *Italian Fever*.

Was there something about not being surrounded by your own language that might have caused that difficulty?

Oh, it was shocking. I did pretty well with my Italian when I was studying in the U.S., and I thought when we got there I'd pick it up, but I didn't. In fact, my tongue was tied. I could understand quite a bit, but I really had to struggle to speak. At a dinner party I would have to apply every bit of energy to trying to understand what they were talking about, and then I'd finally get my little phrase together that I was going to try to add to the discussion, and they'd be on another subject.

So it really was silencing.

Yeah, it was. And then I started writing a book, and a different kind of voice started coming out. I wrote a hundred pages of a novel about New England. It's called *Property*. It's about a man who gets involved in a utopian community and then by a strange error, though he never ever wants to own property, he inherits lots of it. I hope to finish that book.

And then you wrote Italian Fever. *Where does that fit in?*

Italian Fever is almost a mock gothic. It's kind of like E. M. Forster and Jane Austen smushed together. Not that I can write like E. M. Forster and Jane Austen, I'm not putting myself in that company, but their influence made me want to try this particular innocents-abroad topic. It's about a young woman who goes to Italy and doesn't have a good time, though she does have some incredible adventures and a romance, such as it is. She's quite a nice character, Lucy—Lucy Stark. It's a very carefree, rompy book. It was fun to write. I had a great time writing it. I wrote it with real ease.

....

REUNITED WITH LANGUAGE
Lorrie Moore, interviewed by Jim Schumock

—————

Do you find any advantage to being outside the country when you're writing about it?

Sure. To some extent, it is very freeing. Your subject is not there before you, so you don't take any of it for granted. You're forced to re-create it when you're in a country where they're not speaking English. This, however, is not really the case on Lake Como, with numerous American and other English-speaking scholars. But if you go to Paris or Madrid or some other place where you're surrounded by people speaking another language, immersing yourself in that is interesting, because it makes you very homesick for your own language, and then your writing becomes the way you're reunited with that language. And you have this great, intense relationship, like a buoy in a stormy sea. It's something that you don't feel in the same way when you're writing in your own country.

PAUL THEROUX
interviewed by Jim Schumock

I knew that wherever I went I would be writing something. I never stopped writing. As a matter of fact, I wrote even when I was a pre-med student in college. I was writing short stories and poems, and starting novels and abandoning them.

When I was in Italy the summer after I graduated, I was writing. When I was in Peace Corps training, I kept a very detailed diary of what was happening, because it was such an odd thing. It was in Puerto Rico. We were there for a couple of months for Outward Bound training. I remember keeping up this diary, this running account of the camping, the rock climbing, and the relationships.

Once in a while in my life, in my early life especially, I ran across people who knew that I was writing, and they would express surprise. For example, in August in 1963, I was in Fano, Italy, on the Adriatic coast near Urbino, where I had a job. I was standing on the beach there—I remember the day, I remember the time of day—and I was talking to a college professor that I'd had. He taught the nineteenth-century English novel.

He was there visiting another college professor and he said, "What are you doing, Paul?"

And I said, "Oh, I'm here just having a good time."

He said, "How do you spend the day?"

I said, "I'm writing."

He said, "You're not!"

And I said, "What's wrong? What's wrong?" I started to get a little anxious, annoyed.

And he said, "It's just that I see you in that room staring at a blank page, with these beautiful blue skies, all this lovely country. Lovely blue skies and sunshine outside, and you're sitting in a room staring at a blank sheet of paper. I find that so sad."

Well, if I'd had a very big stick, I would have hit him over the head with it. I actually thought to myself, You son of a bitch. But I said, "Oh, well, I'm working on something."

His image of me was: This is a deluded dreamer.

An English professor! In other words: "Here you are in Italy. It's a sunny day. Why aren't you out—" God knows what I'd be doing. "Why aren't you out swimming?" I suppose he was threatened by the thought that I was inside in an Italian summer, working on something. And he imagined that I was looking at a blank piece of paper. And it wasn't a blank piece of paper!

That was thirty-one years ago, and I can remember it as if it was yesterday. Because I remember the feeling of: All my life I've tried to get away from people who have dismissed the idea of writing; I go to Italy to write and I run into this guy who's a college professor, and he's disdainful.

So that was another of the reasons I went away. That attitude. That was a very prevalent attitude: People saying what are you doing; why are you doing it; how are you going to make any money; how are you going to support a family? What he was saying, more or less, was, "You're wasting your time." Well, everyone knows you're not wasting it! This is a craft; this is an art. This is something you have to work at.

You were in the Peace Corps. Were you there to avoid soldiering in Vietnam?

Probably to avoid going to Vietnam. But it was more positive than that. I really did want to go. I wanted to get away from the States. I had a worthy ambition of going to a Third World country and being useful. I didn't know quite how to accomplish that. The Peace Corps was a way of doing it.

I knew also that I wanted to be a writer. I felt that by staying around, by being home, I'd have people asking me questions— What am I going do with my life, how am I going make a living? If I had told them that I was writing, they would ask, What was I writing, how was I going to sell it? I could imagine all the questions. I didn't have answers to these questions. So I thought the best way was just to go away.

Ha Jin: In the beginning, there was a longing for home. But as I continued, I realized that I couldn't continue to write about China for long. That's why my next book is set in Korea, and my book after that is set in the States. I'm an expatriate, but I'm also an immigrant. There's a big distinction between the two.

as interviewed by Sarah Anne Johnson

THE PLACES THAT RESONATE

Lynn Freed, interviewed by Sarah Anne Johnson

⟫⟩⬥⟨⟪

How does your writing relate to your sense of home? I'm particularly interested in this because you are a person who writes away from her home of origin, and in fact travels quite a bit to do her writing. Maybe I should start by asking you, where is home?

Home is an idea, and it is past tense. I am someone who makes a home out of a hotel room. The minute I arrive, I start arranging things to make the place my own. I have felt at home on a dhow on the Nile, and I have not felt at home in a house in which I lived in San Francisco for fourteen years. There is something beyond reason in the places that resonate. I am more likely, for instance, to feel at home with the sound and sight of the sea than in the most idyllic setting inland—which is where I happen to live now. I long for the sea. Why don't I just pack up and move? There is a question I can't seem to answer. Ennui, I suppose.

There is a sense of loneliness, sometimes accompanied by a distance from home, that pervades your characters—loneliness even when surrounded by family.

To my mind, loneliness is at the heart of the human condition. Being at a distance from home is only part of this. There is also the distance from those we love, and from those among whom we live and work. Not to mention the distance from childhood itself, the distance from the places of childhood. Home is an enormous concept. I always think of Carson McCullers saying, "I must go home periodically to renew my sense of horror." I love that.

You've said that travel is part of your writing life, that estrangement is a necessary ingredient to your work because it gives you the perspective of another world from which to examine your own.

I am a natural foreigner. I find home all over the place, and not always where I expect to. I suppose travel, for me, is a sort of search for home. And also for romance. And also for hope. When one travels, one has a sense of living in the moment. For just over a decade, I traveled obsessively, and to wonderfully remote places. Or at least they were then. Now I travel a lot to teach and so forth, and it has become more of a Greyhound experience.

SHEDDING THE MASK

Karen Swenson, interviewed by Susan McInnis

Travel is a vital thread in life and work for you. What has made you a traveler, rather than a woman who takes vacations?

I come from traveling women. In 1930, my mother did something odd for a nice, well-bred young lady from Fargo, North Dakota. She took a friend with her to Europe. Once there, she quickly talked this woman into traveling with her from Paris down to southern France, then on to Sicily, and from there onto a boat bound for Tunisia. A few weeks after they landed in Tunis, my mother convinced her companion to go home. She stayed on, and spent four months alone in Tunis. Neither Sicily nor Tunis were exactly "travel destinations" in 1930, and certainly not for young women on their own. So it was a bold step.

She never urged me to follow her lead. There was never any "You must go to North Africa," but she communicated clearly that, although going to see the world's museums and its lovely places was part of travel, essentially travel has to do with adventure. It has to do with being in an alien environment, and with taking risks.

The poems in this collection, The Landlady in Bangkok, *are about the particulars of life in Southeast Asia, but they also transcend land and culture, and shrink the distance between West and East. What part do the universals you explore play in your thinking and writing?*

I think that inclination to see the universal has been automatic with me, though I didn't really set out to do it. It just became apparent as I traveled that, underneath a certain glaze, a certain veneer of culture, we are very, very similar.

Did your sense of what we all hold in common precede or grow out of your travels?

Both, I suppose. I think I suspected the common thread. But it really began to come clear to me once I was out there, traveling and talking to people who live under very different conditions than I'd ever known.

When you travel, you lose your societal roles. You are no longer enclosed. The shell just drops off. Of course, you aren't totally free. You acquire constraints in the other culture, but they don't really inhibit you much. And you might smack into a cultural wall once in a while, but, still, you think you're free, and that's what's important. We talked earlier about my mother, and my sense that I come from traveling women. I am sure my mother felt imprisoned by the cultural roles available to her. Traveling for her was a way out, and I am sure it is a way out for me, too.

I have used travel to break through constraining roles, but also to work on fear. Women of my generation and culture were taught to be afraid. It was "appropriate" to be afraid then. Timid women were thought to be appealing women. Men felt braver around them, and the timid woman was more likely to get a husband, among other perquisites.

But on reflection, it's clear that when you put on that mask, it adheres to your face. It must be worked off. For me, going to strange places was a way of working the mask off. Southeast Asia. Nepal. Tibet.

TIME FOR REFLECTION
Kent Haruf, interviewed by Jim Nashold

What caused you to go into the Peace Corps?

I wanted to get out of the United States. Since I had no money, the Peace Corps was a way to see different parts of the world. I wanted especially to go to the Middle East.

You were teaching English as a second language in Turkey. Where specifically did you live?

I was out on the Anatolian plateau in the very small village of Felahiye. It was a place of about two thousand people, very much like the places I grew up in. I taught English to kids in the middle school. It was of great value to me since it was a time of reflection and self-examination. I was alone and read a lot, and began to keep a regular journal and to try and write fiction and figure out some things about myself.

CHAPTER

2

EARLY ROOTS

*Elisabeth Burmeister, daughter Helga,
and baby Anneliese Brauner ca. 1937*

CHRIS OFFUTT
interviewed by Rob Trucks

When I was a kid, my hero was Johnny Bench. He was a catcher for the Cincinnati Reds and they won the World Series in the late seventies, and he was my hero. I played Little League, but I was the shortest catcher in the league. In the meantime, they finally got a library in town and my mother would take me in. It was a very small library. You could only check out four books per card. So I got library cards in my name, my brother and sisters' names, and my dog's name. That's a fact. I would go in there with five library cards, check out twenty books a week, every Saturday. My mother would drop me off at the library, and she would go to the grocery, and come back to pick me up. She'd leave me a grocery sack. I'd fill it with twenty books and get out of there.

Finally, I went to the librarian and I said, "Look, I want a book on baseball." There are a lot of baseball books aimed at children that are sort of like, There's a new kid in town. He's great at baseball. Everybody likes him. That's all I wanted to be. Everybody would like me because I was good at something. So I said, "I want a book on baseball." And she goes to the card catalog and she says, "Is there anything you like?" And I said, "I like Johnny Bench." And she doesn't know who that is so I say, "He's a catcher." So she looks up "catcher" and says, "Oh, come here. I have a book for you." She takes me to this part of the library I'd never been in. She pulls out this book and hands it to me and I say, "Oh, great." I check it out. I go home. I start reading it. It's *Catcher in the Rye*.

I stayed up all night and read that book when I was twelve years old. I could not believe it. I'm getting a funny feeling right now just remembering it. It tore me up. It just made my hair stand on end. I could not believe that you could write that way. That book probably had more influence than any single book I ever read. I never read another juvenile again. I couldn't believe you could write like that. I went from Hardy Boys to *Catcher in the Rye*.

THE ACTIVE PURSUIT OF WRITING
Lynne Sharon Schwartz
interviewed by Nancy Middleton

I didn't grow up among writers. I didn't have mentors. I was really not in a milieu that had anything to do with writing, although my parents respected books. I never knew a writer. I just knew I wanted to do this. It was as if that life was somewhere and I had to find it and enter it. I had to break into it.

How did you break into it?

Well, I had always written. Since I was about seven, I had planned to be a writer. But it was an imaginary thing, you know? I would do this. It would happen to me. And I wrote. But I rarely did anything practical about it like sending my work to editors. I was brought up at a time when women were very passive. The idea was that your life would happen to you, that a girl didn't have to do anything. You would get married, you would have children. And these things do tend to happen—well, not so much anymore, but they did then. We lived in the passive mode. We didn't go out and make our lives.

I did editorial work. I worked in Boston at *The Writer* magazine. I worked in Harlem at a fair-housing program. I did public-relations writing. I did proofreading. I taught freshman comp at Hunter College. And I did some translations. I did lots of things. But none of it was writing. And then I went to graduate school. My almost-doctorate was in comparative literature.

When the women's movement began I was in my late twenties, early thirties. And I watched the way my husband pursued a career. It came over me that if I was going to be a writer, I would have to do something about it. Go out there and do it. So I dropped out of graduate school. I decided now or never. I knew that I was not a scholar; I was getting ill at the thought of writing a thesis. I thought I'd drop out for a year or so and write a novel. And I did, and I liked it so much I never went back to school.

ABDELRAHMAN MUNIF

interviewed by Michael Upchurch

At a young age I was a very good reader, and it seemed to me that novel writing was a horizon in which I was interested, and which I could reach. Gradually, as other horizons were closed off—and since I didn't have very much interest in being an employee in a larger context—I tried novel writing. So, I imagine, it really was my first choice.

When I was editor-in-chief of the magazine *Oil and Development* in Baghdad, I told my employers that you could find at least fifty other people who could be editors-in-chief of the magazine, doing what I did—but you couldn't find fifty novelists. And it was my wish to persevere and to pursue novel writing. Of course, I think it's part of the mission of any artist, no matter what kind, not only to depend on his gift, but to depend on himself and on hard work. If he has a gift, if it is there, he can improve it with effort, enlarge it, and build upon it.

What connection did working in the oil industry have with your writing gift?

There is, in our country, a punishment of being an employee without actual employment. It was my punishment. After having spent nearly two years in this shaming condition, of being an employee without work, there was this gap for which I thought the novel might be a solution. We have a saying: In love or other matters, it's like smoking—it starts as a game or flirtation and ends up as an addiction. When I had written my first novel, I had the feeling that this may have been the right path after all, and that I could continue doing this.

Annie Proulx: I was writing fiction when I was a kid, but, you know, not seriously. Every now and then I'd write a story, and then I wouldn't do it for years, and then I'd write another story. Some of them would be published, but I didn't try very hard, didn't actually start doing it seriously until fifteen years ago. Then I knew I really wanted to write fiction at that point.

as interviewed by Michael Upchurch

Henry Louis Gates Jr.: My father subscribed to Alfred Hitchcock's magazine. He's still a detective-novel junkie. *TIME* would come. *McCall*'s would come. My mother got a lot of magazines. We had those *Reader's Digest* condensed books and other books. My father did crossword puzzles. Every day, he still does the *New York Times* crossword puzzle. We were two hours west of D.C., so we'd get the *Baltimore Sun*, *The Washington Post*, the *Cumberland Sunday Times*, the *Cumberland Daily Times*. Reading? It was a culture of reading.

as interviewed by Jim Schumock

DEVELOPING THE PASSION
Bob Shacochis
interviewed by Linda B. Swanson-Davies

⇒◆⇐

When you hear people talk about talent, I have no idea what that is. All I know is that at a certain age, some kids fall in love with language.

What age do you think it is?

Well, I think it's quite early. I'm not sure, but certainly by the time you're six or seven things are cooking and you're suddenly one of those kids who needs a book in hand. Eventually, that develops into wanting—at least for people who are destined to be writers—to contribute to what you've been taking, taking, taking, and you think, Well, I'd like to give back.

Almost altruistic.

Well, I would hate for it to sound that altruistic because, by that time, it's become a passion of yours.

....

A DREAM OCCUPATION

Antonya Nelson, interviewed by Susan McInnis

Given the questions that hum in your mind, was writing an inevitability for you?

Well, I really like to read and always have, and I was raised by English professors, so I'm sure that had an impact. But of the five kids in my family, I'm the only one who pursued literature and writing as a life work. So perhaps it wasn't inevitable. I was my mother's first child, and they lavished a great deal of attention on me. I remember reading flash cards when I was three or four and being encouraged to read and write very early. I took to it, and I was always rewarded for it. So I think it was just a combination of things. I did not expect to be a writer. I thought of writers as being a fairly distant group of beings—like movie stars. Out there. Celebrities. Somehow unreachable. It was a dream occupation, not a reality. My daughter says she wants to be a fairy when she grows up. A fairy princess. I think that's how I must have thought of writers. As otherworldly. But if it was a dream for me, it was one I took more and more seriously as time went on. I guess you have to if you're going to dedicate your life to it. A dream like that has to mean something pretty large to you.

JIM GRIMSLEY

interviewed by Jim Schumock

━━◆━━

I was born in North Carolina to very poor parents. I grew up in eastern North Carolina, which is a notably poor part of that state. It is mostly tobacco farms and tobacco farms, cotton fields now and again. I grew up in one little town called Pollocksville. We lived there all of the first eighteen years of my life, and then I went away to the University of North Carolina at Chapel Hill to attend college.

I started writing little books when I was eight or nine years old in imitation of the books I was seeing in elementary school—you know, the Peter Rabbit books where the rabbit's getting in the garden and the human's got to keep him out of it and all that stuff. I'd take little cards and make these books up and tie them all together, and basically that told me what I wanted to do. And I really never changed my mind, and stuck with it through all the next twenty years.

. . . .

THE VALUE OF AN HONEST CRITIC

Lynn Freed, interviewed by Sarah Anne Johnson

━━◆━━

When did you know you wanted to write?

I can't remember ever wanting to write. I just wrote. At first, as a child, and for a number of years into adolescence, I seemed to write partly to show off. I'd write a story or a play—I wrote a lot of plays, mostly awful—and I'd run downstairs to read it to my mother. She was a completely honest critic: harsh and fair. If she came forth with praise, I knew that what I had written wasn't fake.

....

WRITING AS SUBVERSION

Jayne Anne Phillips
interviewed by Sarah Anne Johnson

How did you get started writing?

I was always a reader, the kind of kid who read constantly. Very early on, it seemed to me a way to be bigger than I was, know more than I should know, travel more than anyone I knew had traveled.

I came from a small town in West Virginia, and people there were very stationary, much less mobile than the rest of the country. Most of the people I knew—and I think it's still true of that place—tend to move in and out for jobs much less. They tend to be really connected to the land and the region, and they tend to have had several generations of their families there. It was a very isolated, intense type of world. Early on, I saw reading as a way of both escaping that, and deepening it. Reading seemed to be very subversive, and writing later became the same. Reading led to writing for me. I started out writing poetry in high school, and by the time I was nineteen or twenty, I'd started writing short prose pieces. Those developed into the one-page fictions in my first book, *Sweethearts*, which was published by a small press. I taught myself to write fiction by writing those very compact, spiral-shaped pieces.

TWELVE LICKS WITH A PADDLE
Chris Offutt, interviewed by Rob Trucks

It was always there. I drew and wrote stories since the second grade. I constantly drew pictures in school. I was an A student who was bored out of my skull in school, and I would get in trouble a lot. I realized the way not to get in trouble was to draw. I drew all the time and I wrote stories in grade school for spelling class.

You had to define twenty spelling words a week. So I wrote the definitions and the teacher said, "Chris, this isn't right." And I said, "Oh yes they are." She said, "No, they have to be dictionary definitions." What she wanted me to do was open a dictionary and transcribe what was in there, which I thought was stupid. I said, "Look, I know these words. I don't want to do that." And she said, "Well, why don't you just write a story and use all the words to prove you know them." So I thought, Okay, great. I started writing a story a week in spelling class. I had her for two years' worth of spelling. I hated her guts.

What about now?

I still hate her guts. She gave me twelve licks with a paddle once. It was a school record. She gave me six for misbehaving, then six more for laughing. It was either laugh or cry. She beat the hell out of me. It's not one of those, Oh, she did me a favor. She didn't. That was not the favor I needed.

Do you still have any of those stories?

Yeah, I have them all. I have everything I ever wrote.

Nomi Eve: Writers were always my heroes. They were always the most magical thing that one could be, and I read voraciously as a child, like a lot of writers do. I have memories of stacks of library books.

as interviewed by Linda B. Swanson-Davies

ANDREA BARRETT

interviewed by Sarah Anne Johnson

I know that you were a biology student. How did you go from science to writing fiction?

By a long, confused road. I initially went to graduate school in zoology, which didn't work out at all. Later on, I studied medieval history for a couple of years in graduate school, but I didn't stick with that, either. In and around those two things, I had about thirteen jobs in ten years, none of them related to each other, and none but the last two related to writing. It took me a long time to figure out what I wanted to do. It really wasn't clear to me. I kept trying awful jobs and fumbling around.

I did finally just start writing and I can't actually account for that, except that I've always been such a passionate reader. I loved reading and loved books and wanted to write, but I didn't understand how anyone became a writer. I didn't know any writers, and I didn't know about graduate programs in writing. But one day, I started writing a novel. I worked on that for about six years, and eventually had to throw it out, but in the process, I learned something about writing and I began to meet other writers, and all that was helpful. It was a long road, though.

....

UNTIL IT BECOMES SECOND NATURE

John McNally, interviewed by Stephanie Kuehnert

≡≈◈≈≡

When did you start writing? And when did you write the first story that you really felt was a keeper?

I started writing in the fourth grade. I was an overweight kid who watched a lot of television. We had to write a play and perform it, so I wrote about an overweight superhero who'd go into a phone booth to change his clothes but couldn't get out again because it was too tight of a fit. I remember the teacher and the students laughing. The play was a hit! Sad to say, but I suppose ego is what kept me writing. I wrote a nonfiction book about film comedians when I was in the eighth grade, typed it all out on a manual cast-iron typewriter, and tried to find a publisher, but only one would even look at it. I tried writing a science-fiction novel. When I first started college, before I took my first creative-writing course, I was writing some sentimental crap about a high-school romance.

The first story that I wrote that was a keeper was "The Greatest Goddamn Thing," which I wrote the summer after I finished my MFA. It was the first story that seemed organic from the get-go; it seemed to have taken on a life of its own, even as I was writing it. Before that, everything was mechanical. I tell my students that you have to learn about craft, but it's like learning to play pool: You work on, say, a bank shot or on slicing the ball off the rail and into a corner pocket, and you keep doing that over and over and over, but then one night, it all comes together. It becomes second nature, and you don't have to think about it anymore—you don't have to line up the shot, you just hit the cue ball and everything falls into place. You run the table. I wish I could say that every story that followed has felt that way, but it hasn't. Only occasionally—and rarely—does that happen.

ALLEN MORRIS JONES
interviewed by David Abrams

I published my first short story at the age of fourteen, mostly due to my eighth-grade English teacher, a woman by the name of Billie Flemming, who has really been the only significant academic encourager of my writing. She arranged to have one of my short stories published in a children's magazine. I think it was called *The Children's Album*.

Do you remember what prompted you to start writing in the first place, back when you were a teenager?

Impossible to say, really. I've always been a voracious reader. I can barely remember not being able to read. By the time I was in second grade, I was hiding Louis L'Amour and Hardy Boys novels inside my math textbooks, seeing what the Sacketts were up to when I should have been memorizing multiplication tables, a math handicap that exists to this day—I can barely balance my checkbook. For a certain personality type, it seems that writing is a natural extension of reading.

THE STORYTELLING ATMOSPHERE
Valerie Martin, interviewed by Janet Benton

In what sense do you think your childhood in New Orleans was advantageous for you as a future writer?

Well, it's a real spooky-story place. Everybody tells stories a lot, though I think that whole Southern storyteller thing is a myth. I think people tell stories all over. In New England, in small towns, everyone's got a weird little story. But I guess the atmosphere here is kind of gothic. And of course if the weather's warm, you can sit outside and chat all the time; stories tend to come out of that. The history of the place was interesting to me, and as a child I always was interested in learning about the people who lived here. I read the old stories about pirates in the city, and Madame John's legacy, and Madame Lalaurie, who had the slaves chained in the attic.

....

MARY McGARRY MORRIS
interviewed by Linda B. Swanson-Davies

How did you become a writer?

My parents were both avid readers, and so from them I learned a great respect for the written word. In grammar school, I was taught by nuns who expended every bit as much devotion and energy on writing and reading skills as they did on catechism. I had nuns in high school as well, but there were a few lay teachers. One of these was Walt Moore, who spoke of symbols, irony, the reasons for living and loving, the soul, tragedy and folly, heroes and fools. He was the most demanding and interesting teacher I had ever had, and I always hated to have the bell ring at the end of his classes.

....

THE SECRET THAT BECAME A LIFE
Alberto Ríos, interviewed by Susan McInnis

In an essay in *Ironwood*, you wrote that you've always written, even as a little boy, but when you were young you "called it nothing," and you didn't tell anyone about it.

I think if I had been writing something and I called it poetry, I might have gone to a poetry book or a poetry teacher—even though we didn't have any—but I might have tried to do that. And I think that would have been wrong. It wouldn't have been my poetry.

Could it also have been tainted by the boys on the streets? By your buddies? Was there an urge not to appear bookish?

Profound! A profound urge. It was more than not wanting to appear bookish. Whatever our perceptions are, they're strong, they're social, they're what guide us through life and let us do all those things that we do. I know that in growing up, as I was writing in the backs of my notebooks, it felt like I was getting away with something. I did homework in the front, and when I would turn my notebook to the back, I was doing what nobody had told me to do. There was no explanation for that. I was getting away with something. Because I couldn't show it to anybody. I couldn't turn the back part of the book in to a teacher, and I didn't know what that stuff was. If I gave it no name, I also didn't know where to take it.

We didn't, in fact, have a poetry teacher. I lived in a very small town. I would call it a tough town, whatever that means. But the most immediate thing it meant to me is that if you're doing something at school that nobody tells you to do, you're different, and different isn't good to a child. And I was clearly doing something nobody else was doing. They did their homework and they were out of there—if they even did their homework. So I couldn't show it to a teacher, and neither could I show it to my friends. I'd be exposing myself in some way as something I couldn't explain even to myself. How could I explain it to them?

It's interesting that a secret became a life.

Well, I think it is.

You know, I couldn't show it to my parents, either, because kids can't do that. So there was some sense of hiding, and they would ask me, "Well, shouldn't you be doing your homework?" It was not that I was afraid of my parents, but I knew they worried about me and what I should be doing.

As I got into high school, it's not like I couldn't figure out what I was doing, but I didn't change the mechanism. I knew that if I showed this work that—first of all, I would still be different because I was doing something others weren't doing—but if I showed it, I'd be writing, which was a curiosity, period. And I'd be writing poetry. Given the stereotypes, there was nothing to be gained. I wasn't threatened by it, but it wasn't going to help for me to show my work and to have it be labeled. If I wasn't going to use adjectives for it, I certainly wasn't going to let anybody else use adjectives for it. And so I think my writing became forcefully mine.

PERFORMING AS YOURSELF

Lynn Freed, interviewed by Sarah Anne Johnson

⟾⬧⟾

How did growing up in the theater help shape you as a writer? Did it influence your desire to write?

I didn't grow up in the theater itself, but as the daughter of parents who were in the theater. There is a difference. I could never stand to be on stage, at least not literally. But when you grow up in a family like mine, in which performance, both formal and informal, is prized, you're never quite offstage. As the youngest child, I soon found that the way to attract and keep attention was to perform as myself. Not necessarily the self I was—whatever that was—but the self that I divined they might wish me to be. In this case, it was clown—not an uncommon role for the youngest child in such a family.

Writing was as natural as playing. In addition, we had to write a lot for school—and from a very early age, five or six years old—essays, stories, plays. Every week, there was a story to write for school. My sisters, of course, paid no attention to what I wrote. They were involved in their own tumultuous lives. And my parents worked like mad. When I had a chance, usually before supper, I would take my efforts to my mother.

Robert Olen Butler: My first publication was a poem about the sun that I wrote when I was in the third grade. It was put in an anthology of children's poetry; I won a contest for it. I've always thought that writing was something I could do and something that I wanted to do.

as interviewed by Jim Schumock

ROY PARVIN

interviewed by Linda B. Swanson-Davies

You said that your mother was a storyteller.

I remember going to the Jersey Shore as a kid, and, after a meal, when we couldn't go into the water—that magic hour and a half?—she would tell stories about her family. Her family is a very large family. I would always ask her about the stories, ask her to tell it again. She would tell them over and over—she had a lot of good stories. I would ask her about the stories from very weird angles. Like about a person who's only tangentially involved in the story. And she would answer me, and I think that she knew that I was asking about point of view. Things like that, and she enjoyed it as an intellectual exercise. She could, of course, also have said, "Roy, I've told you this story fifty times. Go in the water, the hour and a half is up." But she enjoyed it. She loves stories. I grew up in a household where *The New Yorker* was read.

For a long time, all I really wanted to do was write one successful short story. I mean, that was my life goal. I think that it takes a certain kind of reader perhaps—I was talking about this with another writer, a more sophisticated reader—to understand short stories. You don't have three hundred pages to get to know the character. A lot of times, you're left with feelings, sometimes unsettled feelings. And the reader is just getting warmed up after thirty pages. Anyway, my mother, I think—from reading short stories, from always loving stories—understood what I was doing. I would ask her, "Well, what would happen, what would have happened if that story happened in Florida instead of New Jersey?" I was finding out writer tricks about how to tell stories. She went with me on all that stuff.

How marvelous. That's a great gift.

It was. It was a wonderful gift. I remember my first year in college, in 1975, a book came out called *Beyond the Bedroom Wall* by Larry Woiwode. It's a wonderful book, and it was a very influential book in my personal history. I thought, This is wonderful. This is what I want to do. I remember going home, and my mother had read him in *The New Yorker*, and it was a sort of shared thing. We didn't each have the vocabulary to talk about the material, but what we could talk about was how moving it was. Which is sometimes more important than being able to talk about craft issues. And we had that. It was sort of being understood in the world by somebody else. It's really very, very nice to have it happen with somebody within your family.

So even though my brothers were perhaps making fun of me for writing from time to time, I did feel rooted in the idea that writing was a good endeavor to pursue.

What good fortune.

Yeah. It really was. We did that even in high school because we went to the beach every summer. By then I was surfing and everything, but I'd come in and I would make her tell stories. And she would tell them slightly differently, you know, things she would remember, perhaps some embellishments. It was really a lesson in storytelling.

THOMAS E. KENNEDY
interviewed by Linda B. Swanson-Davies

I tried a little bit in my high-school quarterly, a poem or two. I wrote a lot in my journal, and thought of myself as a writer for many years before I had a right to. By the time I was about twenty-four, for a year or two I had made a real try at it and I had some encouragement. I was an undergraduate at the time. I had a break in my education while I was in the army, and had some encouragement from my teachers. But then for one reason or another, I didn't consistently try for some years, sort of set it aside a bit, always taking notes and writing in my journals and such. Then by the time I was in my thirties and had moved to Europe, I really started to try.

. . . .

THE NECESSITY OF PRETENSION
Siri Hustvedt
interviewed by Jennifer Levasseur and Kevin Rabalais

I was very proud of terrible poems I wrote in the third grade, verses in which I rhymed "true" and "blue." In the fifth grade, I wrote a novel, which shouldn't impress you too much. It was forty-two pages of huge handwriting. My parents saved it. The story was straight out of English novels for girls and was called *Carrie at Baxter Manor*. Its middle chapter had the exciting title "Danger." Martin in *Lily Dahl* has a book called *Baxtor Manor* among the volumes that clutter his apartment—a private joke for me alone. By the time I was fourteen, I was loudly declaring to everybody that I was going to become an "author." I was a pretentious little idiot, but I think pretension is necessary for all writers. You have to get over it later, but it's good to live out various personas. That's what writing novels is—enacting other people.

NOT IN MY CLASS

Mary McGarry Morris
interviewed by Linda B. Swanson-Davies

I wrote as a child, all the ordinary and wonderful things children write. I remember writing a story in fifth grade about two children struggling through a blizzard, trying to make it to their cabin. In the story, one child says to another, "We ain't gonna make it, Sister." The teacher circled ain't and gonna in red ink because those were slang words.

"Yes," I tried to explain, "but that's how that character talks."

"Not in my class," she said with the finality of authority. But I knew without doubt that I was right and she was very wrong.

I guess what happened is I never outgrew the play acting, the make-believe that was constantly in my head. You know, Now you be Julia, and I'll be the king. It wasn't just stories, but voices, characters that not only needed to be expressed, but were a way for me—as a child and certainly now—to reduce horror and beauty, disorder and joy, to more manageable elements in order to make some sense of the world. Or at least take a little of the sting out of it.

CHAPTER

3

HOW READING SHAPES OUR WRITING

Susan reading on Skyline, 1994

KENT HARUF

interviewed by Jim Nashold

When I was in college, I began to read Faulkner and Hemingway, two writers that changed my life. I hadn't read anything so shockingly wonderful as those two writers, and what they could do on the page stunned me. I've never gotten over that shock, and don't want to. So I began to know—about my middle college years—that I wanted to do something with literature, and I began to write. But I didn't become intense about writing until after college when I was in the Peace Corps. I was in a pretty isolated situation, and I began to write on my own in Turkey.

Were there specific stories of Faulkner's and Hemingway's that made a big impact?

Hemingway's Nick Adams stories were important. "The Snows of Kilimanjaro," "The Killers," and "In Another Country" made a huge impact. Then we read *The Sun Also Rises* and *A Farewell to Arms*. With Faulkner, "The Bear" made a huge and immediate impact on me, and *The Sound and the Fury*. It's hard to explain, but it was almost overwhelming, like a religious experience, to have read those kind of things at that age.

Was it the stories or the language that impressed you the most?

Both. In Hemingway's case, the language and that cleanliness of prose, and that absolutely clean, precise way of telling something was evocative and interesting. In Faulkner's case, it was his style and his writing about rural America, which I had never read before. I was bowled over by the stories and by his enormous skill.

....

FINDING YOUR TUNING FORK
Mary Gordon, interviewed by Charlotte Templin

How do you start a work?

I think I have an intense relationship with writers whose voices can be what I call a "tuning fork." There's a funny period before I really get started in a work—you know how dogs run in circles until they can figure out the exact spot where they need to lie down? I'm kind of like that until I can find the writer whose tone of voice really gets me going, and for each little project (a part of a book or a whole book or a story), I need almost to hear the tone in my ear. I have a very dependent relationship on the writers, but it's not like I'm going to copy them, or like I can't do something different from them. It's like having an older sister or brother start you on the road, because the road is dark, and you don't know where you are going. I feel like I have a very dependent—and mainly oral—relationship to the writers who have gone before.

....

Chitra Banerjee Divakaruni: I'm very proud of our literary heritage in my mother tongue. I read fluently in Bengali, so I'm in touch with a lot of wonderful writing being done in Bengali, which I know influences my own work. I see myself as part of that literary tradition.

as interviewed by Sarah Anne Johnson

ABDELRAHMAN MUNIF

interviewed by Michael Upchurch

What Western literature has had an effect on you? Who are your influences? Was there any one writer who helped you find your way?

In public debates, I always say the same thing: A writer should always read a lot—and forget a lot. If he's unable to do that, he will become a prisoner of a certain writer or a certain style.

Of course, if I'm asked about the writers whom I've read with interest or with love, there are a great many of them. I don't want to give you a long list, but, for example, there's Faulkner—I like him a lot. Dostoyevsky—I love him to the same extent that I'm afraid of him. Tolstoy's the same.

We Arab writers have to do this reading, but at the same time create the character of the Arab novel, taking into consideration our countries and our circumstances.

FLANNERY AND FAULKNER

Chris Offutt, interviewed by Rob Trucks

It sometimes seems as if every Southern writer of the last thirty years has Faulkner hung around his or her neck, but I haven't seen his name appear in any of your reviews.

Yeah, I don't see that with me. Flannery O'Connor was a much bigger influence on me than Faulkner.

THE SIZE OF THEIR VISION
Beverly Lowry, interviewed by Stephanie Gordon

⟹◆⟸

I come from the Mississippi Delta, from a literary town. William Alexander Percy, Walker Percy's uncle, was the patron saint of the town; he had a salon, and Shelby Foote lived there, and so did Josephine Haxton, who writes as Ellen Douglas. English teachers were always pushing us to be the next major Greenville writer. They gave us a sense that being a writer was honorable.

I wrote a lot, so my teachers thought I might be the next writer from there. Then I went to college and got involved in the theater and acting, even though I also ended up with a degree in English. After I got married and had a child, I continued pursuing acting and lived in New York. I had a friend, Bert Britton, who worked at Strand Bookstore in New York, and he pushed a lot of books on me. He was shocked that I had never read Faulkner, not only because I was from Mississippi—I had attended Ole Miss for a while, the University of Mississippi, which is in Oxford where Faulkner lived. Because of Bert's encouragement, I started reading a lot of fiction that I had never read before. This was in the early to mid-sixties, and women as a literary force had not really happened yet. So when I say, for example, that Doris Lessing was a big influence, it wasn't so much her writing style as it was the fact that she sometimes wrote about women who had traditional women's concerns, in the Martha Quest books, in particular. And she was certainly considered a serious writer. As far as I knew, if you didn't deal with men's issues then you were considered a fluttery, non-serious female writer. And Hortense Calisher was another influence, her sensory prose and great descriptive powers.

Virginia Woolf was another; so was Grace Paley. It was partly how they wrote, it was also the size of their vision, but it always started with the fact that they were women. And I had to find myself as a writer who was a woman. I also blazed through Faulkner, although I resisted him at first, because I didn't want to identify with Southerners.

BRAD WATSON
interviewed by Robert Birnbaum

Can you give me some of your thoughts on Southern writing?

Hmm. Well, it's always been hard for me to give what I thought was a coherent and worthwhile answer to that question. I don't think that the Southern literary tradition is a burden or an impediment, really. I kind of go with Eliot in *Tradition and the Individual Talent*, which says basically that you build upon, that you cannot escape, a tradition if you come out of it. If you deny it, it is self-defeating. I love the Faulkner I've read, the Robert Penn Warren, the Eudora Welty stories, Flannery O'Connor stuff. Some people have said that this book [*The Heaven of Mercury*] reminds them of O'Connor. I'm not sure how, except in the sense of there being some morbid humor in it. I'm very aware of those writers, when I write, as people who taught writers from the South today something about how to see the place they are from. As long as you don't try to write their stories, I think you are okay.

Could your book have been set in Las Cruces, New Mexico?

I wouldn't have been able to write it. [Both laugh.] That's the thing. You are of your place and from your place.

....

ELIZABETH COX

interviewed by Sarah Anne Johnson

Do you consider yourself a Southern writer?

Well, I'm Southern. My stories are set in the South. The rhythm of the language, the plant life, the speech—all these are Southern. I grew up reading the King James Version of the Bible, so I know I use phrases and rhythms from that biblical background. I know that many writers do not want to be called Southern writers, but I don't mind. It's the material I use, but the themes, I hope, are more than Southern.

Where do you see yourself in the tradition of Southern writers?

I don't want to presume to place myself among the great writers of the South, but I can say that they have been my teachers. I respond to the language in both the stories and poems of Robert Penn Warren, to Eudora Welty's sharp humor, Faulkner, of course. I love the wordiness and the archetypal images Faulkner uses. I wish I understood more of Flannery O'Connor's way of putting a story on the page. I study the way she creates a story through three to five scenes. Ernest Gaines is someone I admire for the way he tells a story and the peregrinations that are taken, the labyrinthine way of getting to the final page—I see that as Southern storytelling. I also see that truth is usually told with more complexity in the peregrinations. Paths which lead away from the main road, then come back, create more complexity, more truth, than a line that goes from beginning to end.

....

LITERATURE THAT ROCKS

Frederick Reiken, interviewed by Eric Wasserman

As much as I was profoundly influenced by Joyce, Woolf, Faulkner, Munro, Chekhov, García Márquez, and many other writers, I can equally say that I was profoundly influenced by the Beatles, Pink Floyd, Yes, the Grateful Dead, the Doors, Simon and Garfunkel, Bruce Springsteen, Rush, CSN, Neil Young, Led Zeppelin, and many other rock groups that I would consider literary, or at least of having literary pretensions. I would say the same is true for most writers of my era, and the reason seems pretty obvious to me.

Literary rock music—which now tends to fall under the heading classic rock—more or less started in 1967, when the Beatles put out *Sgt. Pepper's Lonely Hearts Club Band*, and it was only when groups like Pink Floyd and Yes followed suit in the late sixties that this kind of literary influence started to become available. I was not the kind of kid who sat home and read *Moby Dick* for fun, and so the books I read were only those that were assigned for English classes—and I was usually speed-reading them on the bus. Now and then, I would have strong reactions to a book—as was the case with *Huckleberry Finn*, which I recall having vivid dreams about; *The Catcher in the Rye*; *The Sun Also Rises*; *The Great Gatsby*; and even *Wuthering Heights*—but equally as important to my understanding of literature were those Saturday-night parties where we'd sit around analyzing the dark metaphors lurking in Pink Floyd lyrics, or feel the mystical elevation that comes from listening to an exalted, grandiose Yes song such as "And You and I" or "Siberian Khatru."

JIM GRIMSLEY

interviewed by Jim Schumock

Which writers have most drawn you to become the kind of writer you are?

I'm one of those rare people who still likes Hemingway, and I think that's mostly just a fashion trend for him to have been badmouthed the way he has been over the last decade or so, but I think he's an extraordinary stylist. I think I am interested in a wider range of style than he is. I do think, having read nearly everything that I could get my hands on of his, that that style does become predictable and repeatable in some of what he's written, and I don't want that to be true of me.

Other writers I adore: Flannery O'Connor is amazing, especially in terms of content. She can take a fairly simple situation and complicate it and complicate it and complicate it until you think you've read a story about the whole world all balled up in one place. I love Ford Madox Ford. *The Good Soldier* I think is one of the greatest books ever. It's a book I was reading at the time I was starting *Winter Birds*, and it gave me a sense of voice I wanted to repeat—that pristine voice full of danger, very civilized but full of danger all the way through. I could go on naming them—Dostoyevsky, Tolstoy, George Eliot, the nineteenth-century people.

Any other Americans?

Well, these days, yes. Kaye Gibbons is somebody I read a lot. William Maxwell I've just discovered and I think he's extraordinary. Reynolds Price is great. Doris Betts, who's an old teacher of mine, is a very fine story writer. Max Steele. It's an endless list.

....

LEARNING HOW TO LIVE LIFE
Elizabeth Cox, interviewed by Sarah Anne Johnson

I do believe that we learn how to live life through stories. I was raised in a boys' private school where my father was headmaster. Everyone in that community was a teacher—a huge family of teachers—talking about literature, not in a pretentious way, but in a way that made me love the stories of Shakespeare, or the tale of the Odyssey or the Iliad—letting me know these stories were real, and relevant.

An English teacher who lived on the campus saw me reading Austen's *Pride and Prejudice*. I was very young and didn't really know what I was reading, but he talked with me about it and made me confident about my reading. I began very early to learn that literature was a way of learning how to live your life. I think of writing as a way to deepen my life, teaching me to observe everything, every moment, more closely. Reading does the same thing. I put them in the same box, reading and writing.

CHITRA BANERJEE DIVAKARUNI

interviewed by Sarah Anne Johnson

Some reviewers have referred to your work as magic realism. Do you agree with this categorization?

I don't disagree, because I think that category can encompass a lot of things. I'm sure that I've been influenced by the works of people like Márquez and Allende, but I think what I'm doing, which is a little different, is drawing on the old fables and drawing on the legends of India to inform my characters, some of whom are legendary. That's the world that I want to juxtapose against the very real world of America. That makes what I'm trying to do a little different.

ANDREA BARRETT

interviewed by Sarah Anne Johnson

What drew you to writing about the events of Grosse Isle and the Irish immigrants who suffered from fever?

That was one of those strange, wonderful serendipities. Two things converged. One is that I'm a great admirer of the Irish writer William Trevor. He has a beautiful story called "The News from Ireland," a long story, about forty pages, with multiple characters and multiple points of view, about the famine as the people on a Protestant estate in Ireland experienced it. It's a story I teach often. I was teaching at Warren Wilson and I had a student who wanted to write her critical essay on that story. As her supervisor, I asked her to read some material about the Irish famine so that she'd have a better understanding of both how well and how extremely economically Trevor had managed to work the historical facts into that story. Then I had to read the same books because I didn't know the facts, either. This is what I mean about learning a lot when I'm teaching. I assigned her a couple of books, and then I read the same books, which were largely about the Irish famine in Ireland. One had a brief chapter about what happened at Grosse Isle, though, and it hit me like a hammer between the eyes. I knew I had to write about it.

MARY YUKARI WATERS
interviewed by Sherry Ellis

There are so many writers I greatly admire, but I've never felt that any one person directly affected my writing. I think it's because I started writing so late. I didn't go through that typical process of a young aspiring writer, where you read a lot of writers, pattern your writing after the ones you admire, and finally, after a lot of derivative attempts, find your own voice. When I started writing, I was working as a CPA, so it left me barely enough free time to write, much less read all the writers I was supposed to. I just didn't have that luxury. I was actually a bookworm as a kid, but I didn't do much reading during and after college. The bulk of my "literate" reading came after I had found my own voice. I think this made a big difference in the way I approached other people's writing. Through good luck, or bad luck, I missed out on that stage where I depended on other writers to help me with my own style and technique. Having said that, the writers I admire are Virginia Woolf, Doris Lessing, Edith Wharton, and Gail Godwin, among many, many others.

ONE FAULKNER'S ENOUGH

Ernest Gaines, interviewed by Michael Upchurch

The person whose work had the greatest impact on me in my earlier days was Turgenev. I used that book [*Fathers and Sons*] as my bible. I must have had so much of Turgenev in me! I mean, Turgenev does that himself, writes those little chapters. His books were always very small. And although I love the big, mid-nineteenth-century Russian classics, Tolstoy and Dostoyevsky, my favorite was the least known among the giants because of the structure of the smaller novel. And since then, since *Catherine Carmier*, I've stuck to that form.

Your prose is very clean, very understated, offering a low-key approach to volatile subject matter. As a Southern writer, were you never tempted to wade off in the direction of Faulknerian excess? Did you never say, "Now I'm going to cut loose"?

Well, you know, when I was at San Francisco State, I studied Faulkner and Hemingway, and all the others. And later when I went to Stanford, I wrote two short stories, one that was almost Hemingway and the other was Faulknerian. Malcolm Cowley was teaching at Stanford that year, and he told me, "One Faulkner's enough in this world." So from then on I thought, Let's leave those long, convoluted sentences alone and stick to what you can do best.

But I was and still am influenced by Faulkner—not necessarily the sentences—but his scenes, the characters involved. Mississippi borders Louisiana, of course, and you can see some of the same kinds of physical things: trees and roads and fields and the people. And they eat some of the same food. Well, we have a distinct cuisine in the south of Louisiana, with a lot of Cajun and Creole influence, which you don't have in Mississippi. But when I read Faulkner's descriptions of his farmers and his small stores and the square and all these things, I can see those things in Louisiana as well. And, of course, it was Faulkner's concentration on his Yoknapatawpha County which gave me the idea to concentrate on my parish of Bayonne, and to concentrate everything in one area and develop the stories out of that area. I guess Faulkner could have gotten it from Joyce.

I think the understatement stuff, the short sentences, was Hemingway based. I learned a lot from him. But I studied American literature, you know, and I had a lot of influences. I studied Greek tragedy. I studied Shakespeare. I was reading all of that. And I think when I was writing *In My Father's House*, I had Greek tragedy in mind—of a strong man falling. So it's not only one writer or another, but a lot of writers, and then you find your own voice somewhere along the way.

Askold Melnyczuk: I think religion has a very different goal from literature, uses very different means, and yet the two overlap in many ways. Like religious writing, literature helps us to adjust to the predicament of knowing we are going to die, but not knowing in what chapter.

as interviewed by William Pierce

WRITING ADVICE from Thom Jones

There are some books that I have around, perennial favorites, that if I pick them up, I'll start reading a line and I'll have to read the whole book. You know, I might read it from the middle to the end, and then the beginning. I mean, I do that with *Dispatches*, I do it with *Dog Soldiers*, anything by Larry Brown. Reading for me was always the best thing, going to bed with a book at night is the best thing, like Somerset Maugham said. And when I read books that saved my life or came at the right time—all my life, I used to remember thinking, Wow, whatever this person had to do to write this book or the price they had to pay—and many of them paid some pretty big prices—I would think, Thank God they did it! Thank God they did it! God bless 'em! If I could do that some day, that would be the most wonderful thing I could ever do. And when I first read Dostoyevsky, there was probably no one that was more unlikely to become a writer than me. And yet somehow I did it, and I believe you can do it. I mean, I think the universe will come out and help you once you get yourself straight and get on the right road.

as interviewed by Jim Schumock

KIDS THESE DAYS

Jayne Anne Phillips

interviewed by Sarah Anne Johnson

What are some of the common problems you find in your students' work?

They just don't read. Even if they think they read, they really don't read much. They don't come to it with a background in reading. They haven't read a spectrum of writers, or they haven't read all the works of six or seven writers. Now more than ever, they're very sound and print oriented, that is, very popular-culture oriented. They have less and less of a sense of history, and less and less interest in history. Kids who are twenty now grow up in a world in which emotional literacy is discouraged by the culture they live in. I don't hold them personally responsible. Somebody's got to come along and convince them that it's important to read.

YOU MUST KEEP READING

Pam Durban, interviewed by Cheryl Reid

Who do you consider good story writers, ones that have influenced you?

Katherine Anne Porter. I learned sentence construction from her. I studied her sentences and paragraphs. She is such a beautiful, clean writer. Her ability to describe and evoke detail.

Anyone else?

Alice Munro. Chekhov. I love Munro's wild and free sense of what a story is. What a story can be and how it can come together. She's never coy or cute, or any of the traps women writers fall into. She's unflinching. In a story like "Wild Swans," which is an uncomfortable story to read, she doesn't turn away from the uncomfortable situation. In *Lives of Girls and Women*, there's a story in there about the main character who is taken to the river by a relative who beats off in front of her. It's just one of those things that you can hardly keep reading, but you have to. It's what makes a good story. You may not want to keep reading, but you have to. It's compelling in some way. And in reading for *Five Points*, that's what I find missing in so many stories. They are not compelling in any way. They are empty. I'd rather be disturbed by something than unaffected.

ROBERT OLEN BUTLER
interviewed by Jim Schumock

My period of ravenous reading, and every writer must go through that, included a lot of familiar names: Hemingway and Faulkner and Joyce before *Ulysses*, Graham Greene. There were even some books that I'm hesitant to go back to now just for fear that they aren't all as wonderful as I remember them. I remember several remarkable, hot summer nights in Granite City with the windows thrown open to the dark and smelling the naphtha from the mill and reading Sherwood Anderson's *Winesburg, Ohio*. That had a remarkable effect on me. So it was basically the American pantheon that I was reading at that point.

BEVERLY LOWRY
interviewed by Stephanie Gordon

Which writers do you admire most now?

For the last couple years, I've been directing the nonfiction part of the writing program at Mason, and I've also had to do a lot of research on the book that is coming out next year [*Her Dream of Dreams*]. It's just shameful to be in a place where you read for work, but that's what I've been doing. I can't say that I enjoy it too much. But because Philip Roth just won the PEN/Faulkner Award, and I'm on the board for that award (and because he fascinates me), I read *The Human Stain*. I've thought he was brilliant from the beginning, since *Goodbye, Columbus*. But after reading *The Human Stain*, I went back and read *American Pastoral* and *I Married a Communist*, and I am as impressed by his work as ever. I find him very inspiring, his use of language and politics at once. I don't know if he's an influence or not, since I'm not writing fiction right now, but I do find him very inspiring; he expands my vision. I like Alice Munro a lot. I love Grace Paley, but she doesn't write much anymore. Don DeLillo is great. And I also loved Iris Murdoch.

In nonfiction, I tend to read more book by book rather than writer by writer. I am a big admirer of Philip Gourevitch, who wrote this book on Rwanda called *We Wish to Inform You That Tomorrow We Will Be Killed With Our Families*. An English writer I like is Julia Blackburn, especially her nonfiction, such as *Daisy Bates in the Desert* and one called *The Emperor's Last Island*. I love Adam Hochschild's book about the Congo, but whether or not

I'll be wild about the next book he writes remains to be seen. Another writer I admire is Peter Carey, especially his latest [*True History of the Kelly Gang*]. Rick Bragg's *Ava's Man* is wonderful; it's the continuation of his memoir, but going back to the previous generation. It's set on the border between Alabama and Georgia. Bragg speaks eloquently for his people.

WRITING ADVICE from Kent Haruf

First, you have to be a reader and to have read a good deal. You have to read with concentration and close attention to what's going on on the page, and to be open to the magic of what's happening, and be open to a kind of religious experience of literature that's essential.

After that, the thing to do is to write and write and write. It can't be said too emphatically that the way to learn how to write is to write.

Then you have to be open to being instructed. Either by your own efforts or by other people. Perhaps the most important thing is to be persistent. Most people who have some inclination to write quit before they get good enough at it to get published because it's too difficult.

as interviewed by Jim Nashold

THE ALTERED STATE

Siri Hustvedt
interviewed by Jennifer Levasseur and Kevin Rabalais

You are co-translator of the biography Fyodor Dostoyevsky: A Writer's Life *by Geir Kjetsaa. When did your interest in Dostoyevsky begin?*

I read *Crime and Punishment* when I was a teenager, and it was a cataclysmic book for me. I reread Dostoyevsky in college because I was studying Russian intellectual history and ideas are central to his novels. I began reading *Crime and Punishment* for the third time the day I arrived in New York, which was in September of 1978. I didn't know a soul in the city. I sat in my tiny room on Riverside Drive and devoured the story of Raskolnikov. I finished the book in two days. That obsessive reading was probably an emotional response to my entrance into the urban world.

But Dostoyevsky was also an epileptic, and I feel very close to lives influenced by neurological events. Since I was twenty, I have suffered from severe migraines. Once, I had a migraine that began as a seizure, and I was actually thrown against a wall. I have had auras, hallucinations, and euphoria before attacks, all of which were, of course, far less dramatic than Dostoyevsky's grand-mal seizures. Nevertheless, I am convinced that these altered states have a strong influence on personality. Neurologists have associated epilepsy with religiosity—St. Theresa of Avila was probably an epileptic—and, interestingly enough, also with the urge to write.

A DIFFERENT KIND OF EDUCATION
Thom Jones, interviewed by Jim Schumock

⇒◆⇐

Did you really read a book a day for ten years at one point?

When I was working as a custodian, I would get stacks of library books. Olympia, Washington, has three very good libraries—the state library, a university library, and a Timberland system—so I always had twenty-five books by my bedside, and maybe I'd peruse three or four in a day. If I got something that was really slower reading, I would spend a week on it, but all in all, in eleven years I think, roughly speaking, I probably did read ten thousand books, and I know that was my real education. Because I wasn't working as a professional, I could think. I was doing mechanical work. I thought about what I would write. I would think about the books I had been reading—I had time to think. It's very hard for people who are knocking around in the world to have that kind of leisure.

....

Melanie Bishop: "Strays" by Mark Richard (in *Ice at the Bottom of the World*) is a model short story in just about every sense: nothing extraneous, a killer pace, beautiful language, characters you'll love, tragic situations handled with comic grace, and a perfect ending. I tell my students: "If I could only have you read one story in this class, this would be it." I've never tired of reading it myself, and I've probably read it about thirty times now.

READING WHILE WRITING

Chris Offutt, interviewed by Rob Trucks

Can you read when you're writing?

I read different material at different stages. If I'm writing fresh material, a first draft, I read nonfiction pertaining to the work, with as flat and dull a prose as possible. When I'm revising, I can read.

When I was writing this novel, all I read was third-person novels. And I was very careful who I read. I didn't read Cormac's new book because his style is way too pervasive. I read Cormac and for two weeks, man, I'm writing bad Cormac McCarthy. But with Robert Stone, I could read him because I love his style. I could read Joseph Conrad and Graham Greene. I read writers who I thought were big, expansive storytellers, writers who were very ambitious within the project and achieved a genuine sense of reality on the page.

....

DISCOVERING OTHER VOICES

Julia Alvarez
interviewed by Mike Chasar and Constance Pierce

When you started out writing, who did you look to before the voice of the Latina in literature was out there?

Where did I get the permission to write what I know? It was from Maxine Hong Kingston. It wasn't even from a Latina writer. It was from reading a wonderful and, I think, classic book by an Asian-American author, *The Woman Warrior*. Something about her writing about her culture, and making sense of it, gave me permission to write about mine. I'd never had that experience. I went to school pre-women's studies, pre-multicultural studies. I just read the Great Books, and they were my models. Theodore Roethke as a poet, Yeats … well, who did we read? I have a poem in there [*El Otro Lado*] about discovering Louise Bogan's *The Blue Estuaries* in a bookstore. She was the first female living poet I had read. So those were my models and, hey, they're not bad models to have. But what was crazy was that I was trying to sound like William Butler Yeats, and I can't sound like William Butler Yeats. I sound more like the woman in the "33" sonnets—"Who touches this poem touches a woman" [*Homecoming*]—but I thought that I had to make my voice sound another way if I wanted to be a poet, an American poet. I thought I couldn't write about my material because I had to Americanize it, I had to translate not just language but my characters, so I would never call somebody Tía Rosa, I would call her Aunt Rose. And I would make the few short stories I wrote back then about American families, because I thought they had to be that, because I didn't know that something else could be done.

Maybe I would have discovered it without reading Maxine Hong Kingston, but it would have taken a while.

I learned all about writing from the traditional models—the Great Books—I learned how a sonnet works, and how to write in structured verse. I think we read a little William Carlos Williams in school. I'm not even sure. It was a much more traditional curriculum back in those dark ages. Later, it was a process of discovering other voices—maids at Yaddo, reading Maxine Hong Kingston—and giving myself permission, in part because I saw other women and campañeras doing what I hadn't known could be done.

Do you read many Latin American writers?

More in English—more English writers. When I wrote *In the Time of the Butterflies*, I had to read most of my materials in Spanish. But I read much slower in Spanish because I don't have the training, so it's much more of an effort for me. And, at the same time, García Márquez, Isabel Allende, Borges, certainly Neruda—whom I've translated into English—have been great influences.

I see myself coming out of many traditions—and mostly I read these writers because they're my teachers. I read Tolstoy if I want to learn how to do a dinner party. I also read Gabriel García Márquez to learn how to get that panoramic sense of history in what I write. We're learning all the time from who we read, right?

WRITING AS RESPONSE

Russell Banks, interviewed by Rob Trucks

Rule of the Bone certainly wasn't the first time that you worked from a specific literary reference. I'm thinking that *Trailerpark* is a response to *Winesburg, Ohio*, and that the short story from *Trailerpark*, "Black Man and White Woman in Dark Green Rowboat," came from Dreiser's *An American Tragedy*.

Naturally those are important points of reference for me in the writing of the story and of that book, but there are others as well. *Trailerpark* is in some ways a response to my reading of *The Canterbury Tales*, too, and *Dubliners*. There are various levels of response in, I think, any work of literature. You don't write in a vacuum. You participate. That's one of the great, satisfying things about being a fiction writer or a poet, an artist of any kind. Nobody's dead. You participate in the tradition. You become one with these books, and these texts become part of your immediate daily life, and so you enter into that conversation and hope you become part of the chorus in the course of writing the book. It's inevitable. It's inescapable for me. I've been a compulsive reader since my youth, since adolescence, so how could I not end up having a conversation of that sort? Having my work be a response to the works, the books that I've read?

Can we go to either a short story or a novel and talk about the particular process?

Actually, there's a double source for the short story you mentioned, "Black Man and White Woman in Dark Green Rowboat." Well, not source. It responds to Dreiser, certainly, in terms of the psychology of the characters, but it reverses and plays with it so that the victim is the man, in a sense. But also it's a response to a Hemingway story in how it's structured. So the psychology, in a way, and the erotic component of it come out of Dreiser, but certainly the form of the story and the arrangement—one might even say the architecture of the story—come out of "Hills Like White Elephants." The physical positioning of the characters and the movement of the boat, when they turn and so forth, is very much learned from Hemingway. I mean, I learned how to do that from Hemingway, how to dramatize by moving the characters around physically in relation to each other and in relation to the landscape. Where they are in the lake and in the boat is all very carefully orchestrated or choreographed, and I didn't know how to do that until I read Hemingway's stories.

When you sit down in front of the keyboard, have you just finished reading the Hemingway story, or are you working from some distant memory?

Usually I'm working from memory—and what's retained. I read like a writer, and what stays with me is often what has resonance for me as a writer. It might be a false memory, too. It often is. If I go back and reread it, I say, Well, it wasn't like I remembered it at all.

But if it gets you the story...

Right. It's what I needed from it. So it isn't necessarily a close reading by any means. It's associational and sometimes it's intuited, and if it's strong enough or raises questions for what I really was responding to, I'll go back to the text. I did that with *Cloudsplitter*. As I was nearing the end of it, I was hearing certain tones, you know? I'd orchestrated these various pieces, and I was starting to hear tones that were reminding me of tones at the end of *Moby Dick*. And I wanted to get it right, and I remembered that there's a beautiful diminuendo ending to *Moby Dick*. That was how I remembered it. I didn't remember it as the great, cataclysmic ending. There is a cataclysm and then there is a diminuendo, and I was remembering that, and that's what I was reaching for. I was starting to hear the necessity for that. Coming down from Harper's Ferry I thought, There has to be a diminuendo. It can't just sort of be like, That's all, folks. There has to be a follow-through. I was orchestrating it almost musically in my mind, so I went back and read the last forty, fifty pages of *Moby Dick* to see how he did that.

Really, it was pacing I was looking at, and the rhetoric, to see how the rhetoric kind of cooled down, and how the narrative became more direct at the end, and how the whole voice was lowered. And I studied it consciously, but I was led there by what I deeply remembered, not having read *Moby Dick* in twenty-five years. So I think it operates that way, too. Sometimes you will go directly back to the text and see how it's done, but you're led there because you have this memory of it. You're led there because what's unfolding on the page is leading you there. It's in response to what's unfolding on the page.

ALLEN MORRIS JONES
interviewed by David Abrams

Who are some of the authors—dead or living—who have really had an impact on you over the course of your career?

There's the obvious ones who I think show up in my style. Cormac McCarthy has been pointed out by reviewers. I think that's an easy target, though, because I choose not to use quotation marks in my writing, and everyone automatically thinks Cormac McCarthy or Kent Haruf. I think McCarthy and I also share an influence from Faulkner. I'm an enormous fan of about half of Faulkner's work. I'm also a big fan of Hemingway. But I think anyone writing narrative stories these days ends up standing in the shadows of Faulkner or Hemingway. I'm a big fan of Michael Ondaatje and Annie Proulx.

CHITRA BANERJEE DIVAKARUNI
interviewed by Sarah Anne Johnson

Maxine Hong Kingston really influenced me with *The Woman Warrior*. I'd been ready for that book when I read it, which was when I was doing my graduate studies at Berkeley. It opened up so many things for me, and it made me aware of the importance of her subject matter, and also gave me permission for my subject matter. I love the way that story plays such an important part in her book, and story plays a very important part in my books—telling stories, listening to stories, old stories out of our culture and how they affect us—all of those things.

THE INFLUENCE OF HORROR
Dan Chaon, interviewed by Misha Angrist

Do you find that other writers of literary fiction share your fascination with the macabre? I know that in his last story collection [*Werewolves in Their Youth*], Michael Chabon wrote a story under the pseudonym August Van Zorn ["The Old Mill"], who was a character first introduced in his novel *Wonder Boys*. "The Old Mill" is a very creepy tale written in H.P. Lovecraft style. I thought it was the best piece in the book.

Yeah, it was. I had an e-mail exchange with him about it. I'm not a big Lovecraft fan, per se, but I do think that that was a terrific one. I think that Chabon and I agree that our generation of writers has been very influenced by horror, maybe in the same way the previous generation of writers was influenced by science fiction. I mean, think about it: Growing up, we all read Stephen King, Peter Straub, and those guys. That stuff is part of our reading consciousness, especially since most of us read it at a very malleable age. We've been taught to be ashamed of it, but I'm not. King especially gets at something in the zeitgeist better than a lot of people.

Have readers picked up on the supernatural stuff in *Among the Missing*?

Actually, the two reviews of the book I've liked best have mentioned it. There was one in a Chicago paper that said something about the collection being "Twilight Zone-like." It called me "the Rod Serling of emotional weirdness," which I thought was funny and a nice compliment. And *Entertainment Weekly* said that the book was "two parts Raymond Carver and one part Edgar Allan Poe." I'd like to think that both of those poles are at work.

Speaking of Carver, the book begins with an epigraph from him. And yet, your stories are hardly minimalist. Would you include yourself in the Carver lineage?

I wouldn't, at least not in terms of the way I approach prose and story. I'm less interested than he was in slices of life as material for stories. However, having said that, I would say I share his interest in the daily lives of ordinary people, if I can make that distinction.

Carver is usually thought of as writing about working-class people. I don't know if they're working class—maybe just less educated. Anyway, I don't think I deal with the subject in the same way, but I am interested in class conflict and the way people behave as they move from one social stratum to another. For example, people marrying into or out of one social class.

The thing I've always loved about Carver's work is that he had this real appreciation for mystery in people's lives—that moment when something inexplicable happens. In "Fat," there's a very strange encounter between a waitress and a grotesquely fat man. The story ends: "My life is going to change. I feel it."

As I read your book, I thought a lot about the great Irish short-story writer Frank O'Connor and his study of the short-story form, *The Lonely Voice*. If you'll indulge me, I'd like to ask you a bit about your work in relation to O'Connor's view of the short story.

Please do.

Well, first off, I think it's interesting that you bring up that last line of "Fat." O'Connor cites Gogol's classic "The Overcoat" as a kind of prototype of the form, especially the ending, which is very similar to "Fat." In Gogol's story, we are told, "from that day forth, everything was as it were changed and appeared in a different light to him."

Yes—great story, and classic ending. We all know that Carver was an admirer of Chekhov; I don't know, maybe Chekhov learned a few tricks from Gogol.

....

Melissa Pritchard: When I'm working on a project as I am now, my reading choices usually inform my writing in some way. For example, I just finished a new translation of Tolstoy's *Anna Karenina*. Tolstoy is a master at opening up moments and taking time to leisurely follow a character's thoughts and actions. His contemplative style encouraged me to slow down and open up moments in my own novel.

as interviewed by Leslie A. Wootten

EVERYBODY NEEDS SOMEONE

Frederick Reiken, interviewed by Eric Wasserman

A criticism of writing programs is that students are quite impression-able and are in danger of imitating a certain type of story. Many students are drawn to imitating domestic writers such as Raymond Carver and Alice Munro. Isn't there a risk of promoting a specific kind of literature if instructors refuse to challenge students?

I recently saw folksinger/guitar-virtuoso Leo Kottke play in Northampton, Massachusetts. He told a little story about his mentor, John Fahey, and how at one point he said to Fahey something like, "You know, I have this fear that I'm going to sound a lot like you." Fahey's response was, "Well, everybody has to go through someone."

My sense is that this is true for all artists, and is particularly applicable to writing. That is, I think most, if not all, writers must go through a phase of assimilating and emulating their favorite writers if they're to have any chance of finding their own voice. Simply put, all writers need models of form and technique, and any writer worth his or her salt will go through various authors and come out the other side.

It's true that Raymond Carver and Alice Munro tend to be MFA-program staples everywhere, and this is because they're two of the most important North American writers of the late twentieth century. In the thirties, you had Hemingway, Steinbeck, Fitzgerald, and Faulkner. In the fifties and sixties, you had Cheever, Roth, Bellow, Salinger, O'Connor, Welty. Who do you have of that caliber to come out of the seventies and eighties? Carver and

Munro. They've both, in certain ways, modernized the tenets of Anton Chekhov. And whereas Carver might be thought of as the heir to Hemingway, Munro might be thought of in some ways as an heir to Faulkner. No matter how you look at it, and whatever labels you try to put on them, their work has affected our modern literary tradition. To be a contemporary American literary writer, you need to understand the understatement and scene-by-scene movement of a Carver story, just as you need to understand the elliptical expository methods of Munro. That's not to say one should try to write like Carver or Munro—in fact, Carver and Munro imitations have the same parody-like quality as an emulation of Hemingway or Faulkner, simply because their voices are so distinct.

From what I can see in the programs I've been part of, most MFA students are going to be exposed to a wide range of contemporary fiction, ranging from formalists like Jhumpa Lahiri to satirists like George Saunders, so it's not as if there's really a risk involved in focusing on these two masters of the form for a short while, particularly since their stories become a good and useful model for so many people. And whether or not Lahiri or Saunders gets assigned in your grad class, those books exist, and it's any writer or would-be writer's job to read and read and read.

As far as influences go in general, I've always held the belief that a writer can be influenced for the wrong reasons or the right ones. The wrong reasons are that, as you've suggested, they feel pressure to conform with the thing that is being celebrated at the present moment—and such impressionability typically comes with a lack of emotional maturity. Being influenced for what I'm calling the right reasons means being influenced by a writer whose work resonates with you because you share some aspect of that writer's sensibility. In finding a book that speaks to you, you've usually found a writer who in some way shares your own sensibility, and who has already taken ideas and impressions about form or content that are still inchoate for you, and transmuted them into something tangible and fully realized. In reading a work that influences you, you're essentially reading a work by someone who has mastered some aspect of what you hope to master. And so, by reading that work, you are embarking on the process of going through a mentor.

Like most writers, I went through a period of impressionability in which I was unconsciously emulating writers for precisely the wrong reasons. Just after I graduated from college, I took a night course at the New School and had a teacher who despised everything I wrote, and perhaps me personally. He was a big fan of Carver, and "What We Talk About When We Talk About Love" was one of his favorite stories. Toward the end of the semester, I finally wrote a story he liked. I included it with my MFA applications, and when I got to UC Irvine and sat down the first week with my advisor there, he pulled out the story and said, "Now here's an interesting little piece. I think you should change the title to 'What We Talk About When We Talk About Hockey.'" This is the kind of risk I think you're talking about, but I would say that it was ultimately my responsibility to recognize what I was doing. Thankfully, I did.

That was the same fall I had what I think of as my one and only prophetic dream, which I'll be so bold as to mention, since I think it relates to this discussion. In the dream, I came to a bookstore window and found that the entire window was displaying copies of what was apparently my first book. But the book, instead of being pages bound by a cardboard cover with dust jacket, was, in each little wooden bookstand, a bunch of celery, complete with leaves and stalks. When I awoke, I likened the dream to a Magritte painting, said to myself something like, "Neat," and didn't think much of it. But that afternoon, the dream's meaning hit me full force. What I was writing was the equivalent of celery. I didn't care what it was so long as it would be published, and so it really was interchangeable with celery or radishes or whatever. I would say it took me almost two years after that realization to start writing fiction that I could honestly say was not the equivalent of celery. And I would say to any would-be writer of literary fiction that there are thousands of much easier ways to achieve notoriety and/or make money than by being a writer. So if you're going to do it, you have to give over to what is meaningful and authentic, for both your readership and for yourself. And that means letting go of your need to be like any other writer. The best writers' writing doesn't remind you of anyone else.

MARY GORDON
interviewed by Charlotte Templin

What about Virginia Woolf?

She is very important to me. I started a doctoral dissertation on Virginia Woolf. I never finished it, but she was the person that turned me to prose writing.

THE ULTIMATE SEDUCTION

Stephen Dixon, interviewed by Jim Schumock

⇒◆⇐

It's said that writing is the ultimate seduction of reading. If so, who were the people who seduced you?

The author of *Homerun Hennessey,* for one, when I was a boy. You know, wonderful baseball and football novels. I loved those. Franklin W. Dixon, who is not a relative, but I loved the Hardy Boys when I was a boy. The more mature works came from Dostoyevsky. When I was sixteen, seventeen, eighteen years old, I read every single thing that Dostoyevsky wrote. I was absolutely obsessed by the man. Not by the style, because I wasn't really keen or aware of style as much as the content. This guy was writing about the deepest things imaginable. That really influenced me. Later on, it was Hemingway. I like the conciseness in his work and I like the subject matter. I became so obsessed with his work. That's when I was already starting to be a writer. I knew that I had to divorce myself completely and move to another hemisphere if I wanted to be a writer. I knew that a good writer, a serious literary writer, should not sound like anybody else. Unfortunately, I moved on to Joyce. Particularly *Ulysses.* Not all of it. It's a flawed book. I admire the stream-of-consciousness style in Leopold Bloom. Again, this was my second literary divorce. I left Joyce; I had to, or else I would sound like Joyce. He's certainly a tantalizing writer to emulate. I did it because I had to write in my own voice. This was in my early twenties. I've consciously striven to have my own voice and to have my own style and to write my own fiction, my own things in my own style. Those three were perhaps the most influential.

JAYNE ANNE PHILLIPS
interviewed by Sarah Anne Johnson

Who are some of the writers who've influenced you?

A whole gamut of people. Initially, and still, most of them are writers who broke the rules in one way or another, or who made their own rules. Writers like Faulkner, Burroughs, Bruno Shultz, Flannery O'Connor, a lot of the Southern writers for their connection to the physical world, and for their enslavement to it. A lot of the central European writers, such as Kafka, for their anomie, or that almost existential separation from the world. And a lot of language-oriented writers, such as James Agee, just because language was my way into writing. Spiritually, I'm attracted to writers who seem to have gone somewhere, who've been to the other side and come back to bear witness to that event, that is, writers who can represent other dimensions of being in language, like Katherine Anne Porter, William

Maxwell. For instance, a story like Cheever's "The Swimmer," in which a metaphor represents a whole journey into death, compresses time almost miraculously.

RICHARD BAUSCH

interviewed by Jennifer Levasseur and Kevin Rabalais

Raymond Carver, in jest, said he wrote stories and not novels because he had a short attention span.

Well, he was kidding, of course. The story requires plenty of attention span, a deeper kind of attention, I think. Especially with good stories. They require several readings if you're going to get at what is going on. I don't mean what's literally going on, but what the real matter of the story is. They require attention some people aren't finally willing to give. Sometimes, too, it's just that life is stressful, and there's so much going on. So the average person—hell, anybody, everybody—says, "I want it done for me; I want my emotional responses to be passive, and I don't want to have to invest anything of myself in order to be entertained." But the population of active readers has traditionally been relatively small. That has always been the case, and it always will be the case. It's just that now we have this sense drug, television, blaring at us from every living room, it seems. I'll tell you, I think television is one of the great mistakes in the history of human civilization. It has harmed our ability to concentrate. It is creating whole bands of people for whom violence is just the next thing that happens. It's harmed their ability to be empathetic. It's a terrible thing. And it started out being pretty good, pretty good. For a little while, it was a good thing. In the 1960s, it showed this country its own ugly face during the civil rights movement. Seeing those people being chased down the streets by dogs and knocked down by high-pressure fire hoses outraged the rest of the country, and they saw what segregation really looked like. Made it impossible to ignore, and it was a great thing. It probably had something to do with what happened in Vietnam, too. But now it's gotten down to tabloid shit. Who slept with whom?

Alan Shapiro had a great idea. He said we should write a comedy series. It would be like the Jerry Springer show, only you would have all the great stories of literature on it. Like Oedipus, sitting on the Jerry Springer show, with a caption at the bottom of the screen saying, "Slept with mother, engendered children by her, killed father, doesn't realize it yet." Wouldn't that be funny? Anyway, it has always been a small number of people who read books as a regular part of their day. It is always going to be so.

. . . .

Chitra Banerjee Divakaruni: I tell some of my very talented students, "Stop everything. Don't read so much." Usually teachers are saying the opposite, but there comes a time when you have to shut down all of the input channels, and you have to go into yourself and write what's in there.

as interviewed by Sarah Anne Johnson

LYNN FREED

interviewed by Sarah Anne Johnson

I was a sporadic reader as a child. Most of my imaginative time was spent hurling myself out of trees and onto parapets, dancing on the roof, building myself a tree house, racing down steep hills on my bicycle with my feet off the pedals. It is a wonder that I wasn't killed or maimed, but there it is—I wasn't. If I read, I read Enid Blyton, a much-maligned, very non-British children's writer. And I read plays. My parents' study was jammed with plays. I particularly loved Oscar Wilde and Bernard Shaw, read them again and again. And, as I grew a little older, I adored Ibsen, still do. I also became obsessed with their collection of Holocaust books. I looked into that horror, that nightmare, that unthinkable genocide, with real terror. And with fascination, too, of course. Could this happen to me? And how? And when? Bear in mind that I was the child of Jewish parents, growing up in South Africa after World War II.

Anyway, as I grew more literate—in my teens, really—I memorized huge chunks of Shakespeare. Much of this was required by school, which also required us to memorize chunks of the Bible. I found that I loved having the words by heart, accessible always. If anything got into my blood, it was the wonder of Shakespeare, the wonder of the Psalms. I would prop a book up while I was in the bath and recite a passage in there, over and over, until I had it word perfect. This seemed perfectly normal in a family like mine.

At about this time, I also fell in love with Jane Austen. I read through all the novels and, thereafter, reread them regularly every few years. What a wonderful training in irony, in timing, in pacing and shaping and characterization! Later still, when I was released from the bondage of academe and was free to read freely again, I found myself falling in love with one book—say, Duras's *The Lover*—and reading it over and over. I fell in love with Alice Munro likewise, with particular stories of hers. Doris Lessing, too—that wonderful intelligence, the brilliant descriptions of Africa, the tie to the land. I have to admit, though, that the Great Gods of Influence—Chekhov, Turgenev, etc.—do not live with me. I have read them; I have admired them; I have put them back on the shelf.

Are there other influences on your work?

I suppose so. But I never think in terms of "influence." If there is a book, or a section of a book, a poem, a line that stays with me, I colonize it, make it my own. Two shelves in my study are filled with such books. When I'm stuck, I reach over and read, to remind myself of what the whole enterprise is supposed to be about.

Amy Hempel: More than reading new work, lately, I find I've been doing more re-reading of things I like a lot to get me revved up to work. Barry Hannah once told me it took three trusted friends to tell him a poem was great before he'd read it; otherwise, he stuck to the immortals.

as interviewed by Debra Levy and Carol Turner

TO EACH HIS OWN

George Makana Clark
interviewed by Linda B. Swanson-Davies

You mentioned a few minutes ago that it was easy to look down on other people's tastes, easy to suggest that someone should be reading somehow "better" material.

Yes. For instance, I think if a kid is reading Stephen King, they're reading, doing better than ninety-nine percent of the rest of the world. It's like when people make fun of other people's musical taste, and I think, "They're listening to music, they're enjoying themselves, do they have to listen to experimental jazz fusion?"

....

PARTICIPATING IN THE TRADITION
Russell Banks, interviewed by Rob Trucks

How conscious were you of *Huck Finn* when you were writing *Rule of the Bone*?

Totally.

What term would you be comfortable with? Is it an homage?

It's an homage and a critique. There's an intertextual dialogue that I was trying to set up and participate in with *Huck Finn*. Definitely it was there.

Well, I know the connection wasn't accidental. I mean, the words "light out" do appear at the end.

Absolutely. It's throughout. I want to not only bow down before *Huck Finn* but also to argue with it and to point out, by similarities, the differences between Twain's world and Banks's world, the 1870s and 1990s. He's a middle-aged man writing about a teenaged kid, obviously an adolescent version of himself, and I was doing something very similar these many years later. It would be absurd for me to even begin to write a book about a kid like that without first giving more than a passing nod in the direction of *Huckleberry Finn*, and then going on—by noting the similarities, by seeding the book with plenty of similarities to note that there's a big difference in our worlds. I mean, the world has changed in dramatic and frightening ways in the intervening years.

In what sense are you arguing with *Huckleberry Finn*?

I only mean that figuratively. I think that basically what I mean is, not arguing with it, but adding to it. That's a better way to think about it. That book establishes a tradition in American literature that most writers participate in, consciously or not, and I was conscious of participating in it and wanted to extend the tradition into the late twentieth century, because there's so much in the book that's still valid and applicable. It's a great, classic work of art. But all the best stories—*The Odyssey*, *The Iliad*—have to constantly be retold, can be constantly retold. That's what we mean by classics. They can be retold. Not just updated, but retold so we can hear again and recycle, apply again to our lives with fresh eyes and ears, the essential insights and power that that tradition holds.

THOM JONES

interviewed by Jim Schumock

Who were some of the writers that really stood out ... for you?

Well, there are so many that it's hard to say. I'm thinking now of Dreiser, Thomas Hardy, Larry Brown, Richard Wright, of Joyce Carol Oates, Celine, Robert Stone, Richard Price, Cormac [McCarthy], Hubert Selby Jr., Somerset Maugham, Thomas Mann, let me think ... V.S. Naipaul. Kingsley Amis has always been a big one with me—I like the early British Angry Young Men bunch—Alan Sillitoe, John Braine, John Osborne. I'm thinking ... Brian Moore.

I read the Russians a lot—reread the classics—everything, virtually everything. Robert Stone once said, "Being an author is one of the hardest things in the world, because you have to know everything."

I remember being enchanted and enthralled by Dostoyevsky and all the travails of his life he details in his writer's notebooks: the epileptic seizures, Turgenev avoiding him because he'd borrowed money for gambling. What did Dostoyevsky bring alive in you?

Well, when I was discharged from the Marine Corps, I had a head injury from a boxing match, and I didn't have the classic grand-mal syndrome, but rather a variant of temporal-lobe epilepsy with fugue states, which is extremely rare, so I was discharged as a schizophrenic. They didn't quite know what was the matter with me, and I can't blame them at all—they were good doctors—but when I got home, my own physician sent me to a Russian neurologist.

I presented myself with these very strange seizures, and he handed me a copy of *The Idiot*. He said, "Maybe this will help you figure it out a little bit." And, immediately, I embraced Dostoyevsky, read his whole body of work, and absolutely knew that I wanted to be a writer. I'm in Aurora, working in a factory that seemed to be my life, until this happened to me, and then I was obsessed with the meaning of life, the existence of God, the riddle of existence, the existential business. I read *Notes from Underground*, *The House of the Dead*, *The Brothers Karamazov*, *Crime and Punishment*, everything, virtually. I was a madman—tore into all books.

....

Siri Hustvedt: The funny thing is that when I am writing a novel, it is very hard to read other novels, especially good novels. The more powerful the imagination, the worse it is. I remember reading J. M. Coetzee's *Life & Times of Michael K* and thinking, "Why am I not doing this myself? This is so good." I had to put it away. Between novels, I can read fiction with a lot of pleasure, but mostly while I'm working, I read nonfiction. I like to read books for lay people about the brain and memory. I like to read history and biographies. I read a lot of psychoanalytic case studies. I've done a lot of reading about personality disorders from all points of view.

as interviewed by Jennifer Levasseur and Kevin Rabalais

RICHARD BAUSCH

interviewed by Jennifer Levasseur and Kevin Rabalais

Who are some of the writers you teach?

Tolstoy, Chekhov, the Russians. Especially the short stories of the Russians, and Tolstoy's novels. You can learn how to write everything you'll ever write by reading Tolstoy's novels. I love what Mark Twain says about *War and Peace:* "Tolstoy carelessly neglects to include a boat race." I love that. I believe Shakespeare was the greatest dramatist and poet, and Tolstoy was the greatest fiction writer. And, you know, Tolstoy hated Shakespeare—thought he was way too dirty minded. I would love to know what Shakespeare would have thought of Tolstoy. He probably would have found him too prissy.

Are you an avid reader?

Oh, yeah. You can't do this and not be. I don't think anybody who does this, who writes books, isn't an obsessive reader. I have over seven thousand books at home, and I'm an obsessive re-reader, too. I read some stuff every year. I've read *The Great Gatsby* about thirty-five times. I've read *War and Peace* four times. I've read most of Chekhov many times. Consequently, I'm not as up on what is contemporary. I keep up with my friends, which is a very large and productive group of writers. All of them have a book every year. Keeping up with pals is enough for contemporary stuff. Then, I get about twelve books a month from various publishers, asking for blurbs. It is very hard for me to get to any of them. There is a wonderful novel by Cynthia Bass called *Sherman's March*, which some reviewers misunderstood. It's a really good book. Occasionally, I try to read opening lines to see what's there.

Do you read your own work after it has been published?

I do, because I don't want to repeat myself.

....

THE INFLUENCE OF CHEKHOV
Pam Durban, interviewed by Cheryl Reid

What about Chekhov's work can you point to as an influence?

His point of view. His objectivity. His big, loose stories. The possibilities of the story.

His use of time is very large and sometimes very minute.

Yes. His variety. Whenever I am tired of fiction, I turn to him to refresh my ideas of what I can do.

His point of view is objective—you may not get close into the characters' minds, but you get a sense—

Of who they are. And he's willing to let them see themselves as they see themselves. I've also learned a lot from him about structure. What's possible in a story. It doesn't have to be some tight progression of actions toward epiphany. It can be much looser than that and still get somewhere and be about something, and hold some kind of shape.

THE BIBLE AS A WORK OF LITERATURE
William Styron, interviewed by Melissa Lowver

⋙◆⋘

In an interview with Peter Matthiessen and George Plimpton in 1954, you cited the Bible as one of the works that influenced the emotional climate of your writing. What was it about the Bible that affected you?

Although I was never religious, then or now, I do think that the Bible—since I was exposed to it very strongly as a young person, in both growing up in a moderately religious household, and going to school where the Bible was required in the curriculum—I learned a great deal about it. I think, at its best, it's a remarkable chronicle with great poetic overtones, and therefore really a major work of literature. I seem to regard the Bible as literature, and to that extent, I think it has had a great deal of importance in my work.

....

LYNNE SHARON SCHWARTZ
interviewed by Nancy Middleton

⋙◆⋘

While you were growing up, the allure and the mystery of books was important to you. Once you learned how it was done, once you'd been on the other side, did it lose some of the mystery?

No, although there are some writers for whom I think it does. When you know how something is put together, or you want to find out, you begin to read very carefully and analytically, and you're not as caught up in the mystery and glory of the story. I don't do that. I do read as a writer, but I can always lose myself in that childlike way. I get carried along and either don't pay attention to the technical aspects, or I'm registering them—as in, "Oh yes, she's doing this, she's manipulating this"—but it doesn't interfere. I hope I never lose that ability.

MATTHEW SHARPE
interviewed by Sherry Ellis

The narrator of *The Sleeping Father* is wise, knowing, and ironic. For example, you write, "In the lives of Chris and Cathy Schwartz, hospital and school exchanged roles. Hospital was now the place where they went to be educated and socialized by illness and the resistance to illness; school was the place where they visited their gravely ailing secondary education." How did you determine the personality and level of omniscience you wanted the narrator to have for this novel?

I figured out the tone of this novel by reading *Middlemarch* by George Eliot. I happened to be reading *Middlemarch* while I was starting *The Sleeping Father*, and for a story whose subject is consciousness, among other things, I wanted to be able to inhabit the consciousness of several of the characters. And I thought that George Eliot tone, which is lightly mocking, always very tender, and sort of maternalistic toward her characters, would be well worth emulating for doing what I wanted to do. I'm glad you picked up on that. Until I know the tone of the voice, I can't really move forward with any of the other aspects of a novel.

AVOIDING THE ANXIETY OF INFLUENCE
Siri Hustvedt
interviewed by Jennifer Levasseur and Kevin Rabalais

Beckett was the great literary presence Paul [Auster] had to over-come in order to be himself. I never had a writer-father, maybe because I'm a woman. I think most male writers have to struggle with what Harold Bloom called "the anxiety of influence," and it may be that, like it or not, men find themselves at the center of the culture in a way women don't. We're on the side. This doesn't mean that women don't have to fight influences, but rather that we are less likely to situate ourselves in some great tradition. For example, I love George Eliot, but I never had to get over her.

....

THE AMERICAN POETIC LINGUISTIC
Philip Levine, interviewed by Jim Schumock

I suppose it's safe to say that among your poetic fathers are Walt Whitman and William Carlos Williams. How exactly do you think their work opened up the life of poetry for you?

Well, they are two who are very important to me, but not particu-larly important stylistically. I think what I found in Whitman was that amazing ambition to write a poetry large enough to contain the United States. I haven't tried that. But I have tried to capture Detroit and the landscape of California, which is a powerful and extraordinary experience. There's something in Williams that just struck me from the first time I read him. It was his vision that poems were everywhere if we could just find them. They were just universal and they were available to us all. There was a way in which Williams authenticated me. It was that sense that that place, that Detroit, had earned its right to poetry, too. They felt like my fathers, my literary fathers.

On the other hand, I found other poetry that I thought was more beautiful, more beautifully crafted, more beautifully structured. There was Stevens, for example, Yeats, Hardy, and Dylan Thomas. They influenced me more in the way that I wrote line by line, I think, than either Whitman or Williams, but they were never as important to me. In the same way, a writer like Tolstoy was enormously important to me. You could never tell it by reading me, but there was something in him that suggested the largeness of this enterprise. What an enterprise it was to write. What an extraordinary thing that you could give your life to this writing. You could begin to change people. I felt his works were changing me. I felt that way about Chekhov, too. I was getting a different vision of what human nature was, what people were from writers like that. So they didn't influence me in any specific way that I can point to, but they invaded me in a profound sense and changed who I was.

They were also involved in the creation, along with Wallace Stevens and others, of an American poetic linguistic that brought us away from Europe and gave us a new accessibility to our own life and language, don't you think?

Oh yeah. You take Whitman in one of the prefaces to *Leaves of Grass*. He tells the American poet, "You know you must go among powerful, uneducated people." Well, I'd already done that.

I thought, Boy, I'm fulfilling that. He says, "Take off your hat to no one or nothing. Dismiss whatever insults your own soul." I said, "Well, I've already dismissed the U.S. Army." I thought, I'm doing what he wants me to do, I'm in his tradition. I thought, Okay, you're Pop, you're my pop, Walt. He certainly was a very great poet and he's one that I reread. I read "Song of Myself" every year, and I'm amazed by it. I'm just amazed by the power, the authority, the degree to which it thrills me and makes writing seem so worthwhile.

VIKRAM CHANDRA

interviewed by Jennifer Levasseur and Kevin Rabalais

Who are some of the writers you read growing up?

The first stories I remember hearing are tales from the great Indian epics, the *Mahabharat* and the *Ramayana*, which my mother, my grandmothers, and my aunts told to me. I grew these stories into my bones, and I live with them still.

Once I started to go to school, I read an eclectic mixture of Indian and Western authors. I read R. K. Narayan, Khushwant Singh, and Raja Rao, and, later, Salman Rushdie, Anita Desai, and Amitav Ghosh. I remember reading an abridged version of *The Adventures of Huckleberry Finn* in fifth grade, and went on from there to read Wharton, Fitzgerald, and Hemingway. In college, I started reading British novelists, and I am still a passionate admirer of Trollope and Thackeray.

WRITING ADVICE from Joyce Thompson

Do you suppose there was one moment, say in April of 1927, when every cultured person on Planet Earth agreed on a list of literary classics? Still, a shared frame of reference is a beautiful thing. It's probably useful to read the sacred writings of each of the world's major religions, as well as the top texts on each tradition's Greatest Hits list. That would include the Greeks, the Romans, the Slavs, Latin Americans, the Anglo-Saxons, the Indians, the Chinese, the East Africans, to name only a few. Don't be a Eurocentric snob.

Read those books by members of the just-previous generation that critics and publishers designated "keepers." The bright lights of the last generation are the ones you should aim to shoot out. Read the formal innovators. Incorporate what works. Learn from their mistakes. (For example, no one need ever write *Ulysses* again. It's been done.) Read widely and indiscriminately. Mix trash with "classics." How are they different? What do they have in common? Your answers to these questions will help shape your personal aesthetic.

KENT HARUF

interviewed by Jim Nashold

You mentioned that Hemingway and Faulkner had big influences on your career. What other writers have been important to you?

I read a lot of Flannery O'Connor at one time, and I've read Ray Carver thoroughly. I read all of Steinbeck and went through a Russian phase reading Tolstoy and Dostoyevsky, and more recently I've been reading a lot of Chekhov. Conrad, I like. Eudora Welty's been significant to me. The Canadian writer Alice Munro is one of the greatest living writers. At one time, I thought [Camus's] *The Stranger* was a great novel. I studied Sherwood Anderson's *Winesburg, Ohio*, and liked it tremendously, and also liked Ford Madox Ford's *The Good Soldier*.

What books are you reading right now?

I've just finished reading the new biography that you wrote on Dylan Thomas, which corrected some misconceptions about Thomas. Recently, I read *Snow Falling on Cedars*, and I've just started re-reading Cormac McCarthy's *The Crossing* for the second or third time.

ESSENTIAL READING FOR MODERN WRITERS

Thomas McGuane, interviewed by Jim Schumock

You've given rather broad credit to your literary fathers, among them Malcolm Lowry. Do you think there's any novel more read by novel writers and less by novel readers than *Under the Volcano*?

That's really an interesting way to put that. There's no doubt that it's essential reading for modern writers. It's one of the books you read and go back to your own work and say, "Now, what changes can we make in what we've been doing?" A serious writer could scarcely go through that book without contemplating changes in his own work.

....

TOBIAS WOLFF
interviewed by Jim Schumock

If someone were taking a year off to learn to write short stories...

Just a year? Make it twenty.

What stories or collections would you recommend?

Dubliners. Chekhov's stories, as many as a person can read. Tolstoy's "Master and Man" and "The Death of Ivan Ilych." I would recommend a good selection of Maupassant stories. *Winesburg, Ohio* by Sherwood Anderson, and "In Our Time" and "Up in Michigan" by Hemingway. F. Scott Fitzgerald's stories: "The Rich

Boy," "Diamond as Big as the Ritz," "Crazy Sunday,"and "An Alcoholic Case." Katherine Anne Porter's stories, just about all of them. Flannery O'Connor's stories—stories like "Parker's Back," "Revelation," "A Good Man is Hard to Find," "Good Country People"—classics of the genre. Raymond Carver's stories, and Richard Ford's *Rock Springs*. I would also recommend Dorothy Allison's great collection *Trash*. It's a much-ignored book, which she drew on very heavily for *Bastard Out of Carolina*. I think the book of stories is the better book, myself. Mary Gaitskill's *Bad Behavior*. Thom Jones's *The Pugilist at Rest* and *Cold Snap*. Denis Johnson's *Jesus' Son* and Lorrie Moore's *Like Life*, especially the title novella. I could go on and on.

If you were to be abandoned alone in a cabin in the North Cascades for the rest of your life, and could only take along two books and one piece of music, which ones would you take?

I would die trying to choose.

....

Melissa Pritchard: The stories in *Spirit Sei-zures*—my first collection—were modeled after those written by authors I'd read and admired. I'd say, "Now, I'm going to attempt a Gogol, Tolstoy, Flaubert sort of story." Model-ing my work on the stories of others was how I learned to write fiction. With my second collection, *Instinct for Bliss*, I left imitative writing behind for the most part.

as interviewed by Leslie A. Wootten

....

CHAPTER

WRITING WHAT YOU KNOW

Henry J. Burmeister, 1991

Kathleen Tyau: There are many stories I'm not able to write yet because I just don't know enough. I know you're supposed to write about what you know, but I tend to get obsessed with what I don't understand. The man who died young and looks angry in his photographs. The Chinese woman who came from South Africa to Hawaii to look for a husband. There are others, but I can't talk about them. I need to write them.

as interviewed by Linda B. Swanson-Davies

LYNN FREED
interviewed by Sarah Anne Johnson

You stated once that the real world of your childhood—a large subtropical port on the Indian Ocean, with beaches and bush and sugar cane and steaming heat, a strict Anglican girls' school, massive family gatherings on Friday nights and Jewish holidays, and then your parents' theater world—did not exist in literature available to you, and that you didn't think it should. How did you make the leap from that line of thinking to actually creating fiction that inhabits that world?

I grew up in an ex-British colony, on British literature, with the idea that Britain was the source of all things worthy in the world of letters. By the same token, things South African were considered decidedly second rate. There were a few exceptions, of course—Laurens van der Post, Olive Schreiner. But, in the main, we looked north for received literature, and it seemed right and good to do so.

When I began to write real stories myself, I ventured tentatively into home territory, but the work was very poor, very weighed down by the predictable and the worthy. So I struck out and wrote two novels with an American cast—novels about women breaking out of the domestic mold. My first novel was in galleys when, one evening, I was having dinner with Gail Godwin. I was telling her about my family, my background. Then she asked whether I had written about them, and when I said no, she said, "Well, for God's sake!" So home I went and began *Home Ground*. One finds permission to write when one is ready to receive it, I suppose.

This brings us to the issue of authorial invisibility. In writing material that takes place in your hometown, in a family similar to your own, how do you, the author, keep yourself out of the picture?

I don't. I'm in every picture. But I'm in disguise.

....

PUTTING YOURSELF AT RISK
Russell Banks, interviewed by Rob Trucks

I write books that have an effect on me, and that's the main reason why I write—for how they will affect me. Not thrill me, although I hope that will happen, nor move me, but so that it will make me a more intelligent person, and maybe even, if possible, a more decent person. Writing *Cloudsplitter*, for instance, made me more intelligent about a number of things: about race, about relations between fathers and sons, about sex—Owen, after all, has a sexual identity that plays a significant role—about the interweaving between sex and race in America, about American history. It just made me more intelligent about those things, because I put myself at open-ended risk in the writing of the book, and that's what the book's about. That I'm working within the disciplines of an art means it may connect with other human beings in a way that resembles the way the writing of it connected to me.

JULIA ALVAREZ

interviewed by Mike Chasar and Constance Pierce

That story in *García Girls* is, in part, a critique of the Dominican Republic I grew up in, where there was such a love affair with everything European and American and a real deprecating of our own traditions.

I think our racism is a different kind of racism. In my family, for instance, there are very dark cousins, aunts, uncles. You would never refuse entry to your house to someone because he or she was dark. He or she is also your cousin or uncle or aunt! Everybody's so interrelated. But there is an aesthetic racism, though it wouldn't keep you from getting ahead. Class is what's going to keep you from getting ahead more than color. But then the more powerful classes tend to be the white classes and lighter-skinned classes.

If you look at the Dominican history books and pictures of our presidents, most of them are mulatto, from mulatto to black. Because the Spaniards came and, unlike the American settlers, they didn't bring families and wives to create a new England here. They came as conquistadores and they got involved with native women or with black women, and so they created a mulatto country. That's who we are. But within that, there have been later migrants who came in, and some of them with money, who gave some of us a lighter skin. Racism feels different there, but it's something I haven't yet figured out.

TIM O'BRIEN
interviewed by Jim Schumock

My interest, as a writer, isn't in answering questions anymore. It never really was. Instead, I'm trying to go after—to open up the boundaries of—what we don't know. I think of the end of *Huckleberry Finn*: We don't know what happens to Huck Finn once he lights out for the Territories. And we don't know what happens to Jake and Lady Brett at the end of *The Sun Also Rises* after they get into that cab. There's mystery in the world, things we just don't know.

A. J. Verdelle: When you're writing, you have to write as if you're God. John Oliver Killens said that. It's a technical point, really; write as if you know everything: when, where, what happened in the past, what will happen in the future. Write without tentativeness; write with certainty.

as interviewed by Nancy Middleton

THOM JONES

interviewed by Jim Schumock

Beyond Vietnam, a lot of your stories have to do with illnesses and doctors.

Illnesses … there are so many of them, and I'll sit and read … I like to read tropical medicine because those are the really great ones. I'm astonished and horrified. It's sort of like reading about a train wreck or something. I have a tremendous imagination, am an incredible hypochondriac, but now that I've lived this long, it's all my fears coming true. I'm really sick, so now I read about diabetes, which I have, and epilepsy, which I have, and depression, which I have, and all these things. I wonder how I go from day to day sometimes.

I think doctors are fascinating. A lot of doctors say, "You write like you're an insider. You really know what you're doing."

CHAPTER

5

TABOOS AND SECRETS

*Werner Burmeister with Caroline
and Harold Wyman, 1927*

SAYING THE UNSAYABLE

Vikram Chandra

interviewed by Jennifer Levasseur and Kevin Rabalais

—⋙◆⋘—

In *Red Earth and Pouring Rain*, the characters use stories to say things they would not otherwise disclose. What do you think stories enable us to do?

Stories let us say things that we might otherwise censor, hide even from ourselves. So we tell secrets in stories, but we also say that which is unsayable. Life visits upon us the tragedy of passing days, the inescapable death that comes to us, the unfairness of history and suffering—and in stories, we shape this chaos; we form our relationship with all these inexplicable, unsayable things.

....

BREAKING YOUR OWN RULES

Melissa Pritchard, interviewed by Leslie A. Wootten

—⋙◆⋘—

How did you feel after the story ["The Widow's Poet"] was over?

I felt unhinged, almost crazy for having written it. Self-censorship immediately started swirling in my head. I worried what people would think of me when they read it and whether anyone would publish it. Eventually, I was able to face down my fears, and tell myself that I can write anything I want if I'm willing to take responsibility for it. The decision was liberating. As it turned out, *Boulevard* published the story, and it was nominated for a Pushcart Prize. It was probably the hardest story I've ever written, but with it—as with "Funktionslust"—I was able to break free of inhibiting rules I'd subconsciously set up for myself.

WHEN WHAT HAS BEEN HIDDEN IS REVEALED

Elizabeth Cox, interviewed by Sarah Anne Johnson

In each of your novels, and in many of your short stories, there is a mystery or a missing piece of information that creates suspense. In *Familiar Ground*, it's wondering what happened that night to Drue. In *The Ragged Way People Fall Out of Love*, there is the question of whether the couple will reunite, and then the real mystery surrounding the disappearance of their son. In *Night Talk*, there's the question of who killed Turnbull, among others. Do you have this mystery in mind when you sit down to write, or does it come up as the story unfolds?

It comes up as the story unfolds, and very often what happens is a surprise to me. I did not know who killed Drue until the main character knew. When the young boy in RW was killed, I thought he was dead until he came back. I realized it as he walked toward the house. I discover as I go along, and it seems to be the best way for me. I know that people create outlines and write in an orderly fashion. Any fashion is more orderly than my own process. Secrets have power, and I discover the secrets along with the characters. I don't think about the "mysteries" occurring in my books, but I am aware of the importance of secrets.

What does the mystery bring to the narrative besides suspense?

It connects the reader to whatever secrets they have, and hopefully reveals the true hiddenness of things, or tells us something about the parts of ourselves we want to hide. I'm interested in what happens when what has been hidden is finally revealed, because with revelation often some new secret is unfolded. Maybe the secrets never stop revealing themselves.

Jayne Anne Phillips: All through my work there has been this sense of the confidant inside the parent-child relationship, that double burden of being the one who is chosen or selected for special attention, for secrets, for confidences, the one who holds everyone else's life story. It's the writer-in-the-family idea.

as interviewed by Sarah Anne Johnson

CHARLES BAXTER

interviewed by Linda B. Swanson-Davies

Throughout *The Feast of Love*, you were able to get people to make self-disclosures that were so amazing—I don't really understand why it worked so well. I wouldn't usually believe a story where you have somebody telling intimate things about themselves that they'd rather not even know. How did you do that?

I imagined for myself a scene—let's say a bar around eleven-thirty at night, it's getting late. You know, the fans are rotating in the ceiling. Most of the people have gone and someone is sitting there, telling me things that are amazing and true. The way that an old friend may sooner or later open up to you and tell you some feature of her life that you've always suspected but waited years to hear from her. I think in stories and novels we often wait for that moment, signature statements, signature actions. David saying, "It wasn't that I hunted, I was a hunter. That was my essence. That was what I did. And in some sense it's still what I do." I think it's wonderful when characters open up themselves, because it's as if something that has been hidden has bubbled up to the surface and—because it's been hidden—it's a treasure. And you've waited to hear it.

. . . .

WHAT WOULD MY MOTHER THINK?

Lynne Sharon Schwartz
interviewed by Nancy Middleton

⟹◇⟸

You said that around age thirty-two, you decided that you could either "be good or be a writer."

Yes, well, that's a hard one. I'm getting better at it. You can't be nice and please people and also be a writer. It's very hard to overcome the desire to please. Women are brought up to be nice, take care of things, smooth things over, be ladylike, etc., etc. It takes endless work to undo that. It goes so deep that you can be intellectually quite aware of it and yet keep doing it. It becomes a reflex, like using your fork instead of your hands. You do it, and later you realize what you've done and you can't undo it.

Do you feel this held you back in your writing? Did you worry about hurting people's feelings?

No, I wouldn't say that. I always wrote what I wanted to write. But it was a struggle to feel free enough to write it. During the writing process, I would have to constantly beat back feelings of "That isn't very nice," or "What would my mother think?" I knew enough to say, "Oh, forget all that." But it made the writing process longer, more arduous.

THE RESPONSIBILITY OF REPRESENTATION

Edwidge Danticat, interviewed by Sarah Anne Johnson

⇒◈⇐

In *Breath, Eyes, Memory*, you depict a mother-daughter relationship in which the mother tries to guard her daughter's sexuality. How did you arrive at this theme, and is it something that is primarily true of Haitian women?

I had a lot of trouble when that book came out. Many Haitian women were angry because they felt I was branding them all with this experience, when that practice of testing a girl's virginity happens only in some families, in some milieus, and happened much more in the past than it does now. This is something you encounter when you write from within a specific group, from inside the veil. People feel like you're telling tales out of school or telling stories about them. One of the issues that I learned with this book is that when you write, you have a responsibility to the characters, but when you write from within a community, you also have the responsibility of representation. People feel that everything you write is a kind of anthropology. But to answer your question, I decided to write about this because I knew someone it happened to, and it was something I wanted to explore. And I thought it was something a lot of women could identify with, whether or not their sexuality is monitored in that specific way.

How do you deal with that pressure? How does it impact what you decide to write?

I'm completely uncensored when I'm writing. But I worry to death when a piece is about to come out. I really try not to censor myself and not worry during the writing process, though.

In the moment of writing, I let it be. The voices of dissent are always more vocal than the voices of agreement. At the same time that people were very angry about this, there were people who identified with the narrative, but these voices don't shout, they whisper. When you're writing, you have to trust on some level that your soul knows certain truths. Writing is such a mysterious thing. Language and ideas come to you from the air, and you have to allow for that to happen. You have to let yourself be free to receive them.

How did you decide to include the epilogue at the end of the novel?

After having so many fights with so many people, I was getting frustrated. I did a reading with an older woman writer and someone got up and cursed her out about a book she wrote in 1969, the year I was born. I sat there while she tried to defend herself and the choices she made in that story, and I thought, I don't want to be responding to these questions on *Breath, Eyes, Memory* when I'm seventy-five. I was frightened by that exchange. I decided to put the epilogue as a kind of response to the questions I was getting. There was an opportunity when the book was going into another printing. I wrote something in the voice of the book rather than an essay, so that when people read the book there will be a response to those questions. At the same time, you can't control everything. There are things in a story that you and I aren't aware of but someone can read it and respond to something you didn't know was there. This issue was such a public debate for me though that I chose to address it where it began, in the book itself.

ALBERTO RÍOS

interviewed by Susan McInnis

I think I write a great deal about secrets as well as borders. And this was an exploration of my own questions: What are my secret lives? What are my borders?

I am always looking for some kind of truth, though not necessarily accuracy. It didn't have to happen to me in that way. It didn't all have to happen to me. Nonetheless, what I write about is all mine. It reveals a truth. But I'm not a journalist. I'm not reporting anything that happened. Still, I'm talking just exactly about what happened. Picasso said, "Art is the lie that tells the truth."

The known piece and the unknown piece, the secret and the non-secret: when you put those things together, it's like adding a set of lenses. The act brings that faraway thing, whatever it might be, closer, like binoculars. I love that. I love doing it as a writer. I love looking at the magic of binoculars. I mean, to bring a thing closer is extraordinary, and when I can do that in writing, it just makes me want to do it again.

Secrets are always on the border, on the edge. Somehow, a secret is that faraway thing that is not faraway at all. It's right in front of us, but we try to make it faraway, and there's something both right and wrong about that. I don't know which it is, but the moment you can bring that faraway thing, that secret, up close and look at it, you've done a kind of magic. I don't think I'm capable of looking at a secret and not seeing what is positive about it. That's just in my character. If I have to think about how

I write, it's not to expose something that shouldn't be exposed. I just start writing about a thing, and, in the same way that plot is organic, the thing I'm writing about comes out. I don't have to impose it. I also know I'm going to take care of that secret, even though I might talk about it.

....

TIM O'BRIEN
interviewed by Jim Schumock

I remember reading, in Lloyd and Lewis's *The Tainted War*, a quote from you: "If you want to understand what happened at My Lai, you must first understand what happened on the training fields of Fort Lewis, Washington." What was it that you saw happen?

Well, things being yelled at you, like: "The spirit of the bayonet is to kill." Yelling these things at the top of our lungs: "The spirit of the bayonet is to kill, kill, kill." If you went through basic training and then through advanced infantry training, as I did, there's this sound in your head, the word "kill," that represents the military's effort to make you into what they want you to be—a kind of mindless killer. And when you're transported over to a place like Vietnam, where the enemy's all around you and in the earth beneath you, and where you can't distinguish friend from foe, when you walk into a village and you can't tell who's with you or against, a kind of frustration and rage begins to build up as people die. That is taken out not on the enemy, because you couldn't find the enemy in Vietnam—we didn't know who was the enemy—but instead, you take it out on what presents itself. Trees, hootches, little kids, pigs, and Quang Ngai, the province itself, became the enemy finally; the soil, the paddies, the place became the enemy.

How do you think the men you were in combat with would describe you in terms of bravery or conscience?

Pretty normal, in terms of bravery. I didn't do anything special. I did what we all did—I'd stand up under fire, and go where I had to go, and pull the trigger when I had to pull it. Never aiming at anything, because we never had anything to aim at! Mortar rounds would come flying in, and there'd be flashes out of the hedgerows, and landmines exploding ... In terms of conscience, I was really opposed to that war, and I got more and more opposed the more I saw of it.

That is to say, even in the most physical sense, there was no sense of accomplishment. You didn't gain ground and hold it, as in World War II or Korea. You didn't feel that you'd accomplished, on a given day, anything. You'd get up in the morning, go into a village, search it. Somebody might die, somebody might not die; you'd leave the village. And as soon as you left it, it reverted to the enemy. Then you'd come back a week, two weeks, later, and you'd search the same village. Somebody might die, somebody might not, and you'd leave it again. There was an aimlessness to it, a kind of wandering, chasing-hummingbirds feeling to it. You could never find anything, accomplish anything, and it felt senseless and purposeless even in the physical sense, not to mention the psychological sense.

Without the moral qualms of Ron Ridenhour, we might never have learned about the massacre at My Lai. It seems to me that Vietnam is an anomaly in that there were a lot of veterans who accused themselves of war crimes. Why do you think that occurred?

I think out of guilt, out of a sense of reality, the realities around them. If we took, for example, sniper fire—it got to the point where we would just simply step back, call in jets, and watch the napalm. And we'd hear pigs squealing, babies crying, women screaming. We had firepower to burn, and we used it to burn, literally. You come back from a place like that with a feeling of having accomplished nothing, and you feel like you want to confess to things. You can only bottle it up so long. My character John Wade tried to bottle it up for twenty years, from everyone—that he participated in the massacre at My Lai. Even from himself, he tried to bottle it up. To be loved.

....

THE NECESSITY OF BEING DISTURBED
Toi Derricotte, interviewed by Susan McInnis

I remember, when I was fourteen—I was writing since I was about ten—and my cousin Melvin was in medical school then, and, you know, I admired him. He was taking a course in embryology in Chicago. He took me to the Museum of Natural History where they have the fetuses—the embryos—all the way from conception to birth. Nobody had ever talked to me about these things. So I was really impressed. I just knew that Melvin would be the one to show my poems to—because I wasn't showing anybody at that time. And so I said to myself, He's going to appreciate what's hidden and buried and mysterious.

Because he has all these true things in front of him, right?

Yes. He had shown me these things, and so I showed him my poems and he said, "These are really sick! These are really morbid!" And the point was: I was not writing about the things that made you happy to hear about. One of the burdens that kids have is that they're supposed to be happy. If they're happy, their parents think, or their friends or their relatives think, that they've done a good job and they're being good parents. It's a heck of a burden for kids. That's why I love to teach poetry to them. Fourth graders. Fifth graders. There's so much of this powerful questioning about life and observation that can come out in creative work. So often, it can't come out in our relations with the people we love the most. They don't want us to be disturbed. They don't want us to be unhappy. But that's just a part of experience.

It's an interesting thought that people don't want children—or the people they love—to be unhappy because it's a reflection on themselves.

Exactly. Exactly. And parents worry, you know, if their children are talking about dead birds.

But so in that situation with Melvin, either I could stop writing or I could write about what Melvin wanted—I mean, I would kind of know what he would want me to write about—or I could go back in hiding.

You went and hid somewhere?

I went and hid somewhere.

FREDERICK REIKEN

interviewed by Eric Wasserman

In "The Ocean," you implied the sexual content, but with *The Odd Sea*, you made the choice to graphically depict sexuality. Has your sensibility changed since your first novel?

While writing *The Odd Sea*, my standpoint was that I was dealing with adolescent boys and that naturally adolescent boys think about sex a lot, and hence a very frank—I certainly wouldn't call it graphic—exploration of sexuality seemed a legitimate approach. Looking at it now, I still don't think there are any gratuitous scenes. But in hindsight, there are definitely some things I would cut, one or two images that to me now seem excessive—that is, moments where the novel itself lapses into a bit of adolescent behavior. So, yes, I'm now trying to deal with sexuality in a more subtle way, and that will probably continue.

SUSAN RICHARDS SHREVE

interviewed by Katherine Perry Harris

Several of your novels, including *The Train Home* and *Children of Power*, are based in Washington, D.C. *Children of Power* clearly has a political undertone, with its portrayal of a disgraced Joseph McCarthy at the end of his career. What is it like to be a fiction writer in a political city like Washington, where character is so often compromised?

There are wonderful things about growing up in Washington, D.C., raising children here, and becoming a writer. Anonymity for one.

This is a company town. I don't belong to the company and have, therefore, a kind of delicious freedom. But as a company town, in which character is indeed compromised and most particularly homogenized, "character" as we expect to find it in fiction has only a walk-on part. Oddness, eccentricity, individuality—all that is essential for a compelling story are slipped under the rug in this bureaucratic city. But Washington, D.C., is where I grew up, and like any place of childhood, it is neither ordinary nor extraordinary if you have been around long enough to feel at home.

And for secrets—which is at the heart of a lot of fiction, my own included—this isn't a bad place to live and listen.

....

THE TREASURE OF BANNED LITERATURE
Abdelrahman Munif, interviewed by Michael Upchurch

In most Arab countries, your fiction has been banned. Your books are published in Beirut. You've lived in Syria, Egypt, Iraq, Belgrade, and other places—a very confusing situation for a writer. What audience do you have in mind?

For Arab writers, especially for someone like me, I'm aiming at Arab readers throughout the region. I'm certainly not just aiming at Syria or Iraq or Saudi Arabia. As for the other thing: In our country, a banned book is the most widely read book, which shows that it is not easy to restrict or confine a book. From what I know and what I hear, one of the more common gifts among Saudis and their friends are banned books—and particularly my books.

So a novelist has a wide field in front of him in which to work, with the assumption that it's impossible, on the part of leaders, to prevent a reader from reaching the book. It's stupid of them to think such things, especially now with all of the means of communication and ways of transmitting ideas in this age. For example, the memorandum [concerning human-rights abuses in Saudi Arabia] that I sent to the 1993 Conference on Human Rights in Vienna was one of the most widely circulated documents of these times in Saudi Arabia. But I wasn't the one doing the work—it was the fax machine! It's like a bird; it's like a plane. There's no confining or restricting it.

....

HANDLING A DELICATE SCENE
Ha Jin, interviewed by Sarah Anne Johnson

The rape scene between Geng Yang and Manna [in *Waiting*] is difficult to read, but it also seems well balanced in terms of graphic sexual content, physical details, and emotional responses. Was this scene difficult to render, and how did you maintain restraint writing such potentially volatile material?

It was difficult to write. I paused for a long time to think about it, but then I realized that if the novel didn't have that scene, the whole book would be too gentle. It would be like a Victorian novel. The acts of the two male characters contribute to this. Geng Yang is the embodiment of evil, and there's ambiguity about whether there's attraction from Manna's side. The drama had reached a point where I had to have an emotionally tense scene. Also, in terms of narrative drive, the book reached a point where the momentum slowed down. I needed a very dramatic moment in order to sustain the narration. After all this consideration, I decided to just go ahead and write the scene. Of course, it would be very vulgar if I didn't do a good job. I worked on it many times.

AIMING AT THE TRUTH

Ernest Gaines, interviewed by Michael Upchurch

One thing that struck me while reading the early books is that they deal in a pretty rough, raw way with issues within the black community. "Three Men," in *Bloodline*, has black-on-black violence. *Catherine Carmier* has what's now referred to as the "color complex" as the engine behind its plot, and it's dealt with very openly and disturbingly. Two questions: Did you ever have people saying, "No, you shouldn't really bring these things out in the open—that makes black people look bad"? And did you ever have trouble getting some of your strong language and sexual content past the publisher back then?

I never had any problems with publishers about that. I was told very early on, by family, that I should tell people I came from New Orleans instead of coming from the country, that I should not disturb things, that there were certain things that you should not talk about. But I knew I wanted to be a writer, and if I couldn't get my feet dirty, there was no point in trying to write. If you couldn't go against advice like that, that keeps you from aiming at the truth—whether you get the truth or not—there was no point in trying to write.

SPACE FOR UNCIVILIZED THOUGHTS

Matthew Sharpe, interviewed by Sherry Ellis

⇒◆⇐

Your characters have what are often considered unorthodox sexual relationships. In *The Sleeping Father*, Lila Schwartz has sex with her gardener and then with her ex-husband's physician's father. A speech therapist has sex with her patient's teenage son. In *Nothing Is Terrible*, ten-year-old Mary has a sexual relationship with her thirty-six-year-old female teacher. To what extent do you believe this sub-theme of unusual sexual relationships stretches the boundaries of these novels as a whole?

I think I'm discovering that I am a fairly traditional novel writer, at least in the forms I use. I teach in the graduate program at Bard College and if you really want to see experimental writers, check out some of the Bard authors. They are far more adventurous in their storytelling than I am.

I guess in terms of the content of the novel, I think of literature as a civilized space in which to express uncivilized thoughts and feelings. It's not something that I set out to do consciously; it's not that I set out to stretch the form of the novel by having these transgressive sexual acts. One of the ways that narratologists think about stories is that there has to be some violation of the social norm to get the story going. I was walking down the street when such and such happened. I think one of the ways to understand something about whatever phenomenon you're investigating is to imagine an extreme case of it, something that pushes the limits. So to have a transgressive sort of sex act between an adult and a child, or between a doctor/therapist and a patient, would be ways of defamiliarizing the phenomenon in question.

EXPLORING SALVATION

Jayne Anne Phillips
interviewed by Sarah Anne Johnson

Both Alma and Buddy [in *Shelter*] carry unbearable secrets, and while Alma needs a spiritual unburdening—she "wanted a series of screams that opened out until the earth shook"—Buddy needs a physical salvation. He needs to be left alone by his stepfather. What drew you to exploring the different dimensions and manifestations of this issue in these two very different characters?

We all stand at the apex of our own lives. Lines are intersecting and we're standing at the center. Alma has been a confidante and a witness. She's the writer in the book, obviously. And Buddy has a kind of every-child sensibility. Alma's working with the burden of her mother's life, the burden of the secret, while Buddy's working with not only the burden of the secret, but with the burden of needing to save his mother, which is pretty impossible at age seven or eight. Yet he manages to do it. So they're standing at different points along the same spectrum. That's how books should work. They let the reader inhabit different stages, different movements through a spectrum, through an arc concurrently, so that there's an entire journey that the reader takes that is like different facets of light coming into a point.

CHARLES BAXTER
interviewed by Stewart David Ikeda

Beneath the needs, fears, and desires of the characters, there are the secrets.

Well, I think there are more secrets now than ever before, and one reason is that public discourse in this country is worse than it has ever been. There is less language of common intimacy, I believe, than has ever been the case. Conversation is assumed to be proper only if it keeps the secrets out. Television has probably reduced our ability to converse. It does encourage monologues. Which means that all the secrets are being rushed into recovery programs, twelve-step movements, and therapy in various forms—or conversations that end up sounding like therapy. I think fiction is a wonderful place for the demonstration or dramatization of secrets that are both dead and alive. I'm not the first person to say this. A great, great story like Joyce's "The Dead" is built around a secret; a story like "Bartleby, the Scrivener" is about a secret. A lot of stories have secrets as an engine for the movement of theme, character, and emotion.

CHAPTER

6

WRITING
AS ART

One Sunday in the thirties

ROBERT OLEN BUTLER

interviewed by Linda B. Swanson-Davies

One way I explain the difference between fiction writing as an art form and, say, instructive writing or genre fiction—and I love to read those, too, but there's a difference in the animal, and you have to understand that—is that the genre writers and even the Jean Paul Sartres of the world know, before they begin to write a word, the effect they wish to have on their readers. The horror writer wants to scare the hell out of you. Jean Paul Sartre, well, he wants to scare the hell out of you, but also to demonstrate the cosmic varieties of existentialism as a mode of philosophical thought. Those writers construct an object to achieve a preconceived effect.

The artist, though, does not know. The artist simply responds to the chaos of a life on planet Earth, but has a profound sense that behind the chaos there's meaning and order. The artist is driven to try to articulate that vision of order by going back to the way life is lived, which is in the moment, in your body, through the senses, and pull out bits and pieces of that flow of sensual experience and reshape them into these moment-to-moment sensual objects, which are novels and stories. That process of creating is as much an act of exploration as it is of expression for the artist. The artist does not know until the vision is there on the page. ...

[There's a] problem with the creative-writing programs in this day and age. Now, they teach craft and technique—and absolutely they must—but in so many workshops these are taught to the exclusion of virtually everything else. Writers come out of those workshops believing that if you just willfully apply enough craft and technique to a manuscript, it can be made into a work of art, and it cannot.

Right. Sometimes we see beautiful writing, but it doesn't necessarily engage us in any meaningful way.

Dead in the center. It's amazing how many people writing, teaching, reviewing books—especially reviewing books—have lost their ability to have an aesthetic response. As a result, many wonderful works of art are undervalued, and many works that actually are finely crafted fail as objects that will endure.

....

THE MAGIC IN CRAFT

Stuart Dybek
interviewed by Jennifer Levasseur and Kevin Rabalais

⸺◆⸺

What are some of the things you don't want a student to leave your class without understanding about the craft of writing?

I want the student to realize there's magic in craft. Craft makes us better than we are, smarter, wiser, sharpens observation into vision, quickens reflexes, allowing an intellectual activity to be more blessedly instinctive. The practice of the craft of any art is so allied with not simply the expression of imagination but the very experience of imagination, as to become indistinguishable from imagination.

As a reader, what do you expect from a short story?

As a reader, I hope for a short story to surprise me into a more intense vision of life. But then that's as much a response to what

I expect from art in general. But why be so reductive? Poe demanded an effect from a story. Stories can console, enlighten, seduce, mystify, broaden one's sympathies, enlarge one's experience. I don't insist that a story deeply move me; there are, after all, other kinds of more intellectual pleasures, especially in a medium like language. But by temperament, I do favor stories that communicate strong emotion and strong imagination. And in this age in which agendas and attitude take the place of individual thought, imagination and strong emotion are, unfortunately, not especially typical of either literature or some of the other arts, such as painting.

SUSAN RICHARDS SHREVE
interviewed by Katherine Perry Harris

How do you feel about our culture's attitude toward the arts, and, in particular, funding for the arts? On the whole, do you think these are good times in which to be a writer?

The deep-seated American suspicion of funding for the arts is possibly locked in our Puritan history and persists in spite of our fundamental belief in freedom of expression. There is a fear that the artist is dangerous to the status quo, free from social limitations, by nature a furtive Peeping Tom, on the outside, looking in.

Art is considered a threat to order. The artist is interested in new ways of seeing, is suspicious of institutions, and is stubbornly self-reliant—if not in life, at least in work. Funding for the arts—by this I mean federal funding, particularly—will probably continue to be a source of argument. But we are more sophisticated in general than we were when I was growing up. We have faith in the arts as the center of humanism and civilization. Perhaps there are more true believers now who think that for any culture to fail its artists is to fail itself.

LIFE ON THE GROUND

Robert Olen Butler, interviewed by Heather Iarusso

Have you ever contemplated what your writing would have been like if you had not gone to Vietnam?

If I had been given the power when I was younger to look ahead in my life and have a list of the major events—three broken marriages and being sent off to war in Southeast Asia and several other things—and had been given the power to scratch three things off that list, in an inevitable, human, self-protective way, I certainly would have chosen to take off Vietnam. There's no question in my mind that if I had, I would not be an artist today. I would certainly be an intense and deep appreciator of art, but I would not have created anything like my body of work. That alternative life experience would have been a safer, less painful path. I would have gotten a PhD and taught somewhere. I would have gone from school to school to school to work, and if I had a writing career at all, it probably would have followed a track that you can see in some writers. I might have eventually written a pretty good first novel about growing up in a steel-mill town, as I did. The second novel might have been derivative of that, and the third novel would have been a novel about an English professor having an affair with a student. The fourth novel would have been a novel about a novelist, and that would have been about the end. You can just see the gradual shutting down of the vision of the world, and I think that today a lot of writers have that problem. They have the opportunity readily available to go from one enclosed environment to another enclosed environment. There needs to be a seeking out of life experience. ... It used to be that when you read the miniature biographies in anthologies of famous and highly regarded literary artists, no matter how short the biography was, there would always be a sentence in there saying that he drove an ambulance in Italy and was a newspaper reporter in Toronto, or that he picked grapes in California, or that he worked in a powerhouse in Mississippi and painted houses. The assumption was that those real-world, close-to-where-life-is-lived experiences were a necessary part of the education of a writer. I think that's absolutely true and will always remain true.

MARY YUKARI WATERS

interviewed by Sherry Ellis

Did anyone read your early work and give you feedback?

Yes, I was in a workshop for many years with a teacher named Tom Filer. He held it in his home, with the same group of students every year, and that was where I did most of my early writing. It was a real sanctuary. He'd read us letters from Chekhov, or Faulkner's Nobel Prize acceptance speech. We never discussed publishing, or any of the business aspects of writing; it was always about the art. And after the workshop session, we'd snack on wine and appetizers. Tom opened up a whole new world for me. I consider myself very lucky that I stumbled across him.

....

THE WRITER AS MEDIUM

Lynne Sharon Schwartz
interviewed by Nancy Middleton

I don't like the notion that writers are special people. There's been a democratization of the arts, and yet you do need some talent; on the other hand, I don't believe writers have deeper feelings, more profound thoughts, or that their experiences are somehow more meaningful. What writers have is a particular talent, like a musician, say, of using words. I don't believe in exalting the artist. You can exalt the work—there are books I could worship—but never people. It's almost as if the people were the medium. Once the book exists, they're the medium through which we've received this book, this experience.

....

GETTING PAST THE MIND

Thomas E. Kennedy
interviewed by Linda B. Swanson-Davies

One thing that I find very important—and this might not be the case for all writers, but it is the case for me—is to learn to get past the mind, to get past that sense that everything should have a clear meaning. Some things are complex. Some things are mysterious. Not everything is clearly accessible. Life is a mystery. People were talking for some years about moral fiction, and, certainly, who can say that fiction should not be moral? But what worries me about that idea of moral fiction is the sense of imposing some kind of superior framework on the art of writing, which I do not think is a good thing. I don't think that makes a fiction more moral. In fact, it can be a way of falsifying artistic truth.

....

CHARLES BAXTER

interviewed by Linda B. Swanson-Davies

With Chloé in *The Feast of Love*, the first reaction most readers will have, I thought, would be, Here's this young woman, only about nineteen or twenty, and she's infatuated with this guy Oscar. Oscar's infatuated with her. They're not going to be anything more than comic relief in this book. We don't have to take her seriously, partly because she seems to be flighty. And partly because she's innocent. And partly because we generally don't take young people like this especially seriously. But what if you defamiliarize things a bit? What if it turns out that they actually know something, the two of them? About real passion that the other characters in the novel only dimly understand. What if it's Chloé and Oscar, who look like nitwits at first, who really have got the secret to something? What if you write it that way? So that's what I did.

It certainly worked. I think you're right about how easy it is to dismiss a girl in a coffee shop, who's dressed a little silly and talks funny.

We don't pay any attention to those people, but the whole point of fiction is to make us pay attention. To bring our attention in a society full of distractions back to people we wouldn't have noticed otherwise.

Right. In real life. Is that one of your goals when you're writing fiction? Do you want to change me, as a reader?

Only insofar as I would like you to take the story away with you in your head, to remember it and conceivably to recognize part of your own life in the story, and to recognize the story in part of your own life. So that someday it may happen that you will be in the situation and you'll say, This is a little bit like one of Charlie's stories. In the way that people say, My God, this is like a Hitchcock movie.

Right. Right! Not very often but—

Not very often, and it's not necessarily the kind of experience you want to have, but one of the characteristics of art is to color our experience so that it begins to look or to feel like something we once saw in a book or a movie or a painting. You know? When you're walking downtown now, sometimes you'll say, That coffee shop looks like a Hopper painting. That's what art can do. It can give you a frame of reference for certain kinds of experiences.

Kind of thickens our lives up.

Right.

Maria Flook: The art process itself is the painful thing—the day-to-day struggle to deliver the level of writing I want. In James Lord's *A Giacometti Portrait*, he quotes the artist's recognition about the burden of trying to work at our highest level: "The very measure of our creative drive is that we longingly dream of one day being free of it." I really understand that. I want to be able to stop when at last I'm satisfied with the work on the page. But the thing is, the art spirit never lets you feel you've done as well as you can do tomorrow.

as interviewed by Sarah Anne Johnson

ANALYSIS AS AN ACT OF MURDER
Lynne Sharon Schwartz
interviewed by Nancy Middleton

Nowadays, academics—especially the ones who are into deconstruction and so forth—seem to go so far into the intellectual, cerebral analysis of a book that they lose the sense of what a book is, that a book is supposed to transport you, take you out of yourself, do something to you that you cannot analyze.

Of course you can endlessly analyze a work of art. But the core of art has to be mysterious. That's why it matters to us: because it's something that is new and unresolved every time. It's something you've never experienced before, no matter how many books you've read. And the wonder of it is that you don't know what it is or why it is. It just happens. It's a wonderful thing that happens. And when you try to explain it away, you're performing, really, an act of murder.

....

CINEMA OF THE MIND

Robert Olen Butler, interviewed by Heather Iarusso

A reader's internal experience of literature is like a viewer's experience in the cinema. The early film director D. W. Griffith, who was credited with inventing modern film techniques, credited Charles Dickens with teaching him everything he knew about film. It's because Dickens understood that the reading of literature is rooted in the reader's experience of a continuous flow of sensual experience.

Since the writer creates an ongoing cinema of the mind, the techniques that are used in cinema—the cutting and cross-cutting and longshots and close-ups—are also used by writers, though often without artistic control. All literary writers project these images into the reader's mind, with a beginning, a middle, and an end, and transitions between them, so inevitably they have a direct relationship with the things that we think of as filming techniques. The idea of montage, which comes out of film—where powerful and inevitable meaning emerges from the simple juxtaposition of things—is also a crucial phenomenon in literary fiction. But this isn't considered by most writers, especially student writers.

Once you understand the writer's role as an inner filmmaker, you can clearly see how destructive abstract language and ideas, analysis, and rational thought can be. For example, if we were watching Jack Nicholson in *Chinatown* and he's told a lie about the case he's investigating, and instead of him arching that marvelous left eyebrow of his, the screen goes blank except for the word "skepticism" and then goes on to the next shot. You know what your response would be. Exactly the same thing happens over and over in so much of the writing that I see. Literature, like all the arts, must be a direct, sensual experience.

David Long: I'm thinking in terms of making a painting, an art object, and I'm trying to make it the most interesting art object that I can make. Now, unfortunately, words convey meaning, so you're suddenly in the realm of meaning, but meaning is a byproduct. I'm not trying to write about life as much as I am trying to make art. There's a line that William Gass used: "The aim of the artist ought to be to bring into the world objects which do not already exist there, and objects which are especially worthy of love." When I ran into that, I felt very akin to it, very at home with that idea.

as interviewed by Linda B. Swanson-Davies

CHAPTER

7

WRITING AS RESPONSIBILITY

*Henry J., striding
in NYC, 1940*

Elizabeth Cox: The story I'm writing focuses on the violence young people do to other young people, and what kind of world we've created where that can happen. I keep wondering, What are we doing? I don't have an answer for it. I mean, any answer finally seems presumptuous or trite, but I do want to present the problem in a way that makes the reader want to react. It was Rilke, I think, who said, "Art makes you want to change your life." If I don't do it right, people will just be offended; if I do, then they will be encouraged to look differently at something vital.

as interviewed by Sarah Anne Johnson

ANTONYA NELSON
interviewed by Susan McInnis

Do you believe as an artist you have any obligation to society?

There are several ways obligation manifests itself. When I'm teaching, I am under an obligation to present students with the world of literature, and to say to them, "These stories are significant for what they tell us about the past and what they tell us about the present." In the best works, stories present a world, withholding judgment from it, allowing the reader to consider and judge and gain perspective on it, and through it to gain perspective on their own world and its events, to become more aware as they consider the world around them.

There's nothing like reading James Baldwin and suddenly understanding what it means to be a heroin addict. It can be a very liberating, exciting process for middle-class, sheltered, anglo students of the 1990s to think about being black and a junkie in Harlem in 1950. That sympathy can begin to generate sympathy for present-day people for whom they otherwise might feel absolutely no kinship. My own work isn't as far reaching as Baldwin's, but I do think that I'm trying to tell the truth as he did. I see that as another of a writer's obligations.

In my own work, I'm trying to get at what is honestly happening to real people. My characters generally are people without a lot of money. Frequently they're suicidal or depressed, or trying to make sense of bad things that happen in the family or in the world. A principal subject for me is self-hatred. I think readers who struggle with this issue might find in a self-hating character some comfort. They may feel less alone, may even find a way to take steps toward something more positive in life.

For me, this kind of writing is a reaching outward, a small service, as well as being a subject matter that is personally important for me to reckon with. I think a lot of what I'm doing is trying to figure myself out, and, because I'm a writer, that's what makes it onto the page.

WRITERS PROTECTING WRITERS

Siobhan Dowd
interviewed by Linda B. Swanson-Davies

At the very heart of all our activities is the Freedom-to-Write Committee, which looks at writers in general, wherever they are, anywhere in the world, including America; and if they've been in prison or their books have been banned, or they've suddenly disappeared or been abducted, if they've been killed, we send protest letters to heads of state. We're kept very busy by this.

So it's a watchdog group to a large degree—watching and reporting.

Watching and reporting and, because we are writers, we have good access to the media, and there is very much a feeling that it's writers protecting other writers. At the moment, we believe that there are between four and five hundred people who have either been recently killed, kidnapped, abducted, imprisoned, or otherwise threatened.

I have been through days when I sit in my office and I feel as though what I do makes no difference, and I get very depressed. I now believe, and have had this corroborated enough times to be one-hundred-percent convinced, that letters to governments around the world from very ordinary people, writers or whoever, letters saying it's unfair that this person has been imprisoned, really do have an effect. Actually it was Maina [wa Kinyatti] who told me that on one occasion, he had been asked to come see the prison director, and he was brought to the director's office and was shown a whole sack of letters, and the prison director said, "Well, what is this all about, who the hell are you?" And it's quite clear that governments can be very surprised and taken off guard by the response that they get. And I know that the Malawian poet Jack Mapanje said that his government was truly astonished by the level of outrage that his imprisonment caused within the literary community. It couldn't believe the number of letters that came piling in when he was imprisoned. Jack now believes that the fact that he wasn't mistreated in prison, and that he was ultimately released, was due in no small part to all those letters. He could have been detained indefinitely, but he was eventually released, and he believes the international support really played a crucial part.

I would urge the people that read the magazine [*Glimmer Train Stories*] to write letters—I always give an address at the end of each article—saying something like "This person has been imprisoned for exercising his or her freedom of expression; we're really concerned about this and urge you to immediately order his or her unconditional release." If people can write letters along those lines with their own home address on their own letterhead and send them off, it really does have an effect. You should never think that what you are doing ends up in a wastepaper basket. It doesn't. It finds its way to a file and the file begins to bulge, and, finally—action.

MAINA WA KINYATTI

interviewed by Linda B. Swanson-Davies

The Mau Mau movement was an armed struggle against British colonialism in Kenya from 1952 to 1963. After Kenya won its independence in 1963, Jomo Kenyatta rejected the Mau Mau demands, suppressed history, dismissing its struggle as "a disease which had been eradicated and must never be remembered again." From that time onward, the government has attempted to cover up this betrayal. Those who try to write about it are intimidated by the secret police or arrested and taken to a kangaroo court and jailed. I refused to be intimidated.

I was able to secretly publish two books in London—*Thunder from the Mountain* [a translation of Mau Mau patriotic songs] and *Kenyans' Freedom Struggle* [a translation of documents written by the Mau Mau in the forest]…

I had asked for permission to do the research and the government refused. I decided to go ahead.

So you knew what would happen?

I wasn't sure. According to the Constitution of Kenya, they cannot take me to jail just for writing the history of Mau Mau. The police came up with a false story and charged me with it.

What were you charged with?

Possessing a seditious document, which the police had planted in one of my files. They came to my house on June 2, 1982. About six secret police. They searched for seditious publications. After four hours, they came out with books and documents. They took about twenty-three books—one of them was actually my own book [*Thunder*], the others were considered to be Marxist, communist. Then they took twenty-nine files of my research work, the Mau Mau research work. In Kenya, research means collecting oral history—I went to the people and asked them to tell us what happened in their time. So by taking those twenty-nine files, they destroyed all that I was trying to do. There is no evidence. And the people who know this history are old, dying. They take with them this history. I cannot go back and duplicate the work.

After taking such great personal risks to collect that work—it must have been horrible for you.

Exactly. So they took those twenty-nine files and did not give them back. I was taken to the police station, kept incommunicado for three days, being tortured.

My aim was not to divide the country politically. I wanted to expose some of the people who occupy powerful positions in our country and go around saying they fought for independence. My goal is to write that chapter of history so the people of Kenya see what really happened. Especially the young people.

Because otherwise it's lost.

Yes. But I hope this will not be so. Some Kenyans are secretly collecting data for this chapter of our history …

They put me in solitary confinement.

How did this affect you?

It did not affect me. I knew how to deal with it. What really affected me was my arrest. I did not expect it. I had checked everything to see whether I had committed even a small crime. Then to be told I was under arrest, that affected me a lot. And the process of torture. I was alone and I couldn't defend myself. They did not even let me call my wife. According to the constitution, after being arrested, I was supposed to be able to call my family to tell them. And after twenty-four hours, if they have nothing on you, they should let you go or take you to court. They were trying to break me, to force me to renounce my political beliefs.

In what ways did they succeed?

I don't think they did. I came from prison very strong and I was hardened going through those tortures. It was so important to me to know that people outside—my wife, Amnesty International, and International PEN—were all fighting for me. So I decided not to betray them or to break. I saw some people break.

After four and a half months in remand prison, I was chained and taken to a kangaroo court, charged with possession of a seditious publication, and imprisoned for six years. I completed my sentence in October 1988 and left the country in March 1989 to avoid further persecution …

Letters are very important, powerful weapons. A single letter can save a captive's life or force his captors to stop torturing him, and give him food and medicine.

FOR THE INDIVIDUAL SOUL
Andre Dubus
interviewed by Jennifer Levasseur and Kevin Rabalais

In your essay "After Twenty Years," you say you've "always known that writing fiction had little effect on the world; that if it did, young men would not have gone to war after *The Iliad*." What do you feel a writer's role is in society?

I hate to tell you. Somebody wrote me about that essay, and she said, "It helps those of us who do read to help those who don't." And I think that's what reading does, but it doesn't get things done. César Chávez did more than six John Steinbecks could have done. Workers don't own their own lives yet. It must have helped in communist countries, but it doesn't help in capitalistic societies. Have you ever seen any good come because somebody wrote a book of fiction? Individual good, yes. I think it's a limited effort, a beautiful effort that is a gift from God. I think people should do it, and make music and paintings. I just wish the world would get better for everybody and there would be true democracy. Literature touches individual lives. It comforts, soothes, and delights. It turns us on, enrages us.

I think the average life span in Haiti is forty or forty-five. Graham Greene wrote *The Comedians* about Haiti, and that's a wonderful book. When the day comes that a politician picks up a novel and sees the light, I'm just going to walk straight to heaven. I think art is for the individual soul. I never read Thomas More's *Utopia*. A woman I know read it, and she said, "There are no artists in there." I was educated by Christian brothers, and a wise Jesuit once told me, "If there were no sins, there wouldn't be art." At the least, stories are fun to read.

FOREGOING MORAL JUDGMENT
Askold Melnyczuk, interviewed by William Pierce

Given your decisive outspokenness as a nonfiction writer, how do you—as a novelist—keep your mind open to those characters who ignore injustices or, even worse, collaborate with their perpetrators?

There's a wonderful line by Ford Madox Ford that a writer is bound to have political opinions, but he should mistrust them. I claim my right as a citizen to mouth off about matters—but a writer has a different opportunity: to see characters rather than to judge them. Trying to imagine somebody's circumstances forces you to forego facile moral judgments. That doesn't mean that you don't make discriminations in your own circumstances. You do. You inhabit your circumstances and they call for a response.

When Tolstoy set out to write *Anna Karenina*, he was determined to condemn adultery, but then he wound up falling in love with Anna Karenina and in a way committing adultery with her—as he so often did with his freed serfs. There are many variations of this notion. You punish the sin, not the sinner.

....

THE WEIGHT OF PAPER

Edwidge Danticat, interviewed by Sarah Anne Johnson

You write about the political conditions of a volatile country. Do you ever feel torn about exposing harsh realities, or perhaps feel the danger in exploring certain truths?

With the contemporary situation in Haiti, I feel like I need time to process things. I know it's frustrating for people in my community that I'm not more vocal in the immediate moment. But being a fiction writer is a search for nuance. It's this desire to understand all sides.

As a citizen, when you talk to your loved ones you have your own outrage, but when you put things on paper there's a weight to it. That's why I write fiction. I can put all the players together and have them act out a story. In fiction, you can look through everyone's eyes, and that's where I feel most at ease.

You manage to write about political issues from a character-based point of view.

Absolutely. Even if someone is a torturer, you don't have the luxury of writing him off, of not "listening" to him when you're writing about him. You have to live your characters' lives with them. They have to be sympathetic in some way. Understanding the complexity of a difficult character's life is most appealing to me as a writer.

You've said that you felt a tremendous responsibility to those involved in the massacre. How did you honor those memories with your work? Did this pressure at any point inhibit your creative drive?

I hope this does not sound too pretentious, but I feel that in some way the work is a kind of memorial to those who died, a plea to remember them. Some reviewers said the book suffered from that intent. I hope not. But I do hope that each time someone picks up that book, they will think of those forty-thousand–plus people who were massacred.

CAPTURING THE GRAY AREAS IN US ALL
Andre Dubus III, interviewed by John McNally

As someone whose modest goal it was to rid the world of social injustice everywhere, what role, if any, does politics play in your fiction?

That's a tough question about my politics, or political philosophies, and my attempts at writing solid fiction. Tough, because I don't really know the answer! I can tell you what I believe: The fiction I like to read and the fiction I try to write doesn't hit you over the head with any ideological point. I think art is about capturing the gray areas in us all, those that seem to be above or beneath politics.

In writing classes, I quote a lot from Flannery O'Connor's masterful essay "The Nature and Aim of Fiction." Just about every line of that piece is quotable. In it, she says that the writer's beliefs are not what she sees, "but the light through which she sees." So if you're a white, working-class, Marxist twenty-year-old, then that reality cannot help but influence and shape your vision in some way. My hope is that my own political views do not show themselves in my fiction at all. Hemingway wrote, "The job of the writer is not to judge, but to seek to understand." That's an inherently non-partisan act, it seems to me, though the writer probably can't escape revealing her views a bit, whether she wants to or not.

JULIA ALVAREZ

interviewed by Mike Chasar and Constance Pierce

What about a story like "Liberty," which seems to me to be allegorical and which takes politics as its subject even as it's telling the story—the American is named Mr. Victor, and he gives the family a dog named Liberty, and so forth? What about a story like that, where it seems like you're trying to do something overtly political?

Can I tell you a secret?

¿Porqué no?

That's one of my least favorite stories. I think it's flatter when you do that. Re-reading that piece, I wish I had thought of different names. There's always a politic in a story, because a story has a point of view, and if you're trying to create a vision of the world and you have certain politics, you want the world to see it that way. And, certainly, I would call myself a writer that has a political vision of the world. But that's not the way that I want to approach my reader, head on, because I don't think that's the way people change. I like the *Scheherazade* method most, where you engage someone in your characters and in a plot so that they become charged and changed by the experience of reading or listening. When you reduce an experience to polemics, then instantly it becomes easy to reject a different—and therefore disturbing—point of view.

THE CONSCIENCE OF A CULTURE

Jayne Anne Phillips
interviewed by Sarah Anne Johnson

What interests you about the lives of the disenfranchised in Black Tickets, and how are you able to inhabit them so completely?

In the same way that presence is sometimes defined by absence—that is, you don't know what something is until it's gone, until it's absent from you, until you miss it. I think outlaws, outcasts, the disenfranchised, those who are outside the Ozzie-and-Harriet stereotype, often define the values of a culture and a civilization.

Literature is the conscience of a culture, and that conscience should deal with what the culture is trying to reject, or what the culture is not aligning itself with. I also think that in the past, people who read were upper-class people and educated people, and now even upper-class and educated people don't read. It's like the canary in the coal mine idea. They take the bird into the coal mine and when it falls over, there's not enough oxygen. Literature inhabits that same territory. Many times, I don't see these disenfranchised characters as being that far from the mainstream. For instance, in this country, there's the top five percent of people who have a certain income, and there's a much larger percentage of people with a much lower income. I sometimes feel that I'm writing for those who won't write for themselves. I'm articulating thoughts and feelings, or losses, that people won't articulate for themselves. That's a kind of spiritual and political necessity, and art must do that.

....

WRITE WHAT IS THERE

Lynn Freed, interviewed by Sarah Anne Johnson

I find the interplay between the races in your South African setting fascinating. These interactions are so different from what you find in the United States. You do not seem to be trying to make a point about racism, or an overt statement against racism. You simply depict it as a very real fact of life. Can you comment on this?

This is the writer's job: to write what there is. Making a point about anything will shoot the fiction through the knees. When it comes to South Africa—when it comes to anything, for that matter—I write what I know, what I see, what is there. In the case of *Home Ground* and *The Bungalow*, I was writing about a particular time in South Africa (the fifties through the seventies), from the point of view of the white people who, while espousing liberal views, were seldom moved to act upon those views. Which is to say, the vast majority of South African whites, both then and now—although, of course, you'd have a hard time finding any white person in South Africa now who admits to having been anything other than fiercely against apartheid. It's laughable.

The family of which I wrote accepted, as most whites did, the status quo: blacks were the workers, both domestically and industrially. The hierarchy was a given, politically, economically, and socially. Whites at the top, blacks at the bottom, Indians and coloreds in between. Social and economic rigidity is not unique to South Africa—you find this in many countries with large gaps between rich and poor. Many South American countries, for instance. What was unique to South Africa, at least at the time of which I was writing, was codifying this racism into law.

....

TIM O'BRIEN
interviewed by Jim Schumock

Patriotism has to do with a whole constellation of things, but for me the ground of it is being true to my beliefs, even if being true to them will make me unliked, or unloved. It means writing novels that dig into America's past and my own past. Most of us want to just heal and forget. But forgetting and healing are not the proper responses. We've forgotten what we did to the American Indian in this country. Little ellipses appear in our textbooks. And little ellipses appear around what happened at the village of My Lai. I go into high schools and colleges and mention the words My Lai, and I get these blank stares back from college kids. It means nothing to them.

Evil doesn't seem to fit well into our national mythology, our image of ourselves as the White Knight. And part of my job as a writer and as a human being is to make sure that I do my part to remind others that everyone, America as a whole, is capable of committing acts of evil, doing sins, bad things in the world, for good purposes. We went into Vietnam for a good purpose—to save the world from communism, and Vietnam from communism—but good intent sometimes goes awry.

ERNEST GAINES

interviewed by Michael Upchurch

I remember in the 1960s whenever I heard about the atrocities that were going on in the South at the civil-rights demonstrations, I would promise myself that I would write the best paragraph that I could possibly write that day. I felt that that was my political statement. Not just that paragraph, because in all of my stories, I was involved in some way or another—the latter part of *Miss Jane Pittman* is about the same thing. Jimmy [who appears in the final section of the novel] is a civil-rights worker; that's how he's murdered. The last story in *Bloodline*, "Just Like a Tree" [about an old woman who has to move because her young relative's civil-rights activities have put her life in danger], that's what that's all about. So these themes always came up in the stories.

But the political thing was never the main thing in the stories. The characters were the main thing, how it affected these individual characters. None of my people worked out of Washington or out of the state capital, or were FBI people, or whatever. So my political involvement, I guess, is much more indirect.

When I was writing *The Autobiography of Miss Jane Pittman* in 1968, 1969, there were lots of demonstrations going on at San Francisco State University for black subjects to be studied in the university, and I was quite often criticized for not being there. When I told the people what I was doing, they questioned it. They said, "Who wants to read some story about a 110-year-old black woman, when what is happening today is the most important thing?" And I said, "Well, I think if I write it well enough, it will last a little bit." I had to write well, though, because they were out there to get me.

And Miss Jane is still kicking around. She's been around for a while, and she's still there.

....

THE ETHICAL IMAGINATION
Carol Roh-Spaulding
interviewed by Linda B. Swanson-Davies

⟹◈⟸

I teach a class called Creative Writing and Social Change, where I attempt to combine the goals of creative writing with writing with an agenda, but in an artistic way. How do politics and art get combined in ways that aren't so obvious that no one wants to read it?

A lot of my students have real high ambitions to change the world, and I want to honor that. But how do you get that into a story? It's an eternal question, but we try on some ways of thinking about that. In one exercise, I ask them to take any sort of product, like a tube of lipstick, and to set it down in front of them. I have a list of questions that I ask them about the tube of lipstick and most of them can't answer: where was it produced; how was it made; when you dispose of it, what happens to it; etc. We don't know the answers. I ask them to think about the human lives on the continuum of the pre- and post-production of this thing. There are hundreds of people. I mean, it's infinite—the advertisers, the marketers, and on and on. Pick one human life on that continuum and try to describe what it's like to be the producer of this product, or the consumer, or any of the other people involved. We tend to think of ourselves as consumers, as though we have an entitlement or a right, that we're not citizens, we're consumers. Can we consume consciously and humanely? Well, not really, but we could probably do better than we are. We can certainly do it with more awareness. We do exercises that activate one's moral—or maybe it would be called ethical—imagination.

MARY GORDON
interviewed by Charlotte Templin

To go back to the Victorians, people like George Eliot actually thought they could change people's lives.

Well, first of all, they were working in the dominant medium for their time. There were, you know, crushes when the last serial parts of *The Old Curiosity Shop* would come to the docks.

Nobody is going to kill anybody to get one of my novels. We're not the dominant medium; we are sort of flies on the screen of culture in terms of what really hits large numbers of people. Did Dickens and Eliot really change the way people thought? Probably the person who did the most was not a very good novelist—Harriet Beecher Stowe. I think *Uncle Tom's Cabin* probably did change things, but it's a lousy novel. And if you want to ask, "What changed more lives, *Uncle Tom's Cabin* or *Middlemarch*?" it's *Uncle Tom's Cabin*.

INTEGRATING A POLITICAL POINT OF VIEW
Alice Mattison, interviewed by Barbara Brooks

There are co-ops and soup kitchens and feminist women in your work—and in *The Book Borrower*, your sympathies clearly lie with the workers in the trolley strike—yet *The Wedding of the Two-Headed Woman* is your most overtly "political" book, is it not?

I'm glad to hear you say that. I often start out wanting to write a certain kind of book, and it takes a long time to see how to do it. The authors I most admire—Grace Paley, Tillie Olsen—especially Grace Paley—write frankly political work all the way through, and I don't know how to do that. But I hope as I've gone along, book after book, I have moved more in that direction.

You mean integrating a more political point of view?

Yes. I want my books to be fully human, with complex, real, emotional characters, and I also want them to be of a time and place, and to have a point of view. Paule Marshall is a writer I love who writes about full-fledged human beings. They are never just walking signposts for a particular point of view, but there is a point of view.

....

THE POWER OF PATHOS

Robert Olen Butler, interviewed by Heather Iarusso

Do you feel that as an artist you have a social or moral responsibility to society?

Not a preconceived one, not in the sense that I have ideas about society or a moral philosophy that I want to demonstrate to the world. The moral and social obligation of an artist is simply not to flinch ... and to bring out the truest thing she can see about the human condition. The irony is that the artist, in ignoring politics or moral points, potentially has more influence than those who are consciously making political or moral statements. I think it was Jonathan Swift who said that you can't reason a person out of a position that he did not reason himself into in the first place. This fits together with my deep conviction that moral and political positions are, by and large, irrational. They were not reasoned out and adopted. They're being held because of some deep, emotional part of yourself that gravitates to this position, and all the editorial reading and listening to debates is just to rationalize or affirm what you already emotionally want to believe. So most people who write something from a political point of view end up creating objects that then will talk from mind to mind, and only those who already agree with you are going to respond. The artist, by ignoring politics, is the most devastating political force of all, because you are communicating with people at a much deeper, irrational, and emotional level. This is why almost every tyrannical government in the world goes after the artists. So if political consequences are implicit in your view of the world, you are able to communicate them much more effectively by ignoring politics.

FICTION AND PUBLIC INTELLECTUALISM
Richard Russo, interviewed by Robert Birnbaum

Are you in any danger of becoming a public intellectual? Are you being called on to comment on things other than literature and storytelling?

I try my best to avoid such circumstances. People have asked how my life has changed since the Pulitzer and I say, probably too glibly, "I've gotten caller ID." When I went to Spain, right after the Pulitzer, I encountered Spanish journalists, who are very different from American journalists. One way is that they are all very political. They want their writers to be very political. The first journalist that I met when I was there asked, "Are you going to use your prize for political purposes?" I said, "Good Lord, no, I wouldn't trade on it—I'm a professional liar. I tell stories. I make things up." They were appalled. They made it very clear to me that that was the wrong answer and that it was further evidence that what was wrong with American authors and Americans in general was that we were insular. Which we are. And that we were not bearing our responsibilities in the world. And that fame that is ours has been wasted on people like us because we won't use it for good purposes.

American writers are probably far more insular than we should be. Nevertheless, I am very much of the other persuasion. That people should not talk about what they don't know. When they do things publicly—there are those things you do publicly and privately. What I said to a lot of the Spanish journalists was, "If you want for us to have a political conversation off the record, if you want to go out and have a beer or something and talk about the Israelis and the Palestinians, I'd be happy to share what slender wisdom I have with you. If you are interested one to one, person to person. But if you think I'm going to issue policy statements that you are going to run on the page next to Colin Powell"—he was there in Barcelona the same days I was there—"of course not."

I think anybody who has read *Empire Falls* could intuit some of my own notions about globalization. But that's what I do. I write *Empire Falls*; I don't write books on globalization, per se.

Askold Melnyczuk: If I were to pick up a novel and felt that it had my spiritual improvement as its ultimate end, I'd hold it at arm's length and look at it with great skepticism. But, at the same time, I'd also say that every book that's mattered to me has somehow made my life larger, better, and therefore has spiritually improved me.

as interviewed by William Pierce

Julia Alvarez: A novel talks its politics by way of a story. And that's different from talking politics so that everything gets reduced to polemics. That's what's wonderful about a story. It swallows polemics up, and it's more than that. It isn't just a description or a sociology. It's something else. A story does something else.

as interviewed by Mike Chasar and Constance Pierce

NOMI EVE
interviewed by Linda B. Swanson-Davies

I think of my book as already existing. My book exists. It's sort of like the sculpture inside of a block of stone and I have to find it. My work is to find it. So when I'm close, it comes easier. When I'm far, it doesn't. As the writer of it, I have to find it. It's my responsibility.

It's my work in the world. It's why I'm here. Orthodox Jews wouldn't call me religious because I don't observe the Sabbath and I don't observe the Mitzvot, but I do have a pretty spiritual sense of my place in the world, within a Jewish context. And aside from answering to God, I just believe that I, Nomi, was set here in the world to do this specific work, and it's my responsibility and also my joy, but it's what I have to do.

DORIS LESSING
interviewed by Michael Upchurch

Given the social ills that you address in your work, what do you feel is the role of the writer? I was thinking of your political activities. At one time you were—

Yes, I was! I was a Communist. That was a long time ago. Like, thirty-odd years.

Do you have any overt political affiliations like that now?

No. I'm not interested in politics. Wait, that's not true. I'm fascinated by politics. But I don't believe anymore in these great rhetorical causes. I'm much more interested in smaller, practical aims: things that can be done. There was a wonderful cartoon in the *Independent* [a London newspaper] when the Social Democrats were a new party. It had two farmers leaning over a gate. One says to the other, "Well, Giles, what do we stand for?" And the other one says, "Let me see, Bill. Yes, now, we stand for democracy, freedom, justice, equality for women, abolition of poverty …" It went on like this, right? Like the mouse's tail in Alice. And I think that's what I'm not interested in.

There is a line in *The Golden Notebook* that says a novel should have "a quality of philosophy." That's Anna Wulf, your protagonist, speaking. But it seems very much your voice.

No, it isn't really, you know. I can't remember the context. I do think a novel should have that quality that good novels do have that makes you think about life. Forgive me for the clichés, but it should enlarge your mind and not narrow it.

....

BRINGING ART TO THE NEXT GENERATION
Susan Richards Shreve
interviewed by Katherine Perry Harris

⟹·◈·⟸

You have served as the president of the PEN/Faulkner Foundation and have also served on its board. Could you talk about [its] Writers in Schools program, and the importance of bringing books and language into the daily lives of these students?

There's a long history of the artist building his own audience—the street player and mime and poet and songwriter going town to town putting on a show for supper. Essentially, the writer who goes to a school for a day where a book of his has been read by thirty to fifty students becomes a kind of street player spreading the word, building an audience not only for his work but for the book as something to be treasured.

Writers in Schools is a simple inner-city program, which has now become, after fifteen years in Washington, a national program. It is in its second year in Detroit and beginning in Kansas City, Los Angeles, Atlanta, Chicago, and probably New York City. The Ford Motor Company supports it primarily. The premise is deceptively simple. For example, a writer such as Edward Albee goes to a high-school English class that has read one of his plays under the direction of a teacher. He spends the morning or afternoon with the students, many of whom have never held a hardback book or perhaps read a complete book at all. Certainly they have not met a writer. The students ask questions of the author—often disarming, probing, honest questions—and then the author signs each of their books, which have been donated by the publisher. It is astonishing how deeply a student can be affected by this experience—far beyond the particular author or book is the honor given to the book by personally bringing the book to the reader in this manner. The dignity that art brings to human experience is evident in the students' responses. Not only do they feel the importance of language and story, but also they feel important themselves because they know the book and have met the author.

I believe one of the most important ways a writer can contribute to his own profession is to bring stories and poems into the lives of the next generation, in a small way to preserve, as language does, a culture of decency and compassion and order.

....

CHARLES BAXTER

interviewed in 2000 by Linda B. Swanson-Davies

—◆◆◆—

What sort of things shake you, and how do you regain your own equilibrium?

Oh, I suppose, since I'm an American, that the things that shake me up are violence and cruelty. A kind of large-scale acceptance of violence and the idea that violence is inevitable and necessary. And it also shakes me up that we may be beginning, I hope we're not, but that we may be beginning to accept this great gap between rich and poor. There's less and less in between, less and less of a middle class. That shakes me up. And I get very disturbed by what gets done to the environment in the name of business. You know, if you spend time in Europe, or you spend time in Canada, and then you come back to America, you see the omnipresence of violence and the way that we seem to accept the inevitability of that. That bothers me a lot. If you're asking me what do I do about it, what I do about it is to try to make peacefulness start with me. And to write to the degree that I can without masking what I understand the truth to be. I don't know that writers, as writers, can necessarily change things very much. Writers have to tell the truth from the angle that they see it. They can't hope necessarily to change society. What they can do is present society with a picture of itself and then, if that society chooses to change, then that's fine, but if I really wanted to mold behavior more than I'm doing, or to alter actions, I would be in politics. You know, a fair number of writers do have political ends, but I don't. Not in the way they do.

So why aren't you in politics? I'd have somebody to vote for.

Because I, like a lot of writers, am most comfortable sitting in a room, rather than standing in front of crowds.

....

CHARLES BAXTER

interviewed in 2003 by Robert Birnbaum

⇒◆⇐

Do you get angry about the state of the world and the state of the union?

I'm so fit to be tied these days.

I have been thinking that come next year [2004] it's more important for me to be working politically than to be working on another book. That's how angry I am. I have friends who have been talking lately about other countries they would like to move to.

In *Saul and Patsy*, you refer to the president as the "Lord of Misrule." Is that applicable to any president of the late twentieth century?

I wrote that passage specifically about George W. Bush. "Everybody in this country is gun crazy from the president on down" is the line that I think follows that. I was thinking of our current guy-in-chief.

I want to return to the suggestion that you think it might be more important for you to be politically active than to be writing. What does that say about your sense of the value of literature and what it can accomplish against the ambition of improving or saving the world?

If I had an idea for a book that was causing fever dreams, I would probably toss aside the political and begin writing it, but having written this book and having been in public for the last couple of months, I haven't been able to daydream my way toward a new one. So what seems to be compelling to me is the political struggle, even though in that I am just another possible political worker. With these books, I really know what I am doing—or I know what I am doing as well as I can.

How possessed are you by the idea that there is something about literature that perhaps could make the world better, save the world—the idea that literature has some great moral impact?

Literature does change the world, but it does it subversively, it does it invisibly. I like to think that Chekhov has helped more people as a writer than he would have had he gone on to practice medicine instead of writing his plays and stories. And in the same ways, now and then, I hear from readers who have been helped out of clinical depression, people who have been cheered and heartened in some way by reading something of mine. So then I've thought this is a form of changing the world. It may not involve bricks and mortar. It is a change.

WRITING AS THERAPY

Paris, 1983

Antonya Nelson: In much of my life, I think of myself as pretty much in control. But I'm still confused about things, and writing is what I do to try to take away control within the confines of a form. In short fiction, the form controls length, so I'm not making an extravagant commitment to the unknown. I commit myself to twenty pages or so, and try to think through what's bothering me, or what's mysterious. In general, what makes me sit down to write a story is something about which I feel conflicted. If I don't know how I feel about something, it stands out in my mind as being somehow extraordinary. I want to pursue it, to explore what about it bothers me.

as interviewed by Susan McInnis

LOSE YOURSELF THROUGH ART
Thom Jones, interviewed by Jim Schumock

If I didn't have a sense of humor … it's the only thing that saves me. I do have a sense of the absurd, but I can get very serious about things. I can't speak for others because life is … there is no such thing as a normal life; there's just life, and this is my life, and so I don't worry about a normal life. And I think it's true for everyone: there's just life. There's nothing to go running around to find. I tried, and it's right there, right in your own backyard. It's in you. Know thyself—if you can actually do that, pull that off, you begin to have a measure of peace.

When I write every day, I find a kind of wholeness and integration—psychic integration, and if I keep the schedule up, it will sort of carry me the next day. It's the only way I can get high anymore. And I feel well; I feel okay about myself. Basically, I've always hated myself, and I would do anything to escape "me." I suppose that's the reason I took drugs or would get into boxing. I subscribe to Schopenhauer's theory about how you lose yourself through art. You can transcend your own existence through art, and by creating art, too. I have to do it every day, but when I'm out on the road and whatnot, I start screaming at cab drivers or crazy things I still do, and I'm terribly ashamed of doing those things.

DAVID LONG

interviewed by Linda B. Swanson-Davies

Of the many things that you spend your time with, which are the most deeply satisfying to you?

Besides writing?

Doesn't matter—including or besides writing.

I used to joke, you know, when people would talk about writing as being therapeutic—I would say, "Well, there are some of us who need therapy because we write."

So writing is not deeply satisfying for you?

Writing is very difficult for me. Lots of days, it's so hard. The question of being satisfied by it is an irrelevant question. You go and do it every day and it's your job, and lots of days you don't feel like doing it, and that doesn't make you any different from anybody else. I try to demystify the process. Most of the time, once you've begun to work, something happens and work generates more work. In the larger sense, it's very satisfying to have written a book, but, unfortunately, by the time it's published and you're out hawking it, you're on to the next book and you're deeply troubled by the complexities of that work. So the moments of satisfaction are kind of glancing blows.

I use baseball on TV for my therapy.

THE SECOND CHANCE

Paul Theroux, interviewed by Jim Schumock

Certainly the dark night of the soul in this book [*My Other Life*] concerns the breakup of your marriage and your family. You left England, if I read the book as being about you, a friendless man, almost on the edge of a nervous breakdown.

I think maybe I was. Maybe I have been many times in my life on the verge of a nervous breakdown. Perhaps that happens to people. I'm not even sure what a nervous breakdown is. I think it's an inability to cope. You try to cope and you fail. I'm saying that art is an escape, writing is an escape. Certainly I felt that I had to write myself out of the difficulty. The breakup of a marriage is a terrible thing. You feel that all your hopes are lost. Your life is divided; you're left with a fragment of it. You're like someone who's been marooned, like someone who's been cast off a sinking ship. You feel as though you might drown. All these metaphors of ruination and near-doom crowd around you. They did around me. And I found it very hard to write. But then afterwards I thought I'd want to write about this condition when I got to a point where I felt I could cope. I had been traveling in the Pacific and I wrote *The Happy Isles of Oceania*.

That was my, I suppose, transitional book. I wasn't quite sure what I was doing. I knew I was traveling, trying to make sense of my life. I felt I'd lost quite a lot, and I felt guilty. I felt that I had damaged myself. I wondered how I'd get back some sense of sanity. And I suppose just in the course of time, I did regain a kind of equilibrium. Although I will say that time heals nothing. I know that from the breakup of my marriage. I know it from grieving, losing a parent. You can replay that film at any moment. You can replay the moment and be miserable. Maybe it's part of the writer's ability to reach back and to re-create those moments. Maybe that is what it is, a kind of memory—an emotional memory, or the memory of that feeling.

But when I came to write *My Other Life*, I had been mentally working on it for a long time. I suppose I was always looking for alternatives—how might it have been different, what were other breakups like. So, instead of writing about the breakup of my own marriage, I wrote about something parallel. I used it because I think writing about childbirth, writing about death, writing about the breakup of a marriage is mawkish. It doesn't work. I don't like reading about it. It's not that I find it unpleasant. I just find it kind of tedious. I was trying to think of something else to do. But using some of my divorce, some of my alienation, some of the travel in another way. There are a number of episodes which are concerned with drifting—drifting into a psychiatrist and falling in love with her, lying to her. She recommends that I read my own books. She doesn't know who I am. I then fall in with some ne'er-do-wells to whom, in contrast to telling the lies to the psychiatrist, I tell the truth. I bare my soul to these people who don't care. I thought that was clever. Telling someone the truth and they're just deaf to it. So all those things became part of the process and I used them. But I think one of the great things that fiction can do is give us the second chance life denies us. I felt that in a lot of my life there's a road not taken. In this book, I took that road and tried it.

....

SIGRID NUNEZ

interviewed by Linda B. Swanson-Davies

Writing is talk therapy, too. It really is. Virginia Woolf, whose mother died when she was thirteen or fourteen, wrote in one of her autobiographical pieces that, before she wrote *To the Light-house*, she was obsessed by her mother, couldn't get her out of her head. After she wrote *To the Lighthouse* and created Mrs. Ramsey, who was based on her mother, she stopped being obsessed by her mother. She goes on to say in the next paragraph that she supposed what she did was something similar to what psychoanalysis, which was just being invented at that time, tries to do. She saw exactly what it was.

Mary McGarry Morris: Writing is often as difficult for me as it is exhilarating. I come to the desk at the same time day after day, and sometimes I'm discouraged by what I've done, and sometimes the work, the moment, the message are all so right, so close to the bone, that I am transported and never want it to end. While I'm not sure exactly what effect my writing has on me, I do know what happens when I don't write. I feel uneasy and out of synch with all that's going on around me.

as interviewed by Linda B. Swanson-Davies

IT'S NEVER THAT SIMPLE

Tim O'Brien, interviewed by Jim Schumock

I came back from Vietnam thinking I was pretty well adjusted. A smooth glide: one day you're in combat; next day you're sitting in tweed seats, listening to Muzak, and stewardesses are handing out your little dinners. You land in Seattle, say the Pledge of Allegiance, get a haircut, and you're out of the army. Fly to Minnesota and back into the civilian world almost instantly. And it felt for many years in my life that I had come back to America, to this world that I'm living in now, without many problems. And I've learned, both through my life and through my reading, that it just wasn't and isn't that simple.

If you suffer, for example, from cancer—my sister had a mastectomy not too long ago—as much as we can heal on the surface, there's going to be underlying terror and sorrow that's going to find its way like fluid into the remainder of our lives, as it has to. And you can't back the fluid up through deceit or through keeping things bottled up. If you try that, the fluid's going to break out of your skin, it's going to make you do some pretty terrible things. I've learned to be more open about it, to be open about my dreams, to be able to talk about them. When I wake up in the middle of the night screaming ugly, desperate, obscene words, I'm willing now to talk about what the dream was, whereas before, I just couldn't do it. I was afraid of my own dreams, afraid of my own past. I think the only way to break through the terror was partly through talking, and partly through writing this novel [*In the Lake of the Woods*] that focuses on the debilitating effects of silence and secrecy and deceit.

....

GETTING IT OUT OF YOUR SYSTEM
William Styron, interviewed by Jim Schumock

You wrote your novella *The Long March* [the story of a brutal, forced march of Marine reservists just recalled for the Korean War, and of death by friendly fire] in Paris in 1952 during a six-week period. Why do you think this time was so productive for you?

Well, it was a fresh experience. The event I wrote about had happened very recently, only a year or so before. It just had a kind of desire of its own to get written. The savage barbarism of that march, the kind of sadistic quality, was something that was very hard for me to put out of my system. I don't mean to say it was sadistic or savage in the truly grueling way that some military experiences are. There were no deaths or anything like that. But nonetheless, it was a horrible experience. I wanted to get it out of my system. It cried out to be written in a novella form, twenty-five to thirty thousand words. I just sat down and wrote it.

WRITING AS CONSOLATION
Thomas E. Kennedy
interviewed by Linda B. Swanson-Davies

You sent a journal entry that ended with this wonderful question: "Why is it that all our petty misfortunes cast into words become a celebration?" Is this part of why we write, to make sure that something good comes, even from those things that we would have avoided if we'd had a choice? An acting optimism?

I think that's a good and valid point. And I do. I think that it's a consolation, writing, certainly. And it was just that journal entry that made me realize that. I was actually sitting on those steps of that airport in Athens and feeling miserable. You know, broken tooth, petty things, cheated by a cab driver, and writing them in this nice little notebook. And when I got to the end of describing all that, I suddenly realized that I felt fine. I loved having written those things down. Maybe it is just that it's so good to exist. It's so good to breathe. No matter what happens, somehow, it's lovely to be alive. And writing somehow illuminates that sense of being alive—or maybe it's an illusion, that one thinks one becomes a little god who controls all these events by putting them down.

Kent Haruf: I do think you write out of your unhappiness, and out of pain and anguish. I don't think that fixes it or heals anything, but I feel very strongly that that's what a writer does.

as interviewed by Jim Nashold

MARY GORDON
interviewed by Charlotte Templin

You mention that after writing the memoir about your father [*The Shadow Man*], you suffered a loss of faith in memory. That seems like a grave loss.

It is a grave loss, but it's the loss of a romance. Virginia Woolf said that what you are trying to do in writing is to tell the truth and create something of beauty. If, as a writer, what you are doing has any moral significance at all, you are looking for the truth. If memory is a distortion or a work of fiction, you have to witness that. Even if it's painful, it's your job. That's just the way it is. And there is a kind of exultation that comes with the truth-telling.

I felt that exultation in the truth-telling about your father in the midst of the pain.

You don't have to be afraid of that ghost popping out of the closet anymore, because you have confronted the ghost. He can't surprise you; you don't have to be worried about ambush, and that's a liberation.

LEE MARTIN

interviewed by Linda B. Swanson-Davies

At what point were you able to see that your dad's anger was not caused by you, and at what point do you think your father figured out that it wasn't caused by you?

I'll take the second one first. I don't think I can speak for my father on that issue. All I can say is that we eventually came to a time when there wasn't that anger between us, and even though I'm not affiliated with a church, you know, in my adult life, there was that time in our lives when church was very important to us, and I think it had a lot to do with the lessening of the anger. I can't really say whether there was a particular moment when my father knew that I hadn't caused the anger. Maybe he knew that all along.

Maybe he did or maybe he never did.

Yeah, I say that maybe he did, because I'm pretty convinced that people do horrible things all of the time knowing inside that they're culpable and that it comes from them, but not able to articulate that or admit that or—

Or change.

Or change it, yeah. So I'm not really sure what to say about that, as far as my dad. As far as me coming to terms and understanding that it really wasn't me, it was just what life had given us. I don't think it happened in any sort of enduring way until I finished *From Our House*.

When you put it all down and looked at it.

I can remember the day that I wrote the last sentence in the first draft of the book and just sitting there weeping. And my wife will tell you that I'm a much more pleasant person to be around after I wrote this book because, in all honesty, this combination of my mother and father—I had carried a lot of my father's inclination toward anger, and as the years went on, that started to mellow out a little bit, but it wasn't until *From Our House* that I really felt like I had walked through a door to the other side of that whole thing.

UNDERSTANDING WHAT YOU'RE GIVEN
Barbara Scot
interviewed by Linda B. Swanson-Davies

Prairie Reunion has only been out a short while, but I've had people writing and calling, and when they say this or that touched them, it moves me. I'm rather interested in hearing other people's stories back. I think that's what you have to do, if you're going to tell your story, is to listen to the stories of others. The things they mention that touched them are so common. So very common. There are things like, Well, my father left the family and no one ever said anything about it. But the common element is the silence, the silence about shame. That's not something that was just one generation.

I wonder if all the talk shows are a purging for all the silence, a swing in the opposite direction, so that we can eventually come to some kind of dignified and open place.

That might be true. Although I think in a situation like that, where people get only one moment of exposure—I think people get fixated on a revelation like that and they tell it and tell it and tell it, and you know, I think, Oh, there's so much more to it than that. It's such a process to get to the stuff.

I really feel I attained adulthood in that one moment when I went from feeling like a child deprived of her father to a prodigal who hadn't realized how much Uncle Jim had really been a father to her. The essential step is from concentrating on what you were—or imagined you were—deprived of, and understanding what you were given. I did not make that leap until the very end of the writing process.

ROBERT STONE

interviewed by Jim Schumock

What was it that was going on in your life then that sustained such an incredible introspection?

I think I had really spent a lot of my life at that point making things tough for myself. In some ways, I got lucky, but I spent years taking a lot of drugs, doing a lot of partying. Probably no more intensely than a great many people in those years. I saw, I think, this alternative life that I was heading for. So the book [*A Hall of Mirrors*] took on a strange form for me. The very writing of it was a kind of denial, a refusal to go on the road that the characters were going. It became a way of perversely taking myself out of the direction that I was sending my characters toward. The more recognition I got for the parts of the book, the better my life became, the more motivation I had to drink less, to drug less. Although it was coming out of all my troubles, it was the thing that was saving me. That is what art is for, I guess.

MAKING THE MOST OF MISTAKES
Chris Offutt, interviewed by Rob Trucks

I began *The Same River Twice* when I had been dumped by a woman and thrown out of an apartment, and I found myself in a rooming house. I had nothing to show for my life but a bunch of journals. I'd bought a typewriter and I'd tried to write some stories, but I'd failed at it. I thought I would try to write about the most dreadful circumstances of the past several years, which seemed to me like a sequence of errors. I was profoundly depressed. Nothing had worked out the way I wanted. I was alone in a rooming house, you know? I wasn't very happy, and I couldn't believe how I'd gotten there. It wasn't what I'd intended when I left Kentucky.

I thought I'd write about the worst experiences, and the ones that hurt me the most, and I'd try to understand how I went from a guy from Kentucky to a guy in a rooming house in eight years. I wound up with a six-hundred-page manuscript and utterly no understanding of what had happened. I set it aside and several years passed. At one point, my mother typed a draft of *The Same River Twice* before I went to Iowa, because it was just a terrible mess, and she typed it for me. I'd knocked it down from six hundred pages to like a hundred and thirty pages and I took that with me.

So it was handwritten?

It was on all kinds of different papers that I could get for free. What I would do is I would go to copy shops and say, "Look, give me your mistakes," because they always make mistakes on big projects. So I would get their mistakes for free.

Anyhow, it was never intended for print. It was intended for me to understand it.

STEPHEN DIXON

interviewed by Linda B. Swanson-Davies

What would I do if I didn't write, was unable to, in other words? Well, that's too hypothetical a question. What would prevent me? An accident to my hands so I couldn't type? Then I'd memorize stories, line by line, work over them in my head daily, till I was able to write them orally into a cassette player. No, I missed the question. Maybe because it seems impossible that any life circumstances might prevent me from writing. The worse the circumstances, the more I'm motivated to write. I don't look for horrible circumstances, but I've lived through many horrible circumstances by writing. I've come through them, in other words. There isn't a horrible circumstance I couldn't write about, for through writing about it, I'd come to understand that circumstance more clearly.

Writing's finding yourself; that's what I've found. I learn about things, myself, other things, things I go through, things other people go through, through writing. There could be other ways, but to me, this is the best way. Better than painting, better than acting. Many times, I discover not only what I know but, more importantly, what I'm feeling through my writing.

....

DANIEL MASON
interviewed by Linda B. Swanson-Davies

There were a number of really brutal moments in the book [*The Piano Tuner*]. And for the most part, they weren't intentional instances of cruelty, but rather accidents, or cases of coarse disregard that had terrible outcomes. You wrote them with great respect, a lot of tenderness; it was reflected in Edgar's response. His response was pain and horror. Something that kind of surprised me was that he also seemed to be responding with fear. I was wondering what it was like writing those parts.

Some of those parts were very difficult to write. The shooting of the boy, for instance—not the shooting, but the reaction to the shooting of the boy. The rush of the woman afterward. I used a lot of my own journal. It's the only place in the book, really, where I borrowed so heavily from my journal, from a funeral that I'd seen when a friend of mine there died in a plane crash, which was terrible. It was maybe the most terrible thing that I've seen in my life to this point. His body was brought in and his family fell about him and people were holding them back, and I just remember thinking of the geometry of their bodies. I'd never seen human beings in this geometry before. This, this sort of leaning forward against weight and being drawn backward. You don't see people in that position ever. And yet in a way I recognized it, I think from Greek urns, from classical pictures of grief. Where have you seen grief before? Maybe television images of funerals. But this came from something much deeper than that. Like, This is how a human being grieves, in the rawest sense. So that scene ... that scene came from a very real experience.

It was dreadfully real.

For me it was very real. I'd written that on a night when I'd received a letter from someone in Burma that had reminded me of that funeral, and I had gotten upset. Writing that let me deal with this experience I've been wanting to deal with for a long time.

Melissa Pritchard: I truly believe stories repose deep within our flesh, and it's crucial for us to find ways to release them. If we don't let our stories speak, they can create physical and emotional disturbances within us.

as interviewed by Leslie A. Wootten

CHAPTER

9

WRITING FROM EXPERIENCE

Through Venetian blinds, ca. 1938:
The Howland sisters, dancing on a picnic table,
sharing an ice-cream cone

Kent Haruf: You can't help but be influenced by certain experiences. What I try to do is write out of some deep emotion about something. I'll hear something, or see something, or know something that touches some deep emotion that I've been feeling about any number of things, and that new awareness connects up with some older, deeper emotion, and my novels come out of that.

as interviewed by Jim Nashold

EDWIDGE DANTICAT

interviewed by Sarah Anne Johnson

What is the role of autobiography in your work, or how do your own experiences fuel your creative life?

People always ask me about the characters in my books as if they're all living in my house. They'll ask how my daughter is, but they mean Sophie's daughter in *Breath, Eyes, Memory*. They even ask me about a character in a novel set in 1937 as though she were me.

All writing has a certain level of autobiography, whether it's emotional or actual autobiography; we're always drawing a little bit on our own experiences, and I am no different. I don't write pure autobiography because I want the freedom to make things up. However, I do feel like I need something actual, something real to keep me going, a feeling that there's something at stake. Often including actual events along with the fiction gives it a sense of reality. In *The Dew Breaker*, for example, there are actual people in there that others might recognize. For the characters to have actual people next to them lends a kind of reality and gives the fiction a parallel in real life, and that keeps me writing, gives me a sense that the characters and their troubles really matter.

JAYNE ANNE PHILLIPS
interviewed by Sarah Anne Johnson

How do you handle recognizable characters in your fiction?

No one's recognized themselves, because no one character is based on any one person. They're always a combination of people. In *Night Talk*, for instance, the way that August taught his daughter about the world was very much the way my brother taught me about nature, but August is not like my brother, and my father wasn't similar to August. I use bits and pieces of people until a character comes alive in his own right. If I stay too close to a particular person, the character never develops completely.

Machine Dreams was set in what I remembered about my home town, although by the time I wrote the book, my hometown had vanished. That's another thing about autobiography. By the time you write about something, it no longer exists. Memory is so faulty and so selective, that it's like the blind man and the elephant. There may be a certain piece that's very similar to what you remembered existing, but the whole is a very different reality than anything that really happened.

WHAT IS FACT?

Maria Flook, interviewed by Sarah Anne Johnson

Do you find it difficult as a fiction writer to stay true to bare facts?

What are bare facts? There are no bare facts. A fact has all kinds of reasons to be. A fact has a lot of strings attached. The psychological weight of an event or problem is a subjective as well as an objective perception. When I worked as a corrections officer, I used to have to fill out reports, using a form called a SOAP, the acronym for Subjective, Objective, Assessment, and Plan. We had to write up any squabble between inmates or whatever infraction might have happened. The Subjective recorded what the inmate had said. The Objective recorded what had happened. The Analysis was the officer's perception of what happened. The Plan presented what punitive measures or changes the system would institute against the perpetrator. They believed in behavior modification, and sometimes an inmate would have to wear a baby hat or a rattle looped around him if he'd been acting out.

Bare facts have a lot of input and participants involved. There isn't a straight road to the truth. Fact is often merely belief, and we know that belief is a subjective construct. The most common example: Is God fact? Dostoyevsky writes in *Crime and Punishment*, "I like it when people lie. If you lie—you get to the truth. Lying is what makes me a man. Not one truth has ever been reached without first lying fourteen times or so, maybe a hundred and fourteen ...." I think he means that truth is evoked from many teeming human perceptions and emotions.

CHANG-RAE LEE
interviewed by Sarah Anne Johnson

Aloft is a departure from your earlier books in several ways. First, the main character is not Asian-American, but an Italian-American retired landscape business owner and laborer. How did you arrive at the character of Jerry Battle? What drove you into his particular narrative?

Jerry's story is different. I'd been thinking about someone his age, living in this classic suburban landscape. I wanted to write a suburban novel. These days, the suburbs are at the center of what it means to be an American. I was thinking about a guy around sixty years old who is caught between certain points of life, not being a young man and not being too old, and having a lot of pressure from the surrounding generations, and being at a point in life in which the questions should be fewer and the solutions obvious. Part of the inspiration was what I'd seen around me in my parents' and my in-laws' lives. There seemed to be lots of questions about retirement, what to do now that the heavy lifting was done, but feeling as young as ever. This was a time of life that I hadn't heard much about. There are plenty of stories about middle-aged angst and midlife crisis with marital problems and whatnot.

But this book isn't about aging. It's about someone who's been too comfortable in his life and is now trying to figure out what that all means. It's also in a way an immigrant story, but a couple of generations past. I was very interested in that. But I decided early on that the hero wouldn't be an Asian-American character, because an Asian-American character at that age in that setting would have required a very different story. It couldn't be a story about someone who felt like he completely fit and belonged in his context, or felt too comfortable. It just couldn't be. That's why it had to be someone who was white, but not so landed and established. I wanted someone who didn't question his belonging, and yet someone who still had ties to the old world.

The book, I think, also looks at class. There are three very distinct classes in the book. Jerry Battle is squarely middle class, and his father has working-class roots, and his children tend to be upper-middle-class aspirants, his daughter intellectually and his son financially. I liked that Jerry was sandwiched between those generations and could think about the legacies of his working-class father that he didn't fill, and the problems of Jack, his son, and where all those years of family work was heading. He's more like me, too. I have a young family and a life in the suburbs. It's one of the first times I was writing autobiographically, and because it's through Jerry, it surprises people.

....

MOVING CLOSER TO YOUR FEARS
Siri Hustvedt
interviewed by Jennifer Levasseur and Kevin Rabalais

I suppose the use of autobiography is both conscious and unconscious. There is always an autobiographical kernel to my work. It's like an itch I can't get rid of. Whatever it is, it's inevitably something I don't understand, something ambiguous and often frightening. In *The Blindfold*, I kept moving closer to my fears. *The Enchantment of Lily Dahl* began with the true story of a suicide in a restaurant. I was not a witness. I heard about it, and I knew the brother of the person who killed himself. It is a strange thing to commit suicide in front of an audience, and after I finished writing the book, I understood that the whole novel was born of that death performed for others. The play inside the book, Martin's bizarre theories about language and the world, the obsessive questioning about what's real and what's performance, what's art and not art—all of it came out of that single explosion … Writers have obsessions that never get away from them, even if they write different books.

ALICE MATTISON
interviewed by Barbara Brooks

How much of your work is autobiographical?

All through my writing life, in fiction and poetry, I've used the circumstances of my life, but I seem to need to use them metaphorically, so that only later do I realize the connection. I'll write about a family in turmoil because I'm in inner turmoil. The scenarios in the stories embody the conflicts within me, but it's as though all the characters are parts of myself. I've urged my students to do this, too. Sometimes after I've finished writing a book, I realize what it's about, emotionally, for me.

Hilda and Pearl, for example, is a novel about loss and what one loses and what one keeps. It's about a woman who loses her child and who loses a whole lot about her marriage, mostly mutual trust, but she gets a friend, an intensely important friend, who is her sister-in-law. I had started having vision problems in the 1980s, and somebody asked me if I'd ever written about my eyes. Subsequently, I wrote an essay about the vision loss, "The Disappearing Teapot," but at the time I said no. But then I realized that *Hilda and Pearl* was about that loss, and I had never known that. When I lost some of my vision, I began writing better fiction, and I think that was the loss and gain behind the book, though it was probably about other things, too. There are slight connections to my family, but I don't write directly autobiographical stuff, or hardly ever.

In what ways did your fiction improve?

Maybe it became more urgent. I don't know if the vision loss caused the change, but surely it's possible—when outward seeing deteriorates, the imagination could become stronger.

....

HEROES AND MYTHS

Daniel Wallace
interviewed by Linda B. Swanson-Davies

Big Fish is total fiction. There was no dying father, or even particularly ill father, in my own life at the time when the book was written. Obviously the myths and the death scenes are all created. People sometimes think the death scenes are transcriptions of things that happened between me and my dad. But the deeper truth, the more important part, I think, is the emotional truth behind the story, which does exist in my own life. The desire to understand the person—my dad—who probably had more of an effect on me than anybody else. So that is the furnace that drives the book.

You talked last night a little bit about turning an ordinary person into a hero through the telling of myths. What sort of transformation has to take place for a person to change from an ordinary person into a heroic person, a mythical person?

I think that the father-son relationship is one of the only ones that I can imagine being able to withstand that kind of process. I think when you're younger, it could be your mom. As you get older, it could be a lover or someone like that, but to me the dad is such a strong character when you're growing up, so looming and large, that it seems really natural to turn him into a hero. But I think it depends on what kind of relationship you have, the distance—clearly you can't mythologize somebody that you know inside and out, because you can see their faults.

Which can be a good thing. How about that in terms of your own kids?

Do I let them see my faults?

Yes. Will they make myths about you, to fill in the blanks? Or do they know you enough?

Well, I don't just see that—I mean, you think, Well, gosh, I could tell them anything. I could really create a great story. My father, for instance, did lie about things. He told me he made straight A's to encourage me to make straight A's. He never did. He was a terrible student. Said he went to Yale.

Oh my gosh.

He went to Yale cooking school for one year.

And he got you.

Well, yeah. I mean, why not? Why wouldn't you believe him? Even think of somebody like Faulkner. He did that. He lied all the time about his past. Said he had a plate in his head from where he'd crashed as a fighter pilot for the Canadian Air Force. That never happened. He did a lot of self-mythologizing.

And my dad did it, and that's why when you cornered him about things, he wouldn't come clean. He'd go, "Yeah, yeah, yeah, let's talk about …" You know, he was really a very charming person, and that charm gives you the impression of being close to somebody really warm, friendly. But it's like a magician's trick: Look, but don't look at this hand. And then he's doing something with that hand. I think that my kids will know me probably more than they would really like to. Henry, who's my only biological child, and whom I've been with since he was born, and lived with—I don't go to work except at home, so I've been there almost every day since he's been born. So he's gonna know me pretty well, I think. I hope that that's better for him than having a dad that he can, you know, turn into some great—

Untrue person.

Untrue person. Yeah.

David Malouf: Everybody writes a first novel which is vaguely autobiographical, and sometimes what you're doing, without realizing it, is getting rid of that material so that you can be free of it. Of course, everything you write about will be autobiographical in some way, because you've got to test everything against your experience. But fiction is fiction. A lot of modern writing never wants to make the leap into real fiction. There's a certain point when you must do it, though. Getting rid of so much purely autobiographical material in the first book certainly frees you to make the rest of it up.

as interviewed by Kevin Rabalais

FICTION OR MEMOIR?
by Gary D. Wilson

Nearly all of us write stories that are in some degree or another based on "fact" or "what really happened" in our lives. The practice is so ubiquitous that a fellow writer and friend of mine tells his students that the first thing they should do at the beginning of a story is to change the names of the characters so that no one will recognize him- or herself solely on that basis. A problem arises when a writer tries to make a story conform to the external facts that gave birth to it, when those facts may or may not have any bearing on the direction the story is taking. If you were to write a faithful re-creation of the events from your life, remembering as closely as possible their nature and importance, you would end up having created an autobiography or memoir. But those same events infused with the author's imagination result in fiction. Both are viable and defensible genres, and both are true to themselves, but in fundamentally different ways. Autobiography and memoir owe their allegiance to a conscientious retelling of a reality perceived as external to the writer and the work being written—"what really happened"—while fiction must adhere to an imagined, internally driven reality that conforms to its own "truth," rather than one external to it. Therein lies the tension, and therein lies the problem you refer to in your question. Simply put, when you commit even a personal event or a series of events to fiction—that is, you give them over to be recreated through your imagination—you must forget what really happened and open yourself to what might happen. Let go, and see where you end up. It's a wonderful, and occasionally terrifying, experience.

THE UNRELIABLE NARRATOR
Amy Bloom, interviewed by Sarah Anne Johnson

In the final story of this collection, "The Story," you tell a story, and then the narrator tells readers of scenes omitted and names changed and places invented. She says that this is what writers do.

She outs herself as an unreliable narrator.

Right. Do you think this calls into question the reliability of any narrator?

It's clear to me from the way that people respond to the story that it set off all sorts of things for all sorts of people in terms of writing and telling the truth, the nature of fiction, and what it is that people choose to write about.

That the truth is not necessarily what actually took place.

The truth is almost never what happened, not to mention that it doesn't really matter. I'm always telling my writing students that the fact that something actually took place is of no importance at all. On some level, of course any narrator is unreliable, because they're made up! Somebody made them say those things and wrote it down to make you feel like it was really true, which is fun.

What are some of the responses you've gotten to that story?

There was a lovely review on Amazon.com about how I undermined my own reputation for Chekhovian decency. Of course, I'm glad to hear that I have a reputation for Chekhovian decency. But people will take that story sort of literally. In the last paragraph, the character is talking about what she's done. There are people who say, "That's clearly how Bloom feels about fiction," but I would say that's the opposite of how I feel about fiction. But there's a wish for people to believe, especially in this modern age, that your characters represent your own opinions, and represent glimpses into your life and psyche. The narrator is summing up when she says, "I have made the best and happiest ending that I can in this world, made it out of the flax and netting and leftover trim of someone else's life, I know, but made it to keep the innocent safe and the guilty punished, and I have made it as the world should be and not as I have found it." That would not be what I understand the purpose of fiction to be. But that's fine. People found it interesting. I'm glad.

Thisbe Nissen: My mom is a great storyteller, and sort of forgoes truth for the benefit of the story. And, really, who the hell cares if it actually happened that way. I spend much of my life saying, "Mom, I've never said that." She's going, "*Sh, sh*. It's a better story this way, *sh*. This is much funnier."

as interviewed by Linda B. Swanson-Davies

USING FICTIVE TECHNIQUES IN MEMOIR
Maria Flook, interviewed by Sarah Anne Johnson

How much did you have to invent for the memoir [*My Sister Life*]?

I didn't invent events or characters or the chronology of their actions. These were set, and bigger than life. I made great efforts to conform to its authentic map as much as possible.

To create a narrative about what happened, I had to construct scenes, dialogue, and employ all the fictional devices one uses to write a story. My sister didn't carry a dictaphone around when she was working as a prostitute in Norfolk, so I had to recreate that world, make it come alive with voices, faces, with the violence, crimes, and survival tactics that I wasn't witness to in person. These scenes were born from everything my sister had told me, and from my reactions, and from my empathy and anxiety about these events. I also used police reports, hospital records, newspaper clippings, and other materials relating to my sister's disappearance.

We grew up together in the same household so, of course, I knew firsthand the threats she faced when she was still at home, and I saw the unhappiness or defiance that was bred in us as we related to our complicated parents. We reunited when we had our young babies, and those scenes in the book when we are living under one roof, with the threat of her violent ex finding her, were very difficult to relive. As with my fiction, the memoir has importance as a book, not as a personal trial or personal story. The book is its final meaning.

SANDRA CISNEROS
interviewed by Robert Birnbaum

Let's talk about the disclaimer at the beginning of the book *Caramelo*. One might almost think that you didn't want to take responsibility for what was in the story. But that certainly isn't true…

No, I actually wanted to admit that characters were based on real people. But I wanted to also say and be truthful that it's based on real people but it isn't autobiography. Many books that you read, they have those disclaimers that say that none of the events and none of the people are based on real life, and so on. Well, I don't believe that. I think that, as human beings, many people touch us, especially people we love the most, and we can't help but do character sketches when we go to our art. I felt that I was taking some real filaments of my life, some real memories, but I was embroidering from that and departing from that and leaping … especially plot. So much of the plot was invented. Even if the characters were not.

TELLING OTHERS' SECRETS

Mary Gordon, interviewed by Charlotte Templin

Memoir writers have to be willing to tell secrets. Do memoirists worry about that? Do they think about specific readers?

For me, I would feel that I had the right to tell my own secrets. But if I really felt that somebody else's secret was very important to their sense of themselves, I wouldn't feel it would be my right to tell that. Everybody whose secrets I told is dead. I do feel that people have the right to their own secrets, and I don't believe in outing. Were my mother not in the land of dementia so she couldn't be hurt by it, I wouldn't feel that I could write to tell her secrets. I remember a letter of Elizabeth Bishop to Robert Lowell. She criticized him for using some of her letters, which she thought he had no right to publish. She said to him, "Art is not more important than everything." I'm on Elizabeth Bishop's side.

....

USING WHAT LIFE GIVES YOU

Tim O'Brien, interviewed by Jim Schumock

Do you ever imagine what life would have been like for you if there had been no Vietnam War, or if you hadn't gone to Vietnam?

Not really. It's a bit like asking Toni Morrison what life would've been like if she weren't black. You know, life gives us stuff. It gave Conrad the ocean, which he used in his stories. Life gave Updike domesticity and divorce and the suburbs, which he uses as material. And life dealt me the Vietnam card. Yet I don't consider myself a Vietnam writer, any more than Morrison considers herself a black writer. We're writer writers. And we use what life gives us.

THE FREEDOM TO CREATE DRAMA
Ha Jin, interviewed by Sarah Anne Johnson

I haven't written any stories about myself, but I've given a lot of details from my life to my characters. I don't say that this is my own experience, though, and so in that sense I don't write autobiographical stories. I try to avoid that. I think that memoir is quite limiting as a nonfiction form, because if something didn't happen, you're not supposed to create it. You cannot create the drama. The creativity is very limited. In fiction, we can create drama, the order of events, and so on. My next book is a novel in the form of a memoir, but it's fiction.

Alice Mattison: People often think my books are autobiographical. There's a soup kitchen in *The Wedding of the Two-Headed Woman*. I work in a soup kitchen. A lot of people in New Haven know that, so they're going to think the whole book is about me. Well, in fact, the soup kitchen is about the only thing that's taken from my life. Anyway, in the novel it's a supper soup kitchen, and mine only serves lunch.

as interviewed by Barbara Brooks

ON MEMOIR

Patricia Hampl, interviewed by Susan McInnis

You are, at this stage of your career, largely a memoirist, using your own experience and perspective as springboards for your writing. How do decisions about craft, questions of disclosure, point of view, and form, for example, play out for you as you write?

The whole issue of memoir is a vexed one, and therefore particularly interesting. In memoir, a person appears to be writing autobiography—my story—the story of my life. What could be more self-absorbed, more egotistical? What could be more interiorized? But my own experience of memoir has been something quite different. In *A Romantic Education*, my subject was the political and historical reality of another country. In *Virgin Time*, it was the reality of a religion, Catholicism. In both instances, the memoir encouraged me not only to go inward, but to go outward to issues that were far larger than me. Both books seem to be not only about me, but about these subjects in which I am used as the protagonist, although certainly not the heroine. I don't think memoirists are capable of writing themselves as heroes. But the form does require, as does every story, a protagonist, and so you use yourself in that way, or at least parts of yourself.

This discovery surprised me. I was an unwilling memoirist. I didn't want to write—really, it never occurred to me to write—a memoir. When I wrote *A Romantic Education*, the memoir was not being taught as a genre. There were poems, novels, short stories, essays, and that was about it. A memoir was something an old guy with a shelf of novels behind him might write at the end of his life. I intended to write a biography of my grandmother, a Czech immigrant who I thought was an interesting character. But it was very dull writing, and that bothered me a great deal. I couldn't figure out why, if she was so interesting, the writing would be so bad.

Then I wrote the piece about her garden, and I knew it was alive. It took me a while to understand the difference, that the garden piece had a consciousness at its heart. It had a protagonist searching, needing the story, and that protagonist was—alas—my very own self. I realized, "Oh my God, I've got to write the whole book in the first person." I didn't like that. It went against the grain. Later, I learned this was a memoir.

The first-person voice doesn't seem attention-seeking in *Virgin Time*. It carries the book's core questions, and it seems to me that the questions themselves drive the narrative as it moves along.

You know, we tend to think of genre as an "entity." If that entity is called fiction, we understand that people get to make things up. They're free to make things happen. And then there's this thing we call nonfiction. We should probably be wary of any category that comes with the word "non" in front of it. It's really denying the reality of the thing, like calling everybody non-Catholics. When we say nonfiction, it just shows how limited our ability to describe the material before us is.

Nonfiction today is really a great umbrella sheltering a number of different genres. The memoir, which seems to be nonfiction and has allegiances to some of the things nonfiction contracts to do for its readers, at the same time shares with fiction a word that doesn't belong exclusively to fiction or nonfiction, and that is story. At some point, a memoirist must tell a story, and in the telling must find a character who can carry the questions, as you say, and the ideas that are the story's bedrock. They must be carried through a human being, and if it's the first person, guess who that human being is going to be?

This brings us to memoir, to this form among others of the several versions of autobiographical writing. Still, the memoir is a rather flabby genre if it just sits around remembering things. To sustain itself over the long haul, memoir has to have some of the same rigor as a novel, as well as some vehicle for forward movement. So what does the memoirist do? Often the author takes a journey. Travel becomes the spine of the memoir, the way plot acts for the novelist.

I went to Prague for *A Romantic Education*, and for *Virgin Time* I went to Italy, on a journey to some of Italy's pilgrimage sites, on a hike through Umbria, to Assisi—the home of St. Francis and St. Clare—to several monasteries, as well as back home to St. Paul, traveling with groups and alone, back and forth through time and geography, contending with spirituality, religion, contemplation, and prayer, which were at the core of the journey.

The construction of the memoir's story, then, is much like the novel's story—a story that's built from real life, the imagination, and the questions that move us forward.

When we call a piece of writing nonfiction without acknowledging the very difficult work involved in building a reality, rather than simply transcribing one, we deny ourselves the joy, but also the hard truth, which is that we—not just writers, but all people—fashion our lives and our versions of reality.

Even as I say, "fashion our versions of reality," I am not at ease with this. I don't think, "Oh well, I just make it up. Who cares?" I don't think it's responsible or ethical or even interesting to invent in that way. But I do think there is a space between the inventions of fiction and that wished-for land of fact, and that space in between is where most of us live most of the time, where most of our stories—and, in fact, our versions of reality—are embedded. I do think we create them. We don't "find" the truth, as if it were a lost sock. And this is what we have to acknowledge—as readers as well as writers.

JUST DON'T TELL IT STRAIGHT
Elizabeth Cox, interviewed by Sarah Anne Johnson

How much of your work is autobiographical?

Probably all of it, but I change it, or else it comes from something I've heard about. I use events from my life, and then I revise them. My brothers comment on how strange it is to read names and places that are familiar, yet events have been changed, or to see a mixture of both brothers in one character. I take from everything I see and hear, from my own secrets and the secrets of others. I use everything, I just don't tell it straight. I don't use it in a way that is strictly autobiographical. The break-up of a family was written right after my divorce. Some of the things that the children said were from my own kids, but what happened in the book is not what happened to me. The pain of it is true, though. I wanted to put the pain in straight.

MELISSA PRITCHARD
interviewed by Leslie A. Wootten

How does *Disappearing Ingenue* differ from your previous work?

It's the most liberating of the books I've written, both personally and stylistically. With it, I celebrated autobiography, freely embellishing and exaggerating reality to achieve the dramatic—or comedic—effect I wanted. When I began writing years ago, the last thing I wanted was to write about myself. I wrote fiction to step away from my life, and that's why I often went as far afield as possible—fourteenth-century Poland, for example.

....

THE STORY'S IN THE TELLING
Beverly Lowry, interviewed by Stephanie Gordon

Of all your books, essays, and stories, the one that haunted me the most was *Crossed Over*, especially because of the way you wove in discussions of your late son Peter's troubles with those of Karla Faye Tucker. What was it about Tucker that made you decide to write about her?

Well, when I first went to see her, I wasn't planning to write about her. I had seen her picture in the newspaper; I was in Houston during the trial. I read a story about her rehabilitation which went back over the crimes and described her as the personification of evil. Even her lawyers were afraid of her. That paradox of the beautiful young woman whose picture I saw, how soft and kind she looked, right next to this description of her as "evil" struck a chord. It was a writer's response. I couldn't tear myself away from her, or the questions I kept asking. I had to know, to see for myself. It took a couple months of visiting her to figure out that I did want to write about her, but then I wasn't sure what to write. The murders were eleven years old, and anyway, I wasn't interested in writing what's called true crime.

Then a journalist friend gave me the idea; he felt that the story was not just her, but me telling it, the relationship between me and her. The death of my son was also part of the book's imagining—it was never not there. It was never going to be a book only about a murderer on death row, or about a young woman whose life had been turned around; it was always going to be about meeting her, developing a friendship with Plexiglas always between us, and bringing our lives, sadnesses, losses, gains, and loves to one place at one time, and it was always going to be about my son in some way or another.

But I did not want to write about her execution as the climax to the book. I told her I'd be there for her if it happened, but I did not want to be there as a writer, but as a friend. I determined later that she would probably not be executed during the time it took me to write the book. *Crossed Over* will be reprinted this fall, and I just wrote an introduction to the new edition that covers the events leading up to the execution itself.

When you began that book, did you know that it would end up being so personal?

No, I hadn't figured things out to that extent.

Did you have trouble disclosing so many of Peter's problems, and your problems in dealing with him, in the book?

I felt that because I was disclosing so much about Karla, about her troubles and her personal life, that I needed to disclose things about myself and Peter as well. She had asked me not to write about the fact that her biological father was not the man who raised her but who was her sisters' father, and she didn't want me to say that her mother had taken her when she was fourteen to be "trained in the art of pleasing men," which obviously says a lot about why she ended up doing the things she did, but I ended up writing about both of those issues. A lot of times I went along with her requests, but sometimes I didn't because I felt that she was not always acting in her own best interests. She often tried to protect those around her and sometimes this just made her look worse.

I had lots of ethical issues about the whole thing, and nobody was standing over me saying, You can't do this, you can't say that. I wasn't a journalist. I figured things out as I went. We figured it out, Karla and I. However, at the end of her life, she was beginning to open up more about all this, which I found gratifying. It needed to be known if it was to be understood.

Sometimes stumbling along in this way works. Philip Gourevitch, for instance, has an MFA in fiction writing from Columbia. And he was able to apply fictional techniques to, of all things, genocide in Rwanda, and the international politics concerning that genocide.

WRITING TO UNDERSTAND YOURSELF

Mary Gordon, interviewed by Charlotte Templin

⇒◆⇐

I think it was Annie Dillard who said that one challenge for the memoirist is deciding what to put in and what to leave out.

Yes, and in that it's not unlike the shaping of fiction. In the end, there is a form; there is a shapeliness that makes demands, and it's really a formal or almost a rhythmic question.

Would you extend that at all? Is memoir writing not that much different from fiction writing?

It is and it isn't. It has formal demands, demands of shapeliness the way that fiction does. There are some things, which, if left out, would make an untruthful record. Memoir has a responsibility to truth, or the truth as best as you can tell it. That is to say, if you willfully suppressed something—well, there is no point writing a memoir if you don't want to tell the truth as you see it. To deliberately fudge something that made you look better, or made someone else look better—that's the kind of issue that comes up in memoir that does not come up in fiction. In fiction, it doesn't matter if you want to make the character look better or worse; you do that.

One of my students was telling me about a memoir by Toscanini that was distorted to enhance the image of the writer.

I have a lot of trouble with Lillian Hellman. The books work very well as literature, but they are morally flawed. There are moral issues in memoir that don't come up in fiction.

Pentimento is a wonderful book.

It is wonderful, but it's quite untrue.

William Zinsser said one writes memoir to justify one's life—to one-self, presumably.

I think that is very true. I think that if you're a writer, you only believe you've got something right if you wrote it down, and I think it's a way of checking if you have understood yourself correctly.

....

THOMAS E. KENNEDY
interviewed by Linda B. Swanson-Davies

I taught a workshop once where one of the participants was the son of a writer whose work I was very familiar with. The son turned in a story which, as I was preparing it for critique, I clearly saw was identical to a story I had read by his father—a father-son story—with the exception that the father's piece was from the father's point of view, and the son's was from the son's. I called the fellow aside before class and asked whether it was okay with him that I mention this in the workshop, and he said, "What do you mean?" I said, "Your dad wrote the same story, but from a father's point of view," and the young man said, "He did?!" He had never read the story—yet there were incredible similarities. Which kind of renews one's faith in the possibility of an objective reality! Anyway, they were two fine stories.

SUE MILLER
interviewed by Sarah Anne Johnson

I suppose there are people who invent whole national histories, personal histories, which are purely imagined, but most people use their lives in one way or another. They work closer to the bone, or in some cases, a little further away from it. For instance, I have trouble imagining writing directly about someone that I know, and I don't believe I ever have. It would be very confining not to be able to invent a character. I'm working now on a memoir about my father's illness in which I have to write about him. Normally, I think of the act of writing as being fundamentally very playful, and I don't feel that way at all about this memoir. It's hard. I write on it, turn away and write a novel, then work on it again. I've been working on it for years and years, in part because it feels so different and uncomfortable to me to confine myself that tightly to what's real. When I'm writing fiction, my sense is very much of letting myself invent anything, while also using things that I know from my own life, or things that I've lived through. But I feel that at their cores my stories are completely invented in every case.

I remember when my son was little, I'd listen to him playing with his friends actually preparing to play. They'd say, "I'm going to come in and I'm going to say da-da-da-da, and you'll say…" That is in effect what the writer is doing a lot of the time, thinking about what her characters will say or do, and it feels very playful. And open, as though you can do whatever you want with it. I do feel that I can do what I want with my work. In that sense it's not autobiographical at all. Nothing I write is dictated by anything that's ever happened to me, and nothing is dictated by my needing to reproduce any character I've known in my life. Certainly I've used traits or ways of speaking lifted from people that I've known or from myself, but the moment that kind of thing starts to confine me, I have to break the mold.

INVENT AROUND WHAT YOU SEE
Pam Durban, interviewed by Cheryl Reid

You wrote an essay entitled "Layers" for a collection, *The Confidence Woman: 26 Women Writers at Work*, about becoming a writer and working as a writer. Was that a difficult or natural process, to narrate your path toward fiction writing?

It was really difficult. It felt icky most of the way. Any time you're doing that, it's like writing a fiction: You're choosing certain things in order to create a certain impression of yourself. You're writing about becoming a writer, and you've got to pick and choose those things which you think made you, excluding other things that also made you. You can never tell that whole story.

How do you separate autobiography from your fiction, because there is an influence there. It seems to be something hard to escape.

I don't think you ever escape. That's one of those things that made writing that essay so hard to do. You're asked to take this big organic root system and separate these different roots and classify them and say that this was important. Although the stories in my book of short stories are more overtly autobiographical, I've moved away from that as time has gone on.

Is the movement away from autobiography a process of your imagination growing stronger?

Yes, and it's your ability to invent around what you see. I can sit down now and write and just invent these things. I don't know exactly where they come from. And then I'll recognize some strand of experience that I've had or something I've observed. Personal observation is as important as what has happened to you, how you look at things, and how things get stored up over time. I don't worry about autobiography in my work anymore. The longer I write, the less I care where it comes from. Whatever comes out is what's there.

What do you think of scholars/critics who layer the author's biography around their work?

I always try to discourage people from doing that. To me, while it's true, it's also not true. There is some true feeling around which the writer is inventing, and pulling together pieces of what she knows and inventing other things to get at that piece of truth.

IN THE DIRECTION OF TRUTH
Maria Flook, interviewed by Sarah Anne Johnson

How is fiction different from memoir?

Did you ever see the jacket of Exley's *A Fan's Notes*? They call it a "fictionalized memoir." No apologies. People expect a memoir to be about real events and real people, and fiction is supposed to have invented characters. That's a basic expectation. But whether it's memoir or fiction, a story must come from a core anxiety or troubled heart if it is going to matter to the reader. In memoir, a writer uses the same devices used in fiction—scene, setting, characterization, dialogue, rising tension. In memoir, characters and events might be historically accurate, names, dates, etc., but it's not as simple as that. Why is the story important? It's not important because it really happened, but because of what the writer is exploring and examining about the human grain. Characters come to life in memoir in the same way as characters in fiction. My fictional characters should, hopefully, be just as "real" as any in my memoir. They come from the same impulse as when I write about real persons. The seed of both must be this anxiety or heartache I mention.

People worry that if memoir uses invented material, that the story can't be trusted. But in art, I think it's the artist's first task to use invention for further discovery and to reach deeper levels of meaning. One of my favorite instructions comes from Matisse. He would tell his students in his painting classes, "Exaggerate in the direction of truth." One might ask, "Isn't it false to exaggerate the truth?" I think what Matisse is saying is that one cannot reveal or portray the truth without manipulating your medium. The truth in art is not made up of exact reportage, or of concrete and representational elements alone, but it comes from the artist's own mastery of technique in order to deliver the complexity of his impulse. "Exaggerate in the direction of truth" means to use everything at your fingertips to move closer to that core anxiety.

TURN YOUR LIFE INSIDE OUT

Daniel Wallace, interviewed by Linda B. Swanson-Davies

━━━◆◆◆━━━

What would you tell a new writer about the dividing line between fiction and really not fiction? Where is the line, in your opinion?

Well, you know a question like this is like taking a poll of one. It's just one person's experience and opinion.

The only one I'm after.

I know that people have different ways of going about it, and can draw more directly from their day-to-day, tactile experience, and they'll describe the street they lived on. They'll put their fictional character on the street they lived on. Describe the street. I could never do that. For me, what gets me going is when I actually take my life and turn it inside out. One story that I wrote illustrates this point pretty well: "The Story of a Hairy Man." It's about a man whose hair starts to grow all over his body to the point that he can't control it anymore, and he becomes this very hairy man. At first, he's plucking little hairs from his nose, and he's cutting his hair, and he's brushing the hair on his arms, and it's a funny story. It just starts to grow and he can't control it anymore. Now, that was inspired by my fear of going bald. I've always thought I was gonna, and I am. I mean, my hair is thinning as I get older, and I'll have these dreams where I'll be bald. So I took that and I turned it around. It's what I call "going against the grain." I took that same emotion, the same fear, but I made the character experience the opposite reality that I was afraid of facing myself. And I was able to imagine and create something totally new to me, and interesting to me. Writing a story about someone who's going bald just doesn't do it, does it? You know it really doesn't work. It's not interesting. It possibly could've been, but I wouldn't have been interested in writing that. I was interested in writing about this guy who had to go to the bathroom at the office all the time to make sure his hair's okay, because it's growing so quickly. So I think that for me it's much more interesting to take the facts of your life as you see them and distort them. It is like an exercise that I do.

Can I see "My Old Vanity" for a second? The guy in this story doesn't have any hair. At that time, my hair was down to my shoulders. We had cut part of it off and put it in a bag for the birds to use for nesting. That was the basis for this whole story. It became not just a little bit of hair, but all the hair this guy has, and why that would happen. Anyway, for my money, you're usually gonna come up with something a lot more interesting if you take some of the emotional truths that your life presents you with, and then rediscover them through re-imagining them and going from there. That's how I do it. That's what makes it fun for me.

If you stick too closely to your own experience, you have a built-in ceiling to that story. It's not going to go anywhere, or it's not going to go as far as it could.

....

Barbara Scot: Nothing is irrelevant. The strongest temptation is to think, Oh, but they wouldn't be interested in that. But the most ordinary parts of our lives are the very things that tie us to the human condition. The detail of tenderness or pain. We're tempted not to use it because it seems like we're being sentimental.

as interviewed by Linda B. Swanson-Davies

EDITING THE PAST

Kevin Canty, interviewed by Linda B. Swanson-Davies

I see myself and the selves of my characters as being a collage of a lot of different things, of real experiences, and things that were made up, and things that I saw on television, and things that I read—fantasies, memories, desires. It's a patchwork.

I was talking to my mom this summer, and found that neither of the first two things I remember in my life ever happened. I remember them very vividly. One of the things could have really happened when she wasn't around, but she was there in the other memory. I remember it vividly, but apparently it didn't happen. My advice is that if you don't like to hear that, then you should never ask your mom about these things. It's very interesting to see how much we're able to superimpose our own version of our lives on the events of our lives. People say, "The past is the past," but nobody's ever talking about their whole past. Everybody's editing. Everybody's doing what, in a sense, a fiction writer is doing—taking snippets of detail, the ones that seem to matter, the ones that seem to count, and assembling them into a life. It's what I do when I'm putting myself together, take these snippets and put them together into a coherent form.

What's interesting to me about that is that I don't think it's stable or permanent, but always subject to revision. That's one of the things that a couple of people in this book [*A Stranger in This World*] are doing. They're suddenly having to find new versions of themselves because the old persons would never have done that. I've noticed, from watching people, that when you've lost the version of yourself, you really have lost something of value. Whether or not it was particularly accurate, or particularly useful, or particularly constructive, or made you happy—having to move from one version of yourself is essential.

TOI DERRICOTTE

interviewed by Susan McInnis

You've quoted Henri Matisse as saying, "The job of the artist is to turn himself inside out before he dies." Can you elaborate? I think we probably know what that means on the surface—but what does it mean to you when you sit down to write?

Well, I think it means opening yourself to discovering what it means to be human, and constantly finding new material, new theories—things about yourself that at first you may not want to look at, not want to explore. If you believe what's underneath ties us all together as human beings, then really no matter what you find, it's a way of validating human experience. So you keep turning things up, finding a way to take what is buried and turn it into art.

Some part of the skeleton that is you is in me as well?

I wonder if I think of it as skeleton—I guess for me it becomes skeleton when you find a form for it. As it becomes a real work of art, it takes on that kind of reality for me. But there's so much between consciousness and unconsciousness that is of great interest to me: what is almost forgotten. What is intentionally forgotten—like certain times our parents, our grandparents, won't talk about certain things. Trying to find a way to bring those things to the surface is interesting to me … One of the things I do is try to go across boundaries. I'm driven to go across boundaries—boundaries you're not supposed to go across. I can remember when I was very young, there were neighborhood boundaries, lines around neighborhoods, and your parents would tell you, "Don't cross Ryan Road. You'll get hit by a car." There were these practical reasons for you not to go across Ryan Road. But really it was something else. There was a reason you weren't supposed to go across Ryan Road that was not just about the cars. There was something on the other side of Ryan Road that you weren't supposed to go to …

People have said a lot about how light-skinned black people have privileges. I think it's true. Do you know the Andrew Hacker story? He wrote *Two Nations: Black and White, Separate, Hostile, Unequal.* A wonderful book. He did an experiment in the colleges where he said to young college students, "All right, everything about you stays the same, but we're going to make your skin black. What do we have to give you—in terms of money—to make it worth your while?" Their answer was a million dollars a year for the rest of their lives.

To make it worth it to have darker skin?

Exactly. For white students.

In this society you are "dead meat." You don't exist. You are invisible. You are not recognized. You could be an athlete, you know, or a dancer.

A model.

A model. Yes…

Toni Morrison talks about—lots of things she's talked about lately are so wonderful—about how American literature isn't complete until all the stories are there. It's so important is to empower people who don't know how to begin to speak about their experiences because they're ashamed of it.

Writing is so powerful, you see. People who have been—marginalized is a very common word—they feel their experience is not valuable.

BARBARA SCOT

interviewed by Linda B. Swanson-Davies

You were very revealing in *Prairie Reunion*.

You know, I wasn't until the fifth draft.

Why was that?

Well, in writing the book, I lived through all that psychological unraveling and discovery. I just hadn't planned to share it completely with the reader, but I was on my fourth draft when I found my agent and she said, "This is very good, I'm quite sure I can sell it, but this needs more of your pain." I knew she was right—what would make this a marketable book would be to use my own pain, because this is what people would most identify with. But I felt like I'd already sold the bones of my ancestors and now I was going to sell my own soul as well, and when this first started being billed as a memoir, it was rather disturbing to me. I considered the main focus to be social history, using a family as a vehicle to work through social history.

....

WHOSE STORY IS IT, ANYWAY?
Nomi Eve, interviewed by Linda B. Swanson-Davies

I've known for a while now that I've had a story to tell. I'd say for the last four years. Four years I've been actively writing this book [*The Family Orchard*]. And at the very beginning, I wrote hundreds of pages, hundreds and hundreds of pages that no one will ever see. The story had such a complex timetable that I couldn't figure out how to do it. Where does the story start? That was the hardest thing. Where does this story start? Because it's not only my story, but it's a family story, and what does that mean? Does that mean it starts when the people in the family were born, or does it start when I was told their story? Does it start with my birth? How much of it is my story? How much is it their story? Is it my father's story, because he told me part of the story? Or is it my grandparents' story, because those were the people he was telling me about? So does it start with their birth?

I was crazy over this. I remember I would write pages and pages and then I would make lists of the events and try to put them in an order. Nothing worked. I'm picturing myself sitting in my cousin's den making this list. And one day, once again, I was trying to write, trying to write, and I picked up one of my father's notebooks and copied a couple of sentences, and then I wrote the

Esther and Yochanan story, and that was the start of it.

"Esther and Yochanan" was the start? Oh, I'm so pleased to hear that.

Yeah, you have it [in *Glimmer Train Stories* #19]. Suddenly, I combined these times of telling. It was my "I write," and it was my father's "He writes," and it was the family story all at once. I wasn't conscious of this when I was doing it, but that's what happened, and that changed everything.

....

THE MESSAGES WE RECEIVE
Jamaica Kincaid
interviewed by Linda B. Swanson-Davies

The other thing about me and writing is I'm always so interested in getting the thing done that there is no artificiality in it—for me. Maybe it seems so, but I feel I reach into something quite directly. I was just saying to my editor the other day that it will be a while, if ever again, before he got a book like that [*The Autobiography of My Mother*] from me, because I wasn't sure I could go to that area again. It's grim, straightforwardly grim. Unrelenting. I'm not sure I can do it again. Of course, I always say that and then I do it again, when I really felt like I couldn't do it again. When I'm writing, there is no distance between my writing and me.

In your growing up, was there a set of words that you heard regularly that told you the kind of world it was?

Well, it's funny. I wrote a story called "Girl," and … you should read it, it would answer your question quite well. Yes, absolutely.

A litany, over the years, of things my mother said to me about how to be.

Does it boil down to one message?

Yes. Not to be a slut.

Wow.

Which is not to enjoy myself. You should read it. It's really kind of fascinating. Even I think so.

A PARALLEL HISTORY

Abdelrahman Munif, interviewed by Michael Upchurch

Any novel, especially a novel like *Cities of Salt*, depends on a large amount of information from diverse sources. From my connections with the times, the places, the country, and the people who made it, I got much of the detail used in the books. But, of course, there is a lot of work of the imagination that goes into this becoming an artistic work.

Then again, there are events which I did not experience firsthand, but which other people experienced, that would provide material for novels far more provocative than *Cities of Salt*.

In Peter Theroux's memoir, *Sandstorms: Days and Nights in Arabia*, you describe your novels to Theroux as a "parallel history." How freely did you draw on Saudi history in creating the history of Mooran? Did you give yourself any ground rules to follow? And what exactly do you mean by "parallel history"?

A novel is a complete world encompassing things that have happened and things that could happen, plus the imagination. So when I did sit down to write *Cities of Salt*, it may have been as a novel parallel to this political history. In a case like this, the character in the novel may have a much richer personality than the person who did actually pass through history. One does not want to hold a novelist to the logic that would govern a political historian. Of course, sometimes when there's a topic that I can't write as a novel, I write it as an article in the newspaper, as an analysis, or some other way.

I would prefer that people deal with me and approach me as a novelist rather than as a historian. If the novel intersects with history, that's something that happens in many novels. But unfortunately, people tend to oversimplify.

SIRI HUSTVEDT

interviewed by Jennifer Levasseur and Kevin Rabalais

After I finished my dissertation at Columbia, I had the urge to write a story that came out of an uncanny experience I had had as a student when I met someone through an ad on a bulletin board. The true story and the fictional story are very different, but they share what I felt: uneasy and disturbed. It was that feeling that I wanted to turn into a story. I called the piece "Mr. Morning," and after I had written it, I knew I wasn't finished with Iris, and decided to write a book about her [*The Blindfold*].

GEORGE MAKANA CLARK

interviewed by Linda B. Swanson-Davies

When we published "Backmilk," you provided a wonderful picture of your great-grandmother. What gifts do you imagine she would, or has, bestowed upon your children?

It's odd, but it's sort of like a guardian angel looking over us. There's a great deal of ancestor worship in a lot of African cultures, and I wonder if some of that hasn't rubbed off on me, because I feel very aware of my great-grandmother, and yet I know almost nothing about her. Much of what I write is filling in gaps of stuff I couldn't possibly know. That's how I came to write "Backmilk." It's a merging of my life and my daughter's life, because I couldn't really tell you what happened in my own infancy. But I can see my daughter's birth, so I merge the events together … I would like to think that I am getting an idea of the importance of spirituality. It seems so hokey, so corny to us when we're younger, and there's also the if-you-can't-explain-something-it-doesn't-exist idea that so much of our culture has.

Writers often start with autobiographical materials that they are pushed internally to write. Do you have recommendations for people to help them create a piece of fiction that works?

One thing is to try not to embellish too much. I mean, you can add things from other people's experience that relate. I like to throw everything into a story. Someone tells me there's too much going on in a story, I'll throw in more stuff, because life is complicated, and I think a story should be as well. There are so many things that are acting upon us. If you want a simple motivation-action sort of story, then you should go into the juvenile-literature section. Life is not that simple. But at the same time, they should trust their experiences. I ofttimes have my students write down the strangest job or the worst job they've ever had, or whatever seems to stand out in their minds. One person used to clean out chicken cages, which to me would be the most awful job in the world—the stench, and I'm not a vegetarian, but what a cruel existence. I had a professor who used to repossess wigs. If they didn't make their payments, he would go and get their wigs. I had to wear the Winnie-the-Pooh costume. I was claustrophobic, and my head was stuck in a honey jar like in the story. You should just trust the material. That's where I get in trouble. After I first write a story, I spend all the drafts trying to take myself out of it. I mean as a writer, taking out clever little sentences that don't belong, or forced humor, or forced pathos. Though I don't think you ever really succeed …

My stories usually are a combination of my experiences and the experiences of other people. The novel I'm working on is bizarre and darkly comic, and yet almost everything in it either really did happen or nearly happened, or is an exaggeration of something that happened. Yesterday, I saw a pair of very expensive sunglasses in the bottom of a urinal and started thinking of what the story was behind that. Did they belong to a very fastidious person that would never touch them again? And then, of course, nobody else would. There are so many stories going on.

PAUL THEROUX
interviewed by Michael Upchurch

I put in "Lady Max" all the happy moments: my London happiness. That's a story about writing in London, for anyone who's wondered what the writer's life was like in London if you were of that age. It was set around 1978–'79. How old was I then? Thirty-six, thirty-seven. I don't know if that's old or young. I felt very much on top of things, in some respects. In other respects, I was sort of living on Grub Street. Jonathan Raban was part of that life. Martin Amis was just a little guy working as an assistant at the *New Statesman*, and I used to see him every so often. And then there were more grand figures around, like Angus Wilson, V. S. Pritchett, Anthony Burgess.

So I deliberately wrote that story to encapsulate that wonderful experience—the experience of living in London, writing during the day, the winter. I always loved writing in the winter when it was dark.

....

PLAYING WITH HER FOOD
Kathleen Tyau
interviewed by Linda B. Swanson-Davies

Nearly every story in this collection [*A Little Too Much Is Enough*] appears to revolve in some way around food. Why food?

It's not really food but eating that fascinates me. Chinese and Hawaiians are very fussy about what they eat. I know they're not the only ones, but they're the ones I know best. Once my mother came to visit me in Portland. She drove down from Seattle with two of my uncles and an aunt. But they couldn't stay long because they had to drive back to Seattle in time to buy fresh crab before the market closed. I was disappointed, but I didn't take it personally. I mean, you just grow up knowing what's important. One day, I sat down and wrote a list of foods I remembered eating and then just started writing. I turned this list into titles—such as "Uncle Joey's Squab," "Avocado Uncle," "Spoon Meat," and "Fifty-Dollar Pineapple"—and before I knew it, I had started writing a book.

WRITING ADVICE from Monica Wood

By all means, bring in your experience! Those "real" touches are what make fiction seem real and accessible. That's not the same as writing about things that really happened to you. My admonition against doing that still holds. The least successful stories I have seen in my ten years of teaching fiction courses and workshops are those in which the student writers try to force a real-life experience into the shape of a story. Usually it's because they really want to be writing a memoir but want to protect the innocent. Well, guess what? The innocent will recognize themselves anyway, so you lose either way.

SPARING PEOPLE'S FEELINGS
by Melanie Bishop

Anyone who has written autobiographically has faced the fear [of hurting family and friends]. I've had terrible reactions, by loved ones, to stories I've written, and I've also had reactions that were surprisingly reaffirming.

One childhood friend, after reading a story with a character she recognized as herself, wrote me a curt note that basically said, "I'm shocked and hurt at your portrayal of me, that you would see me as such a shallow person. Obviously you've never known me." I was at the very beginning of my writing career at the time, just out of college, and completely freaked out by her reaction. I embarked on an eight-page letter in response, a long, involved explanation of how I come up with a story, how I mix actual events from my life with total fabrication—fiction—and how the character she thought was herself had actually been a combination of three women I know. My disappointment was that in her reaction to the story, she completely missed what the story was about, which was a celebration of our friendship, which had withstood the fact that she and I went in very different directions in our adult lives. When I pointed all this out to her, she was embarrassed and apologetic. She reread the story and admitted she'd overreacted. These days, I would probably not honor such a reaction with the time and effort it took to write that letter. People who respect you and what you do tend to respect the complexity inherent in the writer's challenge.

My father is an example of someone who ends up a character in much of my fiction, and handles this with absolute grace. He knows that my perception of aspects of our family differ from his own, and that some tales I might tell could paint him in a less than favorable light. Regardless, he has never once complained about a portrayal of him, and he has always encouraged me to write what I feel compelled to write, and not to worry about his or anyone else's reaction. I truly admire and respect him for this. He's one of my biggest supporters and fans.

All this is to say that ultimately, if you're going to write, you have to not care who might be bothered by what. If you concern yourself with that, you'll find yourself silenced. There's no autobiographical story that doesn't take on this risk. All we can do as writers is be committed to telling the truth as we know it—emotional truth as opposed to factual truth. There's a good movie, Australian, I think, called *Sorrento Beach*. A woman writes a novel about her family and it becomes a best seller, and in the process, the lid is blown off the family's secrets. She and her two sisters get together, and for a while it's easier for everyone to pretend the book is pure fiction. Eventually, strange dynamics ensue and the women undergo a sort of catharsis. From my experience, the truth, or a truth, however painful initially, rarely results in something totally destructive. As is the case for the characters in *Sorrento Beach*, quite often it can be constructive.

But ultimately we can't concern ourselves with these outcomes. My major professor in graduate school said something I'll always remember: "If you're into the business of sparing people's feelings, don't write. Do something else." And again, more often than not, people will surprise you with the generosity of their response to your work in which they're featured. People, all of us, enjoy at times being the focus of attention, and many folks are simply flattered that they've been a subject in your story.

JIM GRIMSLEY

interviewed by Jim Schumock

What's the family's story in *Winter Birds*? I understand it is somewhat autobiographically your own.

I felt that it was important to own this book in terms of the autobiography in it because it's on very hard subjects. *Winter Birds* tells the story of a woman named Ellen who gets married a good deal too young, because she has no choice, to a man who turns out to be very violent. At the same time that they're trying to work out this very passionate and tender love they have for each other, he is also struggling to deal with psychological problems that cause him to abuse her. I'm making the book sound a lot more psychological than it is; in actuality, it's a kind of single-line tragedy. I tried my best to present the character of the father with some sympathy, but without sheltering myself from the fact that he was a bad man, this man.

He lost his hand in an agricultural accident.

Right. He was cleaning a corn picker and it pulled most of one arm off, or ground it up, depending on whether you're talking about the book version or the real version. This was all stuff that happened to my family. There was never an actual weekend that had this concentration of events in it like I've written about in

Winter Birds, but the essence of the book is very true to what I went through, to what my family went through.

Two of the boys in the family are hemophiliacs as well.

I have hemophilia and my youngest brother also had hemophilia.

I read where you went to your father's funeral just to make sure that he was dead.

Yes. I did say that.

Can you describe how you felt that day?

Yeah. Relieved, actually. It's cruel to say it, but you'd have to know my dad and how much he had done. I got the word—I was at Chapel Hill. I was a junior when I got the call that he was dead. My sister called me. Mom and my youngest brother, Brian, were in Florida and they had decided not to come up, so it was just my sister and my brother and me, and mostly I felt like … at that point, I was having nightmares. I would wake up thinking he was outside the house trying to get in, and I thought if I didn't go, it would be as if he were everywhere, especially knowing that he had died. So I went to the funeral and saw him and really felt nothing for him by that point, not even a great deal of anger. He was simply there and he was finally at some kind of state of rest that I could trust, and that was it.

I know your mother's remarried, and I was wondering how she views that past life now. It must almost be for her as if it were another life.

She's very good with the whole thing. She's read *Winter Birds*. She read it in an advance copy last summer, just before it came out, and was really touched by the book. She told me that it made her remember a lot of things that she probably would not voluntarily have recalled, but that she was glad it was there, and that she thought it was a very beautiful thing.

What about your brother and sister?

My sister's read it; my brother has not. He prefers not to, and I don't blame him.

. . . .

ENTRE LA FAMILIA

Julia Alvarez
interviewed by Mike Chasar and Constance Pierce

My favorite memoir, the one that freed me to write about what I know, was not by a Latino writer but an Asian-American woman, Maxine Hong Kingston. And her book starts out, "'You must not tell anyone,' my mother said, 'what I am about to tell you.'" From the very beginning, she sets out that just by writing she's already overturning her whole cultural programming, betraying her culture. Being a woman, especially a woman of a minority culture where you're trained to have no public voice, that everything is *entre la familia*—already, by being a writer, you are transgressing that cultural norm. Maybe not among the intellectuals, say, in the Dominican Republic, but certainly among my family. My mother's commentary about *The García Girls* is, "Como las gringas." Just like the gringas. "They get on the late-night TV and they tell their secrets to all of America." When you write out of what you know, even if it's not autobiography, but it's based on what you know, it's considered a betrayal of keeping it *entre la familia*.

....

EXPLORING THE 'WHAT IF?'

Tobias Wolff, interviewed by Jim Schumock

⟹◆⟸

I really enjoyed the story "The Chain," where a simple act of minor revenge eventuates the death of an innocent. What's the genesis of this tale?

It's not a memoir. I invented greatly after I started writing it. But the story has its genesis in something that happened to me on a Christmas Day many years ago, when my oldest boy was four years old. He had just gotten a sled for Christmas. I took him to a park in Syracuse that had a beautiful, long hill. He was having a blast. Then, as he was getting to the bottom of the hill, I saw this big, black German shepherd come tearing out of a yard. I could see that the dog was attached to a chain. I kept waiting for the chain to pull the dog up short, but it didn't. The chain was like sixty feet long. It reached way into the park. The dog leaped for my son's face. At the last minute, for some reason—he may have heard me yelling—my son flinched away and the dog caught him by the shoulder and shook him badly. It was a miracle that he didn't have his face torn off or suffer permanent injury.

I couldn't get the police to act; the fact that he could get into the park didn't matter to them, because he was on this chain. I simply could not get them to act. While I was in the middle of all this, a friend of mine offered to kill the dog for me. It was still there, waiting to attack somebody else. This disturbed me greatly. It wasn't just my son. I was afraid that other children would get hurt. I actually entertained this notion. I said, "Well, if anybody does it, it should be me." He said, "You can't do it, they'll know it was you," which was true. He said, "Let me do it, I'll take care of it for you." And I was so furious at the time and frustrated that I actually considered it. I said, "I would be greatly in your debt." He said, "That's okay. Maybe someday you can do something for me." The minute he said that, I knew that this was not a road I wanted to go down. There was no telling where this would end. I cut it off. In fact, I was finally able to get some action out of the dog's owners. They had to move the dog out of the city.

So it was better that I didn't kill it, of course, but the possibility set off a whole chain of circumstances in my mind, a vision of the world we live in where everybody seems to be trying to get revenge for something that went wrong—the Rwandans, the Hutus, the Bosnians, the Croatians, the Serbs, Chechnians, the Russians—they're all trying to get what they think is justice. But one man's justice is another man's injustice. I thought of that as a kind of chain, too. So I started thinking, What if I had let him do this? I recast the story in that way so that this act leads unintentionally to another act and then to another until the very aim this main character had in trying to get justice ends up resulting in the very thing that he was trying to stop in the first place: violence to a child. That's the way it works. We try to right an injustice, and we end up committing more. It's a fable, this story, but it's rooted in reality. That's how I came to write it.

ASKOLD MELNYCZUK
interviewed by William Pierce

How do you navigate the question of what distance to maintain from your own past in your fiction?

I have yet to allow myself the freedom to write "autobiographically." Certainly there are many autobiographical elements in characters and circumstances, but I've always felt a book come alive when I've succeeded in forgetting where it came from, when I've spent enough time writing out characters on the page to have forgotten what memories or sources I may have drawn on. In the new book I've started, I'm trying to give myself the freedom to mix memory more frankly than I have in the first two.

Yet your work amplifies some of the themes presented by the circumstances of your life. In an *AGNI* essay, for instance, you tell the story of a Jewish writer who said to you, "You know, in the old country, your grandparents were murdering my grandparents." And in *Ambassador*, Nick is left to decide how to react to a similar line.

I know things often seem more autobiographical than they feel to me, than I think that they are. In the process of writing a novel, you try to create characters whose lives and concerns grow out of something you have feelings about, but you put the characters into circumstances and situations so far removed from the context of similar real-life experiences that they're really very different things, to be understood in the context that the work has created for them.

Just to work on the thematic example you've brought up here—because I remember the circumstances under which the question in the *AGNI* editorial was asked, and then fifteen, sixteen years later it surfaces as a concern for one of my characters—we see that there's a connection, but what can we say beyond the fact that naturally your fiction will reflect—damn well better reflect—some of the questions that have lodged inside you, that are meaningful, that have not been answered in your own life or in the life of the culture from what you have seen of it? Writing and fiction become a way of exorcising or answering those questions. You try to identify the things that nag at you—obsessions, mysteries that are simultaneously psychological and historical—and approach them as personally as possible, trying to use all the resources of your imagination and intellect to dramatize and come to understand them.

HOW NOVELS ARE BORN
Sigrid Nunez, interviewed by Linda B. Swanson-Davies

When you were writing *A Feather on the Breath of God*, did you discover that certain events or circumstances from when you were growing up had more of an impact on you than you realized before you started writing it?

Yes. It's hard to talk about, because I don't really want to match up experiences in my own life with experiences in the book. But this is a book with a narrator looking back at childhood, and there were many things that I hadn't thought of in years, and, by the time the book was finished, I did understand my own character better. I found it extremely interesting, but I also think that it would happen to anyone. I didn't think it was unique. A woman came up to me at a reading and she said, "You know, I would love to write about my past, but I don't remember anything." I told her that if she sat down and started to write, it would all come back, but she said that she had a feeling that if she did that she would just naturally start inventing. And I said, "Exactly! And this is how novels are born."

THE PESKIEST GENRE
by Monica Wood

I think the techniques for literary fiction and nonfiction are almost exactly the same. You try to pace the piece so that it has an illusion of forward motion; you try to draw memorable, interesting characters; you try to establish a consistent voice; you try to make the "arc" of the piece follow a logical beginning, middle, and end. Creative nonfiction poses a problem, however, because real life is not shaped like a story. In the interest of good storytelling, you are tempted to compress time, combine characters, make up dialogue—all the things you are perfectly free to do in fiction. This is why I consider creative nonfiction a pesky, problematic genre. I read most memoirs with a degree of skepticism, especially when the chronology seems suspiciously elegant. Nonfiction writers take on a terrible burden, because they are bound to tell the truth, which more often than not defies the structural confines of great storytelling. Nonfiction writers have to search for original ways to put "stories" together honestly. They might use letters or diaries to fill gaps in time, or recount a conversation from two different viewpoints, or make other innovations to allow a story to unfold without violating what I believe is their promise to tell the reader the truth. One of my favorite memoirs is *This Boy's Life* by Tobias Wolff, because it reads like a novel, and I believed it all.

THE BOOK OF A LIFETIME

Robert Stone, interviewed by Jim Schumock

You've said that A Hall of Mirrors *contained the sum total of everything you had experienced, felt, or suspected. How were you able to sustain such a high level of creativity during those early years?*

I kept writing in the way that somebody keeps writing the book that they feel they're going to be writing all their lives. I don't know if I actually thought in any real terms that I would ever get this first one finished. I thought I was a guy who was going to be carrying a book around and writing it all his life. Everything that happened to me, everything I knew, as I said, went into it. After a period of time, working one job after another, going on unemployment, coming off it, working my thirty-six weeks, and so forth, to my astonishment and with some help from my publisher and the program that I had been to at Stanford, I got it done. I found it between covers.

JAYNE ANNE PHILLIPS
interviewed by Sarah Anne Johnson

What is the role of autobiography in your fiction?

It's a starting point, much in the way that physical details are a starting point for writing about meaning and time and dimension. The reader should think that whatever you write is autobiographical, because they should be convinced intensely of the reality of the piece. They should feel that it comes from somewhere very deep in the writer. But the minute you work in language, the minute you work in fiction, there's a translation that occurs, like the translation from one language into another, from book to film, thought into speech. There are such different forms of being. The only thing that's autobiographical is the need to write something that has to come from your own life in some way, but it may have very little to do, in a paper-doll way, with the material itself.

10

WRITER'S BLOCK

Jim Mitchell, ca. 1960

GEORGE MAKANA CLARK

interviewed by Linda B. Swanson-Davies

Writer's block doesn't have to be an agonizing experience. Think of it instead as your unconscious telling you to slow down and evaluate where your writing is going. Better to take a breather than become a prolific hack, churning out volumes upon volumes of twaddle.

You might think you're lying in a hammock, idly scratching your pet beagle behind her ear, when actually your unconscious is busy prewriting your next piece. Or maybe it's helping you gain a fresh perspective on a problem story. Start kicking your own backside because you haven't met some arbitrary work quota for the day, then you'll know true paralysis.

When you find you've written yourself into a corner, or you just can't seem to get excited about starting a new project, relax—your unconscious has got it all under control.

WRITING ADVICE from Joyce Thompson

For those times you seem to hit a dead end, take a nap, a long shower, a long walk, cook something complicated, or draw a picture. Pull your brain off active duty and trust that, subliminally, the band plays on.

ALONG FOR THE RIDE

Roy Parvin, interviewed by Linda B. Swanson-Davies

When I'm in the middle of a story, publishing is one of the last things I'm thinking about. I'm trying to survive the story. Someone said to Ron Carlson something about Ron being in the middle of a story right now, and he said, "No, I'm not in the middle; I'm hanging off the edge of it." I think that that's such a wise way to put it. I used to think, Once I get past this one point, the rest of the story will be easy. But there's no coasting in stories. Every single day, it's very, very difficult. Every single day, you're throwing yourself against this object that seemingly will not move, and then one day suddenly budges, and you don't know quite why it is budging. It is. So you jump on and you go along for the ride. It feels like you're creating something that is bigger and smarter than yourself. It's wonderful to see this on paper. I'm surprised by what happens at times. And the connections that you see that you … that they are authoring in one way, but you're authoring in a controlling way.

It comes out of this funny area of our heads that I don't think we understand our connections to.

I don't know if you want to know. I mean you could—

Could screw it up.

Yeah.

RUNNING AROUND IN THE WOODS

Carolyn Chute, interviewed by Barbara Stevens

When you're writing, do you ever get to the point where you get stuck, and it just dies on you?

Yeah, most of the time.

What do you do?

Just keep hitting my head against the wall. I put in between eight and eleven hours every day—even the weekends, if no one comes. So something is bound to happen.

What do you do when you're sitting there for eight hours and it's not coming and you're stuck?

I do try to find a lot of excuses when it's going bad not to go there and do it. But then the time comes when you gotta sit there and keep starting over when it doesn't seem to go well. I probably do that too much.

You go back to the beginning?

Not necessarily the beginning. There's no actual beginning and end in my work until the last few months. There are no actual pages. I don't even number them. If someone asked how far along am I in my novel, I could not even say I even have one finished paragraph.

It's sort of like deer hunting. You spend a lot of time running around the woods wasting your time. You might go out there for ten years and never get a shot off. You might get a shot and miss. More likely, you just blow a deer's jaw off, or a foot. Then you can't find the deer. You hunt for years, just maiming deer. Shooting at a rototiller. A few picnic tables. A woman wearing white mittens. Eventually, all at once, all in one moment, you kill a deer and bring him or her home. That's the way it is for me writing a book. A lot of mess and weirdness, then all at once, I bag it … all in a few weeks. Bang!

JULIA ALVAREZ

interviewed by Mike Chasar and Constance Pierce

I was at Yaddo, where they had given me a residency; I was having horrible writer's block, because I was trying to sound like Yeats, "Turning and turning in the widening gyre"—this huge voice! You can't visit other studios at Yaddo during the day, and so I couldn't even go talk to the other writers, and I was just so anxious. And you know what saved me? I heard the vacuum cleaner outside my door. I discovered the maids. They were all around Yaddo, cleaning up and putting lunches outside of people's doors. And I made my way down to the kitchen where there was an old cook. She had been there for about thirty years and could tell you who was a fussy eater and what so-and-so liked. And she had one of those old cookbooks held together with a rubber band, with Christmas cards and Mother's Day cards and recipe alterations written in and stuff like that, and as she was talking, I started to read her lists … knead, poach, stew, whip, and stir …

And I thought, why not? If Homer can have his catalog of ships, why not a catalog of cooking techniques or of spices? Why not all the ways to iron a shirt, and how to hang out a line of wash?—those are crafts, too. And so I started writing my housekeeping poems.

CROWDED BY WORDS

Louis Begley, interviewed by Robert Birnbaum

Perhaps I should have asked before: are you still lawyering?

I am glad to announce that this is coming to an end. On January 1, I will be a free man. Until now, I only worked as a writer on weekends and holidays. I am unable to write in the evening of a workday, not because I am tired—I am actually quite resilient—but because my head is full of the wrong words.

It really is a question of words. Words on subjects that are not connected with what I am doing. I don't even like to write in the afternoon. I like to start in the morning—when I haven't had contact with people or had real concerns and words crowding in on me. When I get stuck as I write, I find that the best solution is either to go for a walk, or even better is to lie down and sleep for twenty, thirty minutes, and then when I get up I have a whole new view.

I've never been able to catnap.

I'm a specialist.

Any trick to it?

Just lie on your back, close your eyes. Don't make a big deal. Don't pull down blinds. Don't open the bed. Don't make it so that if you don't fall asleep you have failed in some humiliating way.

....

WELCOME TO THE CLUB
by Melanie Bishop

Writer's block doesn't really exist. All writers experience periods of being more prolific than during some other period of time. And most writers have a story about a time when a story was so easy that it essentially "wrote itself." More often, though, it isn't easy for most writers I know. I think people have different definitions of "writer's block." If you're talking about a day when you'd sooner scrub the inside of the toilet with a toothbrush than face the blank computer screen, well, welcome to the club. Very few writers I know face a new manuscript or an unfinished one without trepidation. Some days it's worse than others, when you're struggling with a problem a story has presented you with, a brick wall, a "block." It's harder, no doubt about it, to write on a day like that, but my point is that it's still possible. It's also not a bad idea to take time off from troublesome work; and that doesn't have to mean you're "blocked." Think of it as gestation.

As a teacher, I go through long periods of time where I don't produce any new work. I would not classify this as a time when I'm blocked. At any moment, I can (and sometimes do) sit down, start a new story, revise an old one, or work on something I started and never finished. For me, it's a matter of reserving and respecting the time for my own work. Once I've carved that out, there are good times and bad times at the computer, but never would I say I experience writer's block. I have periods where I'm quite unproductive, but it's not for lack of something to say. It's about being busy, or managing my time poorly; it's not about feeling mute or abandoned by the muse. To the contrary, after a long hiatus, I often gush the next thing out, like all that waiting just made me more fluent once I parked myself at the computer.

I encourage my students to not believe in "writer's block." Writing always takes on a rhythmic pattern, and lows are as necessary as the highs. Refuse to believe in such a thing as writer's block. Allow yourself time off without feeling guilty about being unproductive. Reinterpret the experience of a day when you sit in front of a blank screen for hours and no words come. To me, that's a day when mental work took place, and any writer will tell you that much of a story or novel's development takes place in the writer's head, before it becomes words on a page.

STARTING OVER (AND OVER)
Brad Watson, interviewed by Robert Birnbaum

I had started *The Heaven of Mercury* in the winter of '96. That's when I wrote the first pages. I had a month-long retreat to Seaside, Florida, an artists' retreat. I wrote a hundred pages, which was a pretty good start. Some of that even survived into the book. I was also teaching four classes a semester at Alabama and was looking for a job. It was a hard book to write. I kept running into a wall, knowing I really didn't have a grasp of the story. I started over every year and I'd get maybe one hundred and twenty-five pages, next year one hundred and fifty. Finally, about two years ago, I ended up with something that went from the beginning until the end and was about two hundred and forty pages long in manuscript, and I knew that I had the book.

GIVE IT TIME

by Doug Lawson

I'm learning to pay very close attention to what I have written of the story already, even if it seems weird. Often, I'll find clues to where the story might go by figuring out where the characters would rather not go. We all like to be comfortable, after all, and fiction characters are no different from the rest of us. But a good story is made from drama, and drama arises from change, and change is not usually comfortable.

There's a secret to this, and that's simply this: Give it time. Be patient with your story. When you leave a piece sit for some time and come back to it, you'll likely see all sorts of things in there you can build on. Certain verbs will seem out of place, until you realize what that verb is really telling you—that you'd meant to talk about something else in that spot. Frank Black, Secret Agent, didn't tap dance his way out the door of the bar. But, you realize later, he might have tap danced while growing up, and the memory of that dance might have been in his head in the bar, and that of course is why he shuffled his feet on the way down the street to the dancing school on the corner, where he discovers Imelda, his mother, whom he'd thought dead, working at the counter …

Patience, though, is the hardest thing for a new writer to learn. It's likely one of the most important skills you can teach yourself.

MARY McGARRY MORRIS
interviewed by Linda B. Swanson-Davies

I suppose I've had writer's block in one form or another. But I just kept on going, even if it was lousy.

Often when the writing is most difficult, when a passage or chapter demands attention and rewriting, I've found that these will be the passages and chapters I'm most pleased with in the end. And there have been many, many times when a particular problem with a character's motivation or development was solved because I wasn't just writing smoothly along, but was forced to stop and dig deeper, rework, refashion, strip away, and hold things up to the light in order to find the deeper, clearer, truer meaning.

EMBRACING YOUR ADVERSARY
William Styron, interviewed by Melissa Lowver

How do you feel today, when you sit down in front of that blank piece of paper? Is it ever a friend, or is it usually an adversary?

Well, it's an adversary that becomes a friend, put it that way. I mean, it starts out adversarial, and as you deal with it—of course, I'm speaking only for myself, not for any other writer—as I deal with it, all of a sudden there's a kind of embrace that takes place, and usually after the struggle to get into something, I find that it gets easier, and, in fact, even enjoyable at times. It's kind of unusual.

SOWING THE SEEDS

Jamaica Kincaid
interviewed by Linda B. Swanson-Davies

For me, that thing that writers call writer's block, that's part of writing; I don't think one ought to be writing all the time. You have a dry spot and that's very productive, as productive as the actual writing itself. It's like sowing seeds or something, and it's a while before things sprout, and the ground is bare. It's all barren. I think you need a bare time when you just read and think and walk around, and are even depressed and insane about it, but I consider all that time of not writing a part of writing.

What I don't write is as important as what I write. I often will create large things in my head, and they don't get to the paper because I determine that they're not right for the paper, they are good only for my head. I work through them. It's part of the process. For instance, an explanation for the title *The Autobiography of My Mother.* I wrote a whole chapter about it and then decided not to include it; but I know what the title means, I understand it. I had the title of it before I actually wrote the book, so I knew what it would be; it was just a question of downloading. I downloaded some things and put them in the trashbin, so to speak.

KEEPING THE FAITH

David Long, interviewed by Linda B. Swanson-Davies

The writing was very difficult, but I couldn't give up on it. There were things I wrote in "Perro Semihundido," just passages of description that I was so fond of, that I couldn't give up on the story.

There's a passage early on where Faith is driving and she passes various towns, and passes a truck with round bales on it and then drives alongside a train. And then there's a passage where she's describing her brother's apartment on Queen Anne Hill, and looking out at the container yards and the mouth of the Duwamish. I can't explain why, but it was a little run of sentences that just pleased me, so I had a "faith" in the story for that reason.

Many stories don't get finished. It's like some of those zucchinis, you know. They look like they're going to grow, and then they end up rotting at the end. But when I get a full draft, I'm pretty confident that I can make it work.

. . . .

A WRITER'S SEARCH

Amy Hempel

interviewed by Debra Levy and Carol Turner

The whole book [*Tumble Home*], I probably started six years ago. I do remember more than a two-year block, or, as my former editor, Gordon Lish, calls it, a "writer's search," which is a much more hopeful term, I think. I had too much material to comfortably toss, but I was stalled for a long time. It was a very difficult time. And what was missing, it turned out, was the shape of it—that it was a letter. And a seduction. To my mind, that's equally as important as the fact that it's a letter. It is an attempt at seduction, albeit a clumsy one that can only fail. There's no way in the world that the woman writing this letter is going to capture the interest of this painter. Should he even read the entire letter, he would flee.

....

FOOL YOURSELF INTO WRITING
by Susan Perabo

Everyone who's been through it knows that the worst part of writer's block is that sense of dread when approaching the computer, or typewriter, or notebook. In an attempt to protect yourself from crushing disappointment at the sight of the still-blank page, you've subconsciously already resigned yourself to the idea that you're not going to be able to write, already berated and pitied and mocked yourself into a state of nausea and despair. When you've reached this level of blockage—the "vomit-level"—you must find some way to take the pressure off.

Sometimes I'll work on an old story. Even when you can't write, you can usually revise, or at least tinker. A full page, even if it's lousy, is much less terror-inducing than a blank one. If even tinkering is too much for your fragile state, write a letter. Then, at some point in the letter, try to convey something in scene rather than summary. Write your sister about a fight you had with your mom and give her the actual dialogue. Instead of just telling a friend about your dog attacking the UPS man, show it: the tattered pant leg, the gaping kids across the street, the package burst open on the sidewalk. Basically what I'm saying is that, when all else fails, you must fool yourself into writing. The great thing about this scheme—the reason it usually works—is that you're an easy target; you want to be fooled by that wiser, saner part of you, want to be manipulated by the voice inside that knows you should—and could—be writing.

MARK SALZMAN

interviewed by Linda B. Swanson-Davies

While writing Lying Awake, *you used your working area—moving it to more and more physically restrictive locations—in order to make yourself write. How did you do that, and did it work well for you?*

Well, for the time that I needed it, it did.

And what did it accomplish—what did it do? And maybe describe what you did.

First of all, I found that I was just having so much trouble writing. I felt so lost in the material and was so unsatisfied with what I was producing that it made it hard to sit down and work. You know, I'd sit down and turn on the computer and see what I'd done before, and it all looked bad. Every sentence looked false. Everything looked stale. It made me ask, If everything I've done before is bad, why?

Why write at all?

Remember in the Road Runner and Coyote cartoons, where the Coyote's building a bridge over a cliff with a piece of wood? And then he takes the wood behind him and he puts it out in front of him and all of a sudden he realizes there's nothing holding onto the cliff? That's what I felt like.

I said I was pushing on in the story, but there was nothing at the beginning. It was all so weak. I had trouble concentrating. I would sit down. I'd look at it. I'd feel sick to my stomach and I just had to get up, walk around, make coffee. I had to change the cat litter, anything. Eventually, the only place I found that I simply could not get up from was the passenger seat of my car. So I worked for a year just in the passenger seat of the car with a little notebook, and my poor wife would wave at me every once in a while from the house.

Did she think you were nuts?

No, she's great. She's a much wiser person, I would say, than I am. She always had a bedrock conviction that I was going to pull this through, much more than I did. I was so plagued with doubt throughout this, to the point of feeling almost in tears every day. Thinking that, on the one hand, you don't want to be a quitter, but on the other hand, you don't want to be stupid. You don't want to be one of those people who's unable to acknowledge that you simply made a bad choice, that you've hit a dead end. Time to back up, start over.

That was the most painful thing of all, thinking, Years are going by, I'm not producing. Am I really ruining my career? Am I ruining my love of writing?

All of that was awful. But I think all of us go through that. If not with writing, we go through it with parenthood, or we go through it with whatever—it's certainly not a unique experience. But every time we go through it, we feel as if we're the stupidest person on earth.

....

FINDING THE ANCHOR

A. J. Verdelle, interviewed by Nancy Middleton

I love that James Baldwin quote you cited during your talk: "You don't get the book you want. You get the book you get." You spoke about finding the passionate anchor of a piece.

Yes. Where's the juice? What's happening here? What's good? What is my favorite thing? Having looked this over again and knowing that this is now some sort of story, in whatever shape it's in, what part of it would I not relinquish in any way? This is why my story kept changing, I think.

So I wrote the whole thing about Margarete [*The Good Negress*], and it was not good. It was not what I wanted. And I didn't know what I was going to do. I had wasted, in my mind, a lot of time. So that was tough. But I kept going. This is another thing that I try to talk to people about: understanding the line of observation. Just because you observe something doesn't make it deep. Just because I knew it was wrong doesn't make that the deep thing. The deep thing is the story that is still waiting for my attention. So until I figured out what to do, I had to keep working.

I started to have the idea that Denise was the more appropriate soul, the more appropriate vehicle from which to tell the story. I also went back looking for the passion in the work and found the passion was really around the Denise/Miss Pearson/How-am-I-going-to-adjust-to-Detroit? scenario. So I started expanding that first. I expanded Neesey's educational experience as a way of expanding her. I could have made some other choices about how to expand her, but I didn't, because Miss Pearson was so vibrant and created so much tension. And then it clearly became what people usually refer to as a "thread"—which drives me nuts because it sounds so very thin!—but basically it's a narrative line.

You know, the Miss Pearson story line was so thin when I first noticed it. But it was a surprise and it was something I wouldn't relinquish. So therefore it qualified as something with tension and something that startled me. I built on it.

John McNally: I write my way out of writer's block. I think that when you establish a habit of writing, a routine, a pattern, it's harder to get writer's block, because you're always wanting to return to what you've written, to keep writing on it. Writer's block hits me only when I've taken some time off. Writer's block is like sobriety in that regard: what the alcoholic on the wagon needs is one drink to get going again. The writer with writer's block needs to write a few pages to get it out of his or her system.

as interviewed by Stephanie Kuehnert

RICHARD BAUSCH

interviewed by Jennifer Levasseur and Kevin Rabalais

What was the novel you were having trouble with?

Mr. Field's Daughter. It about killed me. I couldn't figure out the structure of it. In the writing of that book, there were periods of time when the real battle had to do with my attitude toward it. It always has to be, to me, more than the cold application of skill. And that's all it was for the longest time—very craftily putting this novel together. My heart wasn't engaged in it. It wasn't until I started writing the chapters where the characters address the reader in present time that I really became interested. The first one is the daughter saying something about her father's fumbling attempts to be a good father, and I thought, "That is how I can really engage myself in this book." And then it got to be fun.

BEVERLY LOWRY

interviewed by Stephanie Gordon

After looking at a list of your publications—the six novels, two nonfiction books, the dozens and dozens of short stories, personal essays, articles, and book reviews—I'd have a hard time believing that you have ever had writer's block. Have you?

I went through a time, which I discuss in *Crossed Over*, when I wasn't as interested in writing. I thought I was finished as a writer, finished creating, finished seeing life and literature with passion. That was because of a disturbing series of events, losses, troubles in my life which made writing seem not an option at the time. But I don't think of that as writer's block. Writer's block means, as I take it, being unable to put your ideas into words, which must be painful and terrible. I guess I haven't. I struggle a lot. And I rewrite so much that when I start something, I know that it will change ninety-eight times before I get to the final version, so maybe the placing of a word on a page isn't quite as precious an act.

Do you ever begin a long work—a novel, for example—and decide to abandon it because it just isn't moving along properly?

There was a six-year span between the time *Daddy's Girl* came out in 1981 and *The Perfect Sonya* and *Breaking Gentle* in 1987 and 1988, respectively, where I was dealing with a number of very difficult family issues. In that six-year period, my mother died, and my son was in a lot of trouble. The next year, my father had both his legs amputated, then my son was killed in a hit-and-run incident, and all that time I was struggling to write.

I especially had a difficult time with *The Perfect Sonya*, and I tried to abandon it. I remember sitting at my desk, in the days before I had a computer, and I was literally cutting and pasting, cutting a sentence from page three and putting it on page one. I looked on my desk, and there was a stack of page threes and page ones, and other pages waiting, just hundreds and hundreds of them. I ended up with a large laundry hamper full of pages of that book. And I thought, "I'm not writing a book at all; I'm just writing sentences." So I took all the pages and threw them back over my head onto the floor, and then went and mixed up all the pages with my feet so I couldn't go back and re-create what I had done.

Interestingly enough, my old friend Elwyn from Mississippi called and asked what I was doing, in an everyday kind of way. Even though she's not involved in my writing career and I hadn't seen her in years, I told her about the problems I was having with my book. She said in that Delta accent, "Be-ev, promise me you won't throw it away." And I promised her—honor bright, our girl-hood's most serious vow—that I would not abandon the book.

So I put all the pages into a large garbage bag and put it away, and began *Breaking Gentle*. I did not think I'd go back to *The Perfect Sonya*, but after a long time, I changed my mind and decided that I had to finish it before I could finish *Breaking Gentle*. This was before my son's death. After he died, I gave everything up. But after a while, I was sitting at my desk one day, probably months later. I can't remember if I had finished the draft of *Breaking Gentle* or not, but I went back and wrote a completely different version of *The Perfect Sonya*.

In the first version, Pauline was raising a son by herself, an idea that had interested me since so many of my friends had reared sons as single mothers, and also because I think that mothers have a particular closeness to their sons, and they very often work to cut the father out of that relationship, with varying degrees of success. But I abandoned the original book because [my son] Peter died, and I just couldn't return to those themes. I couldn't even bring myself to write about a mother and son for another ten years, in fact. Still, *The Perfect Sonya* is the most melancholy book that I've ever written. But I promised myself that if I could just finish it and get it published that I wouldn't look at how many sold or how much money I made from it. I haven't even read from that book since it was published. Then I went on to write *Breaking Gentle* and *Crossed Over*, which was an opening into a new writing life.

....

BRAD WATSON

interviewed by Robert Birnbaum

How many of the characters in the final version of *The Heaven of Mercury* were in your original idea? Finas, Birdie, the two black women, Earl and his family?

Really, not even Earl and his family.

How do you talk about Birdie without talking about her husband?

At that point, I didn't know who she was. I bounced around a lot thinking that I needed a model from someone in my experience, for Birdie. I didn't know where to start. Or whether I wanted to start from scratch and create her from the dust that was there. I toyed with the idea of using my grandmother, of using my aunt, who ended up being the model for the character Avis.

Is it possible that you wrote four or five novels, or got close to completing four or five novels, in the process of getting this one done?

They were all too abortive. I didn't get far enough along.

I'm interested in this notion that you were blocked for four years. ↑ you been down in Foley, Alabama, or Meridien, Mississippi, down your home country, would you have had that experience?

I don't think it necessarily had a bad effect on me in terms of finishing the book. I was going down there in the summers. Also during the winter break. I didn't feel out of touch with the place.

How about just in terms of your general comfort or ease?

I think that was definitely a problem. It was a big part of the problem in the first three years of being up here. I loved being on the Cape, and actually the first year we were out there, I wrote fairly well. I had a big sprawling house and an attic where I could get away. The second year in Dennis, a beautiful beach house overlooking the bay, didn't help me at all. There was a little bit of a problem in terms of dislocation and comfort, even though it was a really comfortable place. It wasn't so good for the book.

....

THE ILLUSION OF PERFECTION
Richard Bausch
interviewed by Jennifer Levasseur and Kevin Rabalais

—◆—

I love William Stafford's advice. Someone asked, "What do you do about writer's block?" Stafford said, "Lower my standards and keep on going."

That's such beautiful advice. What you get done really doesn't have only to do with how gifted you are, or how much ability you have; it has to do with your own attitude toward it. If your attitude toward it is, "This is my work; this is what I do every day, and I don't have any expectations except that I will have worked today," then you will get a tremendous amount done. Some of it will be really good. Some of it won't be so good. But you are doing it. You're showing up for work, putting in the hours.

And anyway, perfection is an illusion. It's just the way you have to be about it. I don't really teach writing. I teach patience and toughness, stubbornness and willingness to make the mistakes and go on. And the willingness to look like an idiot sometimes. That's the only way any good thing ever gets done, it seems to me.

DIGGING INTO THE PAGE

Richard Bausch
interviewed by Jennifer Levasseur and Kevin Rabalais

If you are writing and don't feel like things are working, do you put it away? Have you ever completely given up on a novel or story?

I've written four novels—and God knows how many stories—that I never let out of the house. I'm stubborn. There's a story called "Where Is John Wayne?" that never did work. I wrote it forty-seven times with a Flair pen before it ever got to the typewriter. And I don't know how many times I typed it. I stayed with it. Sometimes I'll leave it for a while and do something else before I come back to it.

No, writing "Where Is John Wayne?" forty-seven times wasn't fun. After the fifth draft, I started circling the number of drafts. When I got to the forty-seventh, the ink was just digging into the page.

Patrick Tierney: Sometimes you can sit down and the words just drip off the pen. Other times, well, it's more difficult. I have a poem called "Santry Woods" I've been trying to write for many months. I'm having great difficulty because I think it's going to be a very good poem.

as interviewed by Linda B. Swanson-Davies

TRUSTING YOUR SLEEPING SELF

Russell Banks, interviewed by Rob Trucks

You took a break when you were writing *Cloudsplitter*. Is that the first time it's ever happened? That you put something aside?

Yeah. I think so. I think I probably have stopped before in the middle of a novel to write a short story now and then.

How far were you into *Cloudsplitter* before you took a break?

I was probably two-thirds through *Cloudsplitter* when I pulled away from it and wrote *Rule of the Bone*. Then I went back to *Cloudsplitter*, and then the last third I went through pretty fast. I did a lot of revising and changing after that, but just getting it down went pretty fast.

I think I got bogged down and scared of *Cloudsplitter* in some ways, because there was just so much material to organize and to structure into a coherent and compelling story. What to leave out, what to put in, how much to allow myself to digress, controlling the pacing. It was harder work than anything I'd tried before. It's as good as I can do now. I learned a lot and maybe I can do better next time, but I was certainly working as hard as I could.

It wasn't a choice to pull away from it? It was something that had to be done?

Well, you know, it didn't work quite like that. I didn't want to go away from it, but it was just as well and wise that I did. Sometimes your sleeping self is a lot smarter than your waking self, and I just thought, Well, I'll stop and write a short story about this kid, because I was really getting into these kids and the kid's voice, and I was getting into that world, being seduced by it. And I said, Well, I'd love to tell this funny story about this kid stealing his grandmother's coins and using them for dope, and then she doesn't know it until they're all gone because he stole one or two at a time. The story appealed to me, the setup with the kid, the kid's voice. I could hear that, because I really like kidspeak. So I wrote what became the first chapter of the book as a story.

And I said, Wait a minute. This is more than that. This is opening up a whole world here. This is just a door. This is just a way in. It's not a very good short story, but it's really a way in to a larger world that I'm fascinated by, and a character I really, already, love. I've only been with him for ten or fifteen pages, and I already love him. So that's when I decided to go ahead and see how long it would take me. John Brown was going to be around a long, long time anyhow.

There was never any doubt that you would go back to Cloudsplitter?

No. Never. I never thought of abandoning it. I just knew it would be there—I'd already done too much work and I was too committed to it to fear that I wouldn't finish it. But then when I got into the other book, I realized, Boy, it's a good thing I'm doing this, because I didn't know what the fuck I was doing for a while there, for the last six months, on that book. And maybe I'll know when I go back, freshened by this. And it was true. It was the case. When I got back, I was freshened by it. But I didn't deliberately pause and look around, put down *Cloudsplitter* and say, Now what do I really want to write while I'm waiting around? Really, I just got kind of seduced. It was like a little love affair or something.

HAVE CONFIDENCE

Lynne Sharon Schwartz, interviewed by Nancy Middleton

When I began, I knew the beginning and I could foresee the end. What troubled me was the middle. But after a couple of difficult years, it found its shape.

Writing doesn't get easier, because each challenge is new. But I write with a little more confidence. I'm more aware of what I can do. There's a little more relaxation. I know that when I get to those moments, as everybody does, of "My God, I'll never get past this snag," one way or another, a month or two, I'll get past it. I have that confidence.

Alice Mattison: It's true that no matter how much instruction you receive, sooner or later you're home alone with the page. Maybe being a mother home alone with kids did teach me the patience to slog through that.

as interviewed by Barbara Brooks

CHAPTER

11

FAMILY SUPPORT

Carl and Virginia Rozycki, 1958

Daniel Wallace: Unless your spouse or your significant other is also a writer, it doesn't help your relationship to have them tell you what they really think [about your writing]. Because if they like it, you go, Well, you've got to like it. You love me. And if they don't like it, you go, What do you know?

as interviewed by Linda B. Swanson-Davies

BECAUSE IT'S REAL TO SOMEONE ELSE

Carolyn Chute, interviewed by Barbara Stevens

Do you ever get hungry to talk about writing?

Yeah, that's what the conferences and all that stuff are for. But, also, Michael understands. Because he has to hear it so much and he's so close to me that he knows. I talk about it with him constantly.

You talk about the characters in your books, and what's going on?

Yeah.

Does he help? What kinds of things does he do to help?

He'll say, "I just saw Blackstone [a character in *Letourneau's Used Auto Parts*] in town; he was doing this and this." And I'll go, "Wow, that's great!" I'll tell him about characters, and so he's on the lookout for them. So then he adds more to it.

Then does it feel more real to you because it's real to someone else?

Yeah, it gives you a chance to talk about it, and as you talk about it, you bring it out a little more freely than you might if you're sitting there taking yourself too seriously at the typewriter.

CHRIS OFFUTT

interviewed by Rob Trucks

The line in *Same River* about your parents going off to "drop a litter" is one of several personal details. What was your family's reaction to the memoir?

They all loved it, as far as I know. My family is very supportive of my writing, always have been, and I think they are pleased and surprised by the degree of success I'm having. They're glad. Hey, I was the fuckup, you know? I had a juvenile record and an adult record and dropped out of high school to join the army. When I turned thirty, my father said to me, "I'm glad, son. I never thought you'd make it." They thought I was headed for the prison or the grave, and now I have a career, a wife, and two children.

Has any one person had a particular influence on your work as a writer?

My wife. Any success I achieve as a writer is due to her. She provides me with time, space, and support. She and I talk about everything all the time, all the people, all the stories. She's my first reader. If somebody sat and overheard us discussing *The Good Brother*, they would think we led the most unusual lives and knew the most interesting people. We talk about everything as if it's real, because in my imagination it is real.

AN AUDIENCE OF ONE

Paul Theroux, inteviewed by Michael Upchurch

Do you have a person who acts as a sounding board for your writing? In "Lady Max," in the memoir-like element of the story, you read chapters from a book that resembles The Mosquito Coast aloud to your wife, Anne. Is that usual with you?

At that time, from *Girls at Play* to a little beyond *The Mosquito Coast*, so from the mid-sixties to the early eighties, I used to read to my wife—my then-wife. And it was a sounding board; it was something to do in the evening. It was a pleasant experience of just sitting down, having a drink, with something I'd done during the day. Or I'd do it maybe every few days, when I'd finished a chapter.

And whenever I finished, she'd say, "Go on—then what?"

And I'd say, "No, that's as far as I've got."

She'd say, "Oh … I like that. But I'm not too sure about your description of this." Or: "Should he have said this or done that?"

It was a lovely experience. To me, it was one of the most pleasant experiences of my life, reading to her. And I was reading to her because I hadn't seen her all day—she was at work—because I needed encouragement, and because I needed her critical gift. That was very important to me, all of that. And, you see, I worked every weekday, and had something to read to her.

THE SAME, BUT DIFFERENT
Louis Begley, interviewed by Robert Birnbaum

⇒◈⇐

What makes your wife your best reader?

She is so intelligent and honest and has excellent taste, and she is a writer herself. She writes biography, so there isn't a shade of competition between us. What she does is so totally different—not that there would be, even if she were to write fiction. There would not be competition between us, but there could be a divergence in what we thought was the way to go about writing. I know she writes differently and she knows that I write differently. Besides, she writes in French and I write in English.

....

THE IMPORTANCE OF SOUL SISTERS
Barbara Scot, interviewed by Linda B. Swanson-Davies

⇒◈⇐

Is there one person now in your life by whom you feel most truly known?

I, of course, would probably say my husband or my sons, but that's not true. My husband knows a lot about me, but not about the writing part. He's proud and very supportive, but he's just not involved in that part of my life at all. My kids are in their twenties, they're very busy with their own lives, and I love my sons dearly, but there are parts of your life that you really don't—maybe you'll have a nice discussion the way my mother did with me, or maybe you'll leave it in a trunk, but you still won't tell them the whole story. I have a friend that I mention in the book [*Prairie Reunion*] as my soul sister, and I really think she knows me best.

STEPHEN DIXON
interviewed by Jim Schumock

Who are the people that you've dedicated the story collection *I.* to?

This is probably the only book ever dedicated to one's in-laws. The reason I dedicated it to them was that they're very fine people, but they suffered during World War II. They had to flee to America. They've put up with me as a son-in-law for about thirteen years. That is enough reason to dedicate a book to a couple.

....

THE IMPORTANCE OF A GOOD LISTENER
Richard Bausch
interviewed by Jennifer Levasseur and Kevin Rabalais

Does anyone read your work before it is completed?

I read every day's work to Karen. She sits behind me in a chair. Her response is visceral. She's either involved or she isn't, and if she isn't, I have to be very attentive to that, because she's a sharp reader. It's been said that my prose is spare and there's no clutter, and the reason is that I have a listener who just wants the story; she doesn't want anything in the way. Over the years, I've decided that as a writer, that's the way I like to do it. I like to be effaced, so it's just the characters doing whatever they are doing—you're not thinking of me at all, you're not aware of me. I'd like the words themselves to disappear, so it's just the reader and my characters.

Now, of course that ain't the only way to do it. The fact is, as a reader, I sometimes like to feel the presence of the author. I like Dickens. I like the overblown, lush passages of Faulkner; they're fun. I just don't want to do it myself.

EDWIDGE DANTICAT

interviewed by Sarah Anne Johnson

I have had two sets of family my whole life. When I was two, my father left Haiti to move to the United States, and my mother when I was four, and I didn't join them until I was twelve. I had an uncle and aunt who raised me, and I had to go through the what-do-you-want-to-do-when-you-grow-up with my aunt and uncle first when I lived in Haiti. When I told them that I wanted to be a writer, we were still living under a dictatorship, and a lot of our writers were exiled or killed under that dictatorship. That's what it meant to them to be a writer, to put your life in danger.

When I told my parents later in the United States when they asked me the same questions, they didn't see how I could be a writer because there were no examples of other people who'd come to the United States from Haiti and become writers. They thought it was the strangest idea, and they were very concerned about how I would make a living. That concern is valid. Most writers I know do something else in addition to their writing, whether it's teaching or something else.

It's not an unreasonable concern, but also with my family there was this idea that by becoming a writer I would be this rebel outcast that no one would understand or know what to do with. When people have sacrificed so much and left their country, they want their children to conform and lead what they think of as a good, stable life. If you're not doing that, there's fear that not only will you fail, but the whole family, the whole enterprise will fail. I don't think any group of immigrants is alone in that. Especially the newer immigrants who are coming from poorer and poorer situations or fleeing extreme circumstances—stability is a strong goal for us.

A NAME OF ONE'S OWN

Jamaica Kincaid
interviewed by Linda B. Swanson-Davies

When you compare the person that you were born—Elaine Potter Richardson—and Jamaica Kincaid now, in what ways are you different from and in what ways the same as Elaine?

Well, I'm sure it's the same person. I changed my name ostensibly because I did not want my family to know that I'd done this foolish thing, becoming a writer—this foolish, unprofitable thing, at the time, instead of being responsible and having a job as a servant or a nanny. I changed my name. I'd taken this risk and I was afraid that I would fail and they would laugh at me and know who I was.

What I was really doing was giving myself a way of assuming an authority that could never have been given to me by my family: the authority to be the person that I am, that I wanted to be—a writer. Whether I failed or succeeded was not on my mind, just to be that. And that would not have been allowed me by my family, no matter how profitable it was. It still isn't given to me by them. They have no interest in it because it's not connected to them, and that's fine. That's all very honest and fine, but ultimately, psychologically, the change of names was a claim of my own.

ALL IT TOOK WAS ONE LAUGH

Stephen Dixon
interviewed by Linda B. Swanson-Davies

As to someone finally getting what I was trying to do? It wasn't so much that as it was hearing my older brother Jim laughing in the next room in Washington, D.C., when he came down for a visit and I was working there. I'd given him a story of mine to read, one of the first I'd written. I was twenty-three, and he was a fiction writer, and I felt if I could get him to laugh at my story—though I didn't try to get him to laugh; he just laughed—then perhaps I was doing something all right with my budding fiction, since he was a guy whose opinions and reactions I respected.

That's all. I didn't need much. One brother laughing at one of my early works kept me writing for a few more years.

Robert Wrigley: My parents, bless their hearts, will introduce me now as a poet. They used to say, "This is our son, the professor."

as interviewed by Jim Schumock

ALL IN THE FAMILY

Andre Dubus III, interviewed by John McNally

Writing seems to be in your blood. You're also related to James Lee Burke [author of the Dave Robicheaux detective series], aren't you?

James Lee Burke is my father's first cousin, which makes him my first cousin once removed. His kids and my kids are second cousins; I just recently figured out what all those kin terms really mean! I'm a huge fan of his work and have been since I was sixteen or seventeen and first read his second novel, *To the Bright and Shining Sun*.

Did you have much contact with him when you were younger?

I didn't see much of him as I was growing up, mainly because all of my relatives from both sides are from Louisiana, and my mother and father had settled up in New England. I'm pretty sure Cousin Jimmy (as my family calls him) was living in Kansas for a while, then Florida. Raising his four kids with his lovely wife, Pearl, teaching, writing. I do remember him visiting once when I was about eleven or twelve.

When I published my first short story ["Forky," in *Playboy* magazine in February 1984], Jim sent me a handwritten and very generous letter calling me a writer and welcoming me as one more into the family. I didn't believe I was one, but it sure felt good hearing that from him, one of my literary heroes! Over the years, he's been very generous with me, calling now and then to see how we're doing, offering to help out in any way he can. I'm thrilled at all the hard-earned success he's had, and am proud to be of the same family tree.

VIKRAM CHANDRA

interviewed by Jennifer Levasseur and Kevin Rabalais

What was your family's reaction when you decided to leave India and study filmmaking and writing?

They were always encouraging, especially my father. My mother was somewhat more skeptical, having herself been a writer. She knew exactly how hard it would be to make a living from writing. My earliest memories are of her sitting at the kitchen table, writing. She wrote and acted for Indian television during its infancy in Delhi in the sixties. She also wrote for radio and, later, for film in the seventies. She understood my urgent desire to write, but was afraid of how hard it would be.

In India, during the sixties and seventies, it made no sense to think you were going to be a writer. In the eighties, after the success enjoyed by Salman Rushdie and others, everyone began to see it as a possibility, as a viable job or vocation that people could have. Before that, if you said you were going to be a writer, the immediate response was, "That's nice. What else are you going to do?"

....

Nomi Eve: Various people have been generous in my life. It helps a lot. I'm so lucky. I have such a supportive family. When I said I was taking this English-as-a-second-language job, both my parents asked, "Is this going to give you time to write?"

as interviewed by Linda B. Swanson-Davies

LIKE MOTHER, LIKE SON

Susan Richards Shreve
interviewed by Katherine Perry Harris

Your son, Porter, attended the MFA program at the University of Michigan. When did you know that Porter would become a writer? How did you feel when he made this decision?

I think I knew that Porter could become a writer. His sense of order was entirely his own. He had a kind of fearlessness as a little boy, and he certainly didn't mind resisting the institution of school. He was an observer from the start, a looker and listener, wickedly funny about people and with a strong sense of his own voice. But he didn't read for the longest time. And then he did read; not for school, but as his own teacher. I suppose I thought he would be a nonfiction writer or a journalist. He liked being around the house when writers were staying with us. While so many people in the conventional world of school gave him a hard time, imagined a dismal future for him, writers took him seriously. And he always had a passion for something—basketball or statistics or dictionaries or lists—an important quality for a novelist.

He was working at *The Washington Post*, had bailed out of college and then finally finished. When he was ready to be a fiction writer, he persuaded his younger brother to bike across the United States from an island off the coast of Washington to an island off the coast of Massachusetts. After that journey, and as a result of going a long way from one place to another, he planned to write a novel. It made perfect sense to me, so I simply crossed my fingers and hoped, as any battle-weary writer would do when her beloved child is walking into the fire. I wanted him to sell a book. I was never concerned about how he would deal with trouble along the way—he has the temperament for that kind of failure. So when he sold his first book, I was ecstatic.

Porter now has his first book out, *The Obituary Writer*, which came out at the same time as your most recent novel, *Plum & Jaggers*. How was that experience?

The Obituary Writer and *Plum & Jaggers* came out within two days of each other. It was terrifically hard for both of us. I love writing a book and hate it when it comes out—and this was no different, only worse. I was more worried about the reception of Porter's book than mine—I had a lot behind my book, but as it turned out, he received excellent reviews and I did not.

Our family was all together in Massachusetts at the time. Porter and I were appearing jointly at events for one another, stepping gingerly around each other, which we had never done. I was thrilled for him, but that made me no less upset for my own book. When I finally told him that I was plenty sad for *Plum & Jaggers*, things changed for us. That was a conversation with a peer, a serious professional. It isn't easy to have two fiction writers in the family (four, including my brother and Porter's wife), but I think we have negotiated it with a lot of patience and a long history of genuine, hard-won friendship, honesty, and respect. And love—the source of all fiction.

Richard Bausch: I remember my sister saying, "I can't believe it. My own brother's a poet." It felt so good. I was eighteen years old. I walked around for days thinking, "I'm a poet."

as interviewed by Jennifer Levasseur and Kevin Rabalais

OF COURSE YOU CAN

Mary Gordon, interviewed by Charlotte Templin

There are things I am extremely grateful to my father for. Growing up as a girl in the fifties, there were things you weren't supposed to do. Well, I never heard that. I never heard you are not supposed to be smart; you're not supposed to say what you think. You're not supposed to write. You're not supposed to spend your time reading.

You never heard it from him.

He was the most important person in my world. What the rest of the world said came into my one ear, but I felt like the real story was, "Of course you can do this." Anybody who didn't think so was not quite up to scratch, and I didn't have to pay any attention to them.

The thing about my father was whatever I did he felt was fantastic. I think that's what every writer needs—some angel saying, "You're great, you're great, you're great!" twenty-four hours a day. Because there's also the devil on your shoulder telling you that you are completely worthless and your enterprise is delusional.

ROY PARVIN

interviewed by Linda B. Swanson-Davies

My siblings and I are very, very different. My older brother is a successful businessman. My younger brother is a scientist at Harvard Medical School. And the three boys, all born within five years, I think we scattered. I said, Okay, in some subconscious way, I will do writing. You'll take business, Andy, and, Jeff, you'll take care of science. That way we won't compete so much with each other.

We are geographically thrown all over the map, all over the United States. Well, we're all over the map in terms of our interests, and I think my parents did a lot of things right about that, but I think they were scared about the fact that I wanted to be a writer. You know, wondering if I could survive doing that; but they also knew that it was in my blood somehow. It's always been in my blood, and it was something that I had to do.

How old were you when your father died?

I was in my late thirties. I was thirty-eight, and I started writing seriously at thirty-six. It was a nice period; it was an interesting period of time where a lot of things were happening. I have to say that unless someone has a parent who's died, it's really hard to describe that. It was very, very sad; Lou Gehrig's disease is a horrible disease. No way is a good way of dying, but—

Some beat the hell out of others.

Yeah. The experience was intensely sad. But also intensely beautiful. It was extraordinarily beautiful. I felt very alive. I felt all the things that had to have been said were said already, so I could just concentrate on loving my father.

Had he gotten to read any of your work?

He'd only seen one of my stories. I was nervous about showing my stories to my family. I've always written, but also thought it was seen as something less than manly. We three boys were athletes. I'm six-two, and I'm the shortest one in my family. We were big, strapping, young men.

Those are heavy words.

Yeah. Exactly. I was very nervous about it, but I did show him one of the stories that was in my book, and he had an excellent criticism about it. I think that he knew I was writing. He was very proud of the fact that I was doing what I wanted to do in life. It had taken me a while to get to that point in life. It's an eternal sadness that he didn't get a chance to see the end product of the book. See what happened, how it was received in the world. But I also think that the last of the stories in the book have his shadow hanging over them, and that those stories wouldn't have been as good if I hadn't gone through the experience.

So I feel his loss all the time, and yet I feel his presence there all the time. It's very hard. It's a strange thing to explain to people. But you know, I felt lucky. I didn't feel lucky that he had Lou Gehrig's disease, but I felt lucky in who he was and how that formed my life and my work.

And you had the good fortune to have the relationship that you did toward the end. So often, people don't have that opportunity.

I was going through a rebirth, at least career-wise, and he was able to see me go through that. He was able to see me, probably much like seeing a child take his first steps. So that was terrific. I think that I feel his example all the time in my work.

Oh, do you? How?

He knew I was bored, that I wasn't being challenged by life. I was doing a lot of physically challenging things. I've always done physically challenging things, but this writing thing was something that I always warned my friends and family that I was going to do, but somehow I hadn't done it. I finally decided that it was now or never. And his death really hit that home harder.

....

DOCUMENTING A BOND

Maria Flook, interviewed by Sarah Anne Johnson

Your rendering of your sister Karen's voice in *My Sister Life* is striking and passionate, delivered in the first person. It's a vivid and truthful depiction of a young girl with street smarts, innocence, and an unusual wisdom. In these chapters, one feels the writer's efforts to reclaim her sister and pull her up from those lost years.

When I wrote in Karen's voice, I was trying to let her speak for herself because she'd never had the chance to speak up and explain her torment. She had gone missing. Later, when I talked to her about writing the book, she gave me full license to evoke her grim experiences, her pain, and her eventual triumph over so many obstacles. She was very pleased by the story I wrote. I gave her money from my advance because she needed the money; she's still so disenfranchised. I wanted her to have it, but she didn't ask for it. I had to push it on her. She seemed amazed that what had happened to her had mattered so much to me that I would write a book. The book was a document of that bond that she had never recognized fully, how her experience was embedded in me. Her disappearance had changed my life and had actually precipitated my transformation from silent witness to writer. My remedy was to write, hers was to escape. Of course, Sister Life means parallel life.

....

NEVER COMPROMISE THE DREAM

Bob Shacochis
interviewed by Linda B. Swanson-Davies

Why did you go from Pennsylvania to the islands?

I was born in Pennsylvania, but my parents moved to the suburbs of Washington, D.C., when I was fourteen months old. I grew up in the suburbs of Washington, in McLean, Virginia, home of the CIA and the Kennedys—but in the white-trash neighborhood of McLean.

What made you leave?

It's a very banal answer in some ways. It depends on what you mean by leave. Of course, I had to go away to college, so that was one act of leaving. But I had already left before that, to surf. I had brothers who were ten and eight years older than me, so they were always going to the beach. This was the early sixties and the Beach Boys were singing their songs, and I was a kid with a skateboard and a subscription to *Surfer* magazine, and took the beach culture to heart. By the time I was sixteen and had my driver's license, I was at the beach all the time surfing, and by the time I was seventeen and still a senior in high school, I got on a plane and went to the Caribbean, which for an East Coast surfer is our Hawaii.

So you went to surf?

Yeah. That's the first time, why I went. I went back because I felt absolutely spellbound by it—different world, black nations—to see how different reality could be. It was tremendous. I understood, like anybody would who's interested in an education, that that was probably going to be the best education I ever got anywhere. So I was seventeen and went to the Caribbean for three months and surfed, and then came back and went to the University of Missouri journalism school.

Was that a jolt to your system?

Oh, the Midwest, sure. I cried.

But you chose it.

I know—sort of—my parents saw the life they wanted for me and were very good at brainwashing me, making me feel that I was obligated to pursue something more traditional like that.

I'm surprised that they had that hold when you had already left.

What they were able to do was instill in me a value system and a sense of guilt that took years and years to overcome. I was always battling against it, but I won, eventually. They didn't want me to become a writer. Journalist, okay. Professor, even better. But fiction writer? What was that? There was no apparent shape or function to such a life, and the gamble, from a parent's point of view, was absurd.

It's a good thing you were so stubborn about it.

Anybody who ends up doing something like this has to be one of the most stubborn people in the world, because all you get forever is the message: Back away. Don't do this. This is a foolish gamble. You're deluded.

And all of the people who I thought were the most talented people around me when I was in writing schools—one by one, they started compromising on their dream. One by one, they started thinking that the gamble was foolish, and, one by one, they just stopped doing it.

FREDERICK REIKEN
interviewed by Eric Wasserman

Parents are not exactly known for being enthusiastic about their children pursuing careers in the arts.

Actually, my father's opposition to my choice of becoming a writer was something I grappled with for a long time. And it was not as if he was a tyrant about it, nor did he do anything to stop me. But he has always been a very persuasive man, and he simply could not fathom why—when I announced at the age of twenty-two that instead of applying to medical school I was going to pursue becoming a fiction writer—I would choose something that would not guarantee me a predictable income. In all earnestness, he would say things to me like, "Most doctors play golf on Wednesdays. You could write on Wednesdays."

The day I graduated from my MFA program, we were talking on the phone, and he asked me what I was going to do now. I said I had applied for several teaching positions and was also considering a work-exchange position at an artist's colony in western Massachusetts. He said, "Why don't you think about getting an MBA?" and I said, "Hello, Dad. It's me on the phone—Rick, your son."

OPPOSING THE TYRANNY OF REALITY
Askold Melnyczuk, interviewed by William Pierce

You've talked about the émigré community's distance from literature. How did your parents handle your decision to write?

My father had very little use for the fine arts, and was initially freaked and frustrated that both his children pursued them—my sister painting and me writing. He simply did not get fiction or poetry, and was very frank about it. But he has—at first grudgingly, and now, in his serious and enlightened old age, enthusiastically—embraced the practices, and takes an avid interest in them, and reads reviews and reads a lot of fiction.

My mother aspired to be a poet. She published poems in some magazines when she was fifteen or sixteen, and was later invited to submit a book for publication by a press in western Ukraine. She'd sent the book off for publication in Kiev, but had it rejected because it seemed too bourgeois for the communist editors there. Western Ukraine was itself still bourgeois and was willing to go with it, but then the war broke out and the publishing house collapsed. I have the book on my desk, and I'm translating a couple of the poems. My mother has a profound respect for fiction and poetry, and called my father a barbarian for not appreciating it. I had great support and backing from her. It bound us together in opposition to my father's tyranny of reality, of a kind of two-dimensional or three-dimensional reality that was not enough for either of us.

I remember talking about this once with Derek Walcott when I was in my early twenties and had published very little. I said that my father was advising a career shift, and Derek said, "Say to him, 'Did you really have the nerve to do what you wanted?' Maybe he wanted to be a ballet dancer and just didn't have the balls."

CHAPTER

12

THE WRITING LIFE

Lotte Matzen, ca. 1930

KENT HARUF

interviewed by Jim Nashold

What time of day do you like to write, and what are your habits?

My habit is to write in the morning. I start by 8:30 and work till noon. When I'm working on a novel, I will do that six and seven days a week. My practice is to begin by making a few notes in a journal about the weather and about what happened the day before. Then I read something by some classic writer. Most of that reading is of Faulkner, Hemingway, or Conrad. I read things that I've read before and don't have to think about what the story line is or what my feelings are about it. So what I'm trying to do is get my mind into some vein of fiction. Then I begin to look over what I've written the day before and make changes in that, and gradually work up to writing new material. So it's a process of bringing me back in touch with what I've been writing, and inching the novel ahead each day.

Do you produce a paragraph or several paragraphs in that amount of time?

It varies, but if I write several paragraphs a day, I feel pretty good about that. I don't think I've written more than a page or two at a single sitting.

And you're working through these drafts on a typewriter.

I start out making notes on paper with a pen or pencil, and then I use old yellow paper called "seconds" to do a first draft on my typewriter. When I do this first draft, I shut the lights off and pull a stocking cap over my head and eyes, and I'm typing blind. It's the old paradox that you see by blinding yourself. I do that for a couple reasons. One is that the second book, *Where You Once Belonged*, I wrote on a computer, and I never felt good about it, so I wanted to get back to using a manual typewriter. It's also an effort to stop rewriting sentences endlessly. I'm also trying to get in touch with some subliminal or subconscious thinking, and not be distracted by punctuation, grammar, spelling, or sentence structure.

WORKING THE LATE SHIFT
Amy Bloom, interviewed by Sarah Anne Johnson

What is your process like when you're writing? Do you have a set time to work each day?

No, not really. I tend to get really going later in the afternoon. But I can do a lot of puttering. I'm an expert putterer. Plus I have three children, so I can interfere in their lives. I have aging parents. I have plenty to do if I don't want to write. I can keep myself busy for a couple of days without going anywhere near my computer. But basically, when I have work to do, I usually buckle down in the afternoon. Sometimes I'll get a whole day in, but it'll be toward the end of the day. I'll work an eight-hour day, but never more than a couple hours at a time at the desk. I have to walk around, check the mail, make a cup of tea. So it's an eight-hour day that unfortunately starts around four in the afternoon.

THE SPLENDOR OF THE LATE BLOOMER
Roy Parvin, interviewed by Linda B. Swanson-Davies

You have to do it when you're ready to do it. I perhaps was a late bloomer for writing, starting at thirty-six.

But, you know, I hear that from a lot of great writers, who didn't even think about getting started until they were at least in their thirties or forties. Maybe things don't usually gel before that. You don't have enough perspective.

Perspective is a really good word. Things haven't happened to you enough in life. You haven't been left out by life quite enough. A writer I admire enormously, Chris Tilghman, who wrote *In a Father's Place* and *Mason's Retreat*, has a collection out now called *The Way People Run*. His first book, I think, came out when he was forty-six. And it has a feeling of wisdom. I think he's a brilliant person, but I also think it has the sense of wisdom, of seasoning.

WORRY ABOUT THE DETAILS LATER
Kathleen Tyau, interviewed by Linda B. Swanson-Davies

I have to get up at 3 A.M. sometimes, just to save the part of me that doesn't make sense. I try to write my stories from start to finish in one sitting. I call these my "beginnings." For the book I'm working on now, I've written many of these beginnings in longhand. I don't revise until I've found the heart of the story. And that's when I flesh a piece out and rework the language. Of course, it doesn't always happen this neatly, because the stories come to me in different ways. Sometimes I have a character, sometimes just a phrase or title. There's no real logic to it. I freewrite until something gels, and worry about the details later. Probably the images come to me first, because of the freewriting.

OPERATING THE FUNHOUSE
Allen Morris Jones, interviewed by David Abrams

⇒◇⇐

What is it about the writing process which keeps you coming back to the keyboard day after day? What do you love and hate about it?

I write mostly because I can't stop. It's the hinge of my life, and I don't know who I would be without it. It's my identity. I love the potential of it, the possibilities of it. You choose your palette, your subject, your canvas. You can write about anything in the world, or out of it. Fiction is limited only by your own imagination, your abilities. And this is precisely what I hate about it, too. It scares the shit out of me. Any success I'm able to find—and perforce, any failure—is entirely my own.

Also, there's this: You're never entirely sure where it comes from, so you're never sure that it's going to keep coming. Or what to do if it stops. I hate the uncertainty of it—not knowing when I sit down to write if it's going to be any good or not.

It's too bad that the effort you put into it—the daily grind, the research, the struggling, the interior sweat and shake of it—is, if you're doing it right, mostly invisible within the published work. Writers should be the unseen mechanics. As soon as a writer says, "Look at me. Look at how hard this is," the reader is knocked out of the dream, which is the Original Sin of all fiction. This is a particular risk in historical fiction, where there's always the temptation to stuff in a lot of interesting and irrelevant historical detail. With *Last Year's River*, I ended up using a very, very small percentage of my research.

To steal John Barth's excellent metaphor, we should all be the secret operators of our funhouses, "Though [we] would rather be among the lovers for whom funhouses are designed." And so no one—family, friends, people you see every day—ever realizes how hard it is. Which is maybe why we do interviews, so we can holler it out loud: "Man, this ain't easy!"

ANDREA BARRETT

interviewed by Sarah Anne Johnson

What would you say to new writers working on their first stories or novel?

Try to be patient. It's so hard for people to be patient. It was really hard for me. It took me a very long time to get better, and a very, very long time to begin to publish. I wasn't very patient. It's painful. I think people now have even more motivation to be impatient than I did when I was starting out, because the culture is more impatient. Everything moves so fast. First novelists are pushed so hard to produce a second novel, and young people are pushed so hard right out of school to get the first novel done. It takes time to write well. You have to sit with it. You have to be patient with it. You have to trust in your intuition and in your own material, and stay with it for as long as it takes. Writing isn't rocket science—a person can learn this if a person is dogged enough and spends enough time. If you throw yourself at it wholeheartedly and humbly, and you read and work and read and work, and try and try to get better, and stay open to learning and growing, you will get better. People get better. There's so much that I can't do, that I'm still learning to do. It's a wonderful thing to think that you can get established in your career and still have room to grow and new things to get excited about. There is a sense in which you can't get good at this in general, even though you can get good at the specific book or story you're working on. If you sit with it long enough, you will find a way through that has some integrity and that might be good, but when you start the next thing, you're a beginner all over again. You may have a larger toolkit and a few more skills, but the project has its own new problems; it demands new thinking, and it's hard all over again. It's good that it's hard all over again. That's what keeps us challenged and interested.

Daniel Mason: I like always to be working. I like to be doing something, and so if I feel creative and the writing's going well, then I'm just going to put as much as I want on the page. I usually can't get more than a couple hours of that a day, and so then I'll spend time editing or researching. It's nice to balance it out that way. And then when I get tired of researching in the library, I'll try something creative again.

as interviewed by Linda B. Swanson-Davies

RICHARD BAUSCH

interviewed by Jennifer Levasseur and Kevin Rabalais

When I wrote my novel *Rebel Powers*, there wasn't any aspect of the writing that wasn't fun, that I didn't look forward to in the mornings. I never used an alarm clock. I would wake up at sunlight. There was a big shadow of the house on the lawn, and I would know that by the time I was through with that day's work, the shadow would be on the other side of the house. It was a wonderful time. I would go sit on the porch after having worked all morning, and I'd play guitar. It felt so good, I didn't want to finish it.

How do you manage to keep up with reading and writing? You wrote Take Me Back *in five months and* The Last Good Time *in almost the same amount of time.*

I can't go to sleep until I've read. I don't watch any TV. I'm really out of it; you could name five pop-culture figures, and I wouldn't know who you were talking about. I'm always feeling out of it at parties because I'm traveling with people who watch TV, and I don't know the slightest thing they're talking about. I read whenever I'm not writing. I play guitar or I read. I take walks and read. The only time I feel crowded is when I'm teaching, when I have a lot of manuscripts to read.

I waste a lot of time. I had a dream not long ago that I was being forced to serve all the time I had wasted. I was in this gray office with something dripping in the pipes, and I had to just walk back and forth. I knew it was a sentence. It felt like I had so much time to serve. I don't consider reading a waste of time. I'm talking about just fucking around and wasting time. I play video games on the computer. I'm capable of spending two hours doing that.

Being a writer can be a very time-consuming occupation. How does it affect your wife and children?

I made up my mind when I was very young and starting out that the first thing was living. I was never going to go to a colony and write, and I never have. I believed that I should be up to my elbows in life if I was going to write about it. I wasn't going to deny myself any of that stuff. We didn't have any money, and I didn't have a job, and we still wanted to have children because we wanted to have a family, and if you wait until it makes sense, you're never going to do it. So I trained myself early to work in confusing circumstances with lots of things happening. I've written with babies sleeping on my chest. I remember once, I was typing something on the computer and I had my daughter Maggie on my lap. I felt this cold something, and I realized she had fallen asleep and was drooling. So I laid her down and went back to work. I leave the door wide open so the kids can come in any time they want.

I'm not one of those people who believes that when I think of something to say, I have to get it down or it'll escape back into oblivion and be lost. If it's really good, and if it matters enough, it'll surface again. It will surface in a better way than I originally thought of it. I try to teach my students that you have to train yourself to be adaptable to various circumstances in order to work. Working is shaking the black ball and seeing what surfaces, and every time, something different will surface. It doesn't mean that what surfaced before was better. When I was starting out, what I would do would be to have my time with my family, and when everybody went to bed, I would write from about midnight to two or three in the morning. I would read for an hour or two before drifting off to sleep. Now I try to work in the mornings and forget about it, do whatever it is I do all day.

Do your children read any of your work?

They are starting to.

How old is your oldest?

The oldest is twenty-five. He's already read *In the Night Season*. He read *Good Evening Mr. & Mrs. America, and All the Ships at Sea*, and he read *Violence*. But they're starting. My daughter Emily is starting to write. She is twenty-two. She's pretty serious about it. Do you know the Richard Wilbur poem "The Attic"? It's about hearing his daughter rattle off on the typewriter, and it sounds like chains being pulled over a gunwale. Then it stops and starts again. It is addressed to her.

But we've always kept it so separate; I'm just Dad. My publisher, Sam Lawrence, talked me into letting someone come into my house to interview me about my novel *Violence*, and I won't ever do that again. Here's this person writing about our "obligatory lace curtains," and how I don't write about the bucolic pond outside my window. As if any writer, from anywhere, would do that. Hell, even Thoreau wasn't really doing that. So anyway, we've kept it pretty separate. Even if the kids weren't around, I wouldn't spend a lot of time thinking about it. I don't have any ambitions in that way. I want to write. I would like to have the market be good enough, the sales good enough, so I could just keep doing what I'm doing. I don't want to buy a yacht. I don't care about any of that stuff. I want to keep doing this. As long as I'm allowed to keep writing, I'll be happy professionally.

You work with the perfect knowledge and expectation that whatever you do will probably disappear with you. But it's a dignified way of spending your time. I don't think anybody has a right to expect anything more than that. Anybody who does is a fool and is asking for trouble. You can't think about that. When I'm tempted to think that way, I always think about evolution, the future of your work, stars and that stuff. Does anybody on Pluto know about Shakespeare? When the sun dies, it's all going away, no matter what we wrote or how long we were remembered. You just do it. You provide something now to make your life meaningful and to feel like you've done your job. You've showed up for work in the mornings, as Norman Mailer put it once. I try to teach my students to look at it that way, too.

. . . .

LYNNE SHARON SCHWARTZ
interviewed by Nancy Middleton

⇒·◆·⇐

You know that they used to say a woman could either be a writer or have a family. Was that much of an issue for you? Finding the solitude that being a writer requires?

It's very hard. There's no way of glossing it over. It's very, very difficult. At this point, my children are grown, but still they're—of course—more important than my work. And that's how it is. It's a very hard question. When they were little, it was a constant struggle to find time and, even more, the space in my mind. That's still a struggle. I think that a woman who has children can never give herself as totally to her work as a woman who doesn't. I sometimes think back through history: Were there any great women writers with children? I've been unable to find any. Of course, the way history is written, we don't know … but those whom we know didn't have children and families. And in this generation, it's too early to tell who will be the great ones, the enduring ones.

It's hard. It will continue to be hard, because the energy comes from the same place. You give the same kind of profound engagement to the writing and the children. It's not like being a waitress and being a writer. It comes from a different part of your mind.

When did you finally consider yourself a writer?

I don't remember. I guess after a couple of books. It's a constant question. If you're not doing it right now, you don't feel you're a writer. But that's more of an existential issue. As far as professionally—yes, I know I am, and I knew that after a couple of books.

Do you work on a computer? You don't use longhand?

Oh, I mostly write in longhand, especially fiction. But then I put it on the computer. It's easier to print it out. I print a lot! I like to see the work. Seeing it on paper makes a big difference, particularly as I'm very interested in the pacing of things—how long things are. For instance, how long is this description as opposed to that description? I like to see the balance, the proportion, where the words are being allotted, because that's a reflection of their relative importance, their priority in the piece.

What kind of schedule do you keep when you write?

That's hard to answer. I have a studio that I work in; it's about a mile away from my apartment. Ideally, I get up, get organized, and go there for the better part of the day. But lately everything's been so disjointed that I don't really keep to it. When things settle down, I suppose I will. I try to go there as I would go to a job. Otherwise I wouldn't get any work done.

Writing is not something you do when you're in the mood. People always say, "How do you find time to write?" It's really the amateur's question because it misses the point. The point is, how do I find time to do anything else? You don't ask a doctor how he finds time to take care of patients—that's what he does.

Does writing, and living as a writer, help you accept things, give a context to events, as you've said reading does?

Reading does. I'm not sure writing does. I can't compare, because I've never not been a writer. I've always had the need to put things into words. If something happens to me, it's not quite real until I've re-created it in words. I think in words. Reality, life itself, is not quite real to me without the words. I don't think this helps me accept things. Actually, I don't think writers have an easier time, or a harder time. Writing is simply their way; it's a different way.

The writers I know, their lives are not easy. Sometimes I feel it's harder to write than, say, to be an accountant. But in other ways, the accountant's life may be more difficult. Everybody's life is hard.

What advice would you give to writers just starting out?

Well, the task differs for each person. You have to really want to write very passionately. I mean, there must be no question that this is what you want to do. If there's any question like, "Well, do I want to be a writer or would I do better in law school?" you'd probably do better in law school. If you want it badly enough, you'll find yourself turning down other things you want to do. But you have to be kind of ruthless and say no to a lot. You have to have perseverance. It really takes a kind of nerve—not only in what you write. The whole act is very nervy. Sometimes you find yourself sitting there thinking, "What am I doing?" "How can I say these things?" "Why?" and "What for?" And you somehow have to believe that it's worth it.

TRAINING YOURSELF TO BE ACCESSIBLE
Daniel Wallace
interviewed by Linda B. Swanson-Davies

I'm wondering, what is it like when you're getting the voice of a person, a picture of their lives?

The voices that you hear when you're going to sleep are inside of you. They're inside of me. They're louder with some people than they are with others. Some you can't shut up. But I think that there are elements within me that are darker than the brighter elements, which I like to present to the world. Some voices that I discover in my writing, which plug into that dark side, are the things that help me write the story. And it's really hard to talk about that. I don't, because it's sort of the missing link between what happens between me and the page ... or the word processor. You can't say "the page" anymore. Isn't that sad?

Yeah. It is. Yes. Between me and the screen.

"Me and the screen" doesn't sound right.

But there's a training process. Eventually, I didn't work twenty-four hours a day. I had to get a job. Had to get a family. So I worked every morning from 8:30 or 9:00 to 12:00 or 12:30 or 1:00, depending on where I would be able to stop. Every single day, regardless of whether I had a novel or a story or nothing. I would be there at that time, just like you would go to your job at the 7-Eleven, even though you don't know if any customers are going to come. You have to be there, just in case. And so I feel like what had happened is I trained myself to be open or available at that time to make these voices accessible.

I can't just sit down and start writing. I write at certain times now. I really do feel like my creative mind has been trained to be available at that time and kicks in at that time. Otherwise I'm not thinking about writing. It's the same with my drawings. I have to sit down and concentrate on and think about what it is I want to do. I have to design greeting cards for Christmas. I never think about what's a good Christmas card until I sit there and start to think, Okay, what's funny about Christmas? With writing, it's a different state of being at that particular time of day. You let certain things in that you wouldn't normally let in. So that's why I think it's good to have a schedule. Not just because if you don't make yourself do it, you're not going to do it, but also because you will be much more present for it. Because that's what you're supposed to be doing then.

So you give the racket in your head the opportunity to take shape then.

Exactly.

Chris Offutt: I get the house clear and I listen to absolute silence when I write. I listen to my own head when I write. When I'm writing, the words that I write are just screaming inside my skull. They're just roaring in there.

as interviewed by Rob Trucks

....

BRINGING POETRY TO THE PEOPLE
Patrick Tierney
interviewed by Linda B. Swanson-Davies

꘎

I would like to hear, from you, what you do. The label I have in mind is "street poet."

Yes, the bardic lifestyle. As you know, I spent a long time in America. I was an illegal alien, traveled all over, worked on ranches and fishing boats. Then I went across the border and up to Newfoundland. I spent a year there going from village to village writing poetry and songs about various villages, incidents, characters, or just historic events. I had already been interested in the bardic tradition, the traveling bard. It's a part of our history and upbringing in rural Ireland. What actually sparked me off was a poetry reading advertised in the paper. I was going out with a girl and said, "Let's go to this poetry reading." She said, "Okay, how much is it?" I said I thought it was free, and we didn't have any money anyway. When we got to the door, it was five pounds each. "Can't we get in half-price or something?" He said, "No, it's five pounds and that's that."

I decided there and then that I wanted to revive the bardic tradition, to bring poetry back to the people, to allow the ordinary person on the street, the person that's unemployed, anybody and everybody, to have access to poetry. It was about a week later that I got on Grafton Street [in Dublin] for the first time and started reading poetry. I say, "How are ya doin', would you like to hear a good poem?" I'm knocking laughs out of people with the comments I make. "Would you like to hear a poem? It's recommended by the bishop," I joke. They love to laugh over that.

We had a presidential candidate recently, a sure bet to win, but then people found out he had told lies, and he said, when he was defending himself, that on "mature recollection" he had in fact been telling the truth. So the next day on the street, I was saying I'd really like to step up and test my mature recollection. It makes me and poetry, the whole thing, more accessible.

STEPHEN DIXON
interviewed by Jim Schumock

I always wanted to be an artist of one sort or another, be it pianist, painter, or actor, but I was never very good at any of these things. I tried for a while. I became a newsman by default. Two of my three older brothers were newsmen. I was in Washington working as a newsman. In the evening, I would drink too much while reading a lot. I didn't have a car and I was lonely, so I decided that I was either going to become the youngest, best-read, most drunken reporter in Washington, with an early demise, or I'd better do something else in the evening besides drink. So I started writing. I just sat down and tried out a story about a young drunken writer/ reporter. It seemed to work. Although, it wasn't much of a story.

What it did was give me, for the first time, the kind of lift and ecstasy that a creative experience never had before in my life. I tried it again the following night and then the following night. Every night I wrote a first draft of a story until my brother, Jimmy, came around. He read one of the stories and laughed a lot, but he said that I'd better start finishing them. I knew that the writing process entailed not only writing first drafts, but the sweat and labor of finishing stories. That takes a lot longer. That's how I started.

....

LEAVING NO OTHER OPTIONS
Amy Hempel
interviewed by Debra Levy and Carol Turner

I mention the period of time in my twenties in San Francisco when I moved something like twenty-four times in six years or twenty-six times in four years—the punch line being: without ever leaving San Francisco. I described that behavior as a confusion of activity without action, of activity that wasn't getting anywhere. In New York, you can't just up and move quite as easily. I was forced to stand still. And it's not surprising that that's when I started getting some work done, instead of just packing boxes and taking them to the next Victorian house and the next Victorian house ...

Do you remember the exact time when you said, Okay, this is it, this is what I'm going to do, I'm going to write fiction?

I came to New York from California—that was a big part of it. I worked in publishing, which I thought was about writing, which it really isn't. And then I went to Bread Loaf, as an auditor. That was an acknowledgment and a step ahead. I was reading widely. That was in my late twenties. And then there was a general push, acceleration. And really, I was painting myself into a corner; I was never good at saying, "Why, this is what I'm going to do, by golly!" You know, with great gumption. I was painting myself into a corner, leaving no other options. Nothing to fall back on. So it had better work. By the time I took Gordon's [Lish] class at Columbia, I was about thirty or so, and I really believed there was nothing else I could do. I think that signing on for his class really was it. I was saying, I will try to do it. I won't punish myself if I'm unable to do it, but I will try to do it.

ON MOTHERHOOD

Pam Durban, interviewed by Cheryl Reid

I like what you have written about being a writer: "You have to be tough minded if you're going to write at all. You learn to make your own quiet by muscling your daily life aside and clearing a space for yourself. You have to learn not to waste time whining about what you don't have and feeling sorry for yourself. You have to teach yourself that no one is going to give you what you need, that you have to make it for yourself to have it at all. If you're a woman, I think you have to learn to be selfish. You have to teach yourself, hour by hour and day by day, how to do what pleases you, because it pleases you." Is it difficult to be selfish for your writing with your many roles as a mother, wife, teacher, and editor, or has it gotten easier over time?

It's gotten easier. But being a mother is still demanding. It takes a lot of time and energy to be a good parent—which is the only kind of parent I want to be.

In a way, the question is an unfair one, because people don't ask male writers that question.

No, nobody ever asks a male writer what happened when he had children. The answer: "My wife takes care of them." And that's just the reality, as much as we might want it to be different.

Many writers have noted that their writing changed after their children were born. Has your writing or your perspective changed since your son, Wylie, was born?

Yes. I love this Anne Tyler quote. She says before her children were born, she had more time, but after her children came, though she had less time, she had more of a self to write from. Having children enriches things. When you have a child, you see the world in a whole different way. I don't know how I can explain the influences of one's children.

Maybe it's related to time and a sense of an ongoing self?

It's related to time, but it's also related to what's important. I remember early on when Wylie was little, being in line in the grocery store with him. I had this tiny baby and this grocery cart, and I was trying to find my checkbook, which is a real ordeal with a baby. Nobody can explain that until you have one. How everything gets more difficult. Just going to the bathroom in a public place with a tiny baby is difficult. What do you do, lay him down on the floor of the bathroom, or do you hold him?

And if you hold him, how do you take your pants down? I was trying to find my checkbook, and this woman behind me was really impatient.

I realized then that our life as human beings is not made to be hurried and rushed in the way that we live it. Having a child gives you a whole different perspective—on what hurry is and why people do the things they do. I wasn't running on her clock, I was running on another clock that was set with the basics and beginnings of human life. That's where having a baby takes you. And also, that feeling of first seeing him, that overpowering love and this absolute terror. I remember thinking if something happened to him, even right now, it would destroy me. There's a fear that comes along with motherhood.

So motherhood gives you knowledge of your perspective on the world?

And where you exist in relation to the world. Your life becomes more dangerous.

. . . .

Chris Offutt: I'm a fairly superstitious person, you know. I come out of a culture that has a lot of superstitions and old folkways and this and that, but I invent stuff like that all the time, for myself. I have a lucky shirt. I have a lucky jacket. I wore one shirt for *The Good Brother*. I wore it every day I wrote. I had a chair. I have lucky stuff in my pockets right now, around my neck, two lucky objects in my briefcase. My room is filled with objects that I have imbued with powers.

as interviewed by Rob Trucks

DANIEL WALLACE

interviewed by Linda B. Swanson-Davies

It's always easier if you have a natural talent for something. You get that immediate satisfaction if you're fast or you're strong or if you're good at math or whatever. Whatever your talent happens to be. My talent was never writing. I was never good at it, and always avoided it. I never wrote a term paper in college. I took classes. I wrote ten-page papers and twelve-page papers, but not the kind of paper with forty, fifty pages and footnotes and all that. I never wrote one of those, and I think one reason I never graduated was probably that I avoided it so …

Diligently.

Diligently. I'm so good at that.

So what in the world made you, at the age of twenty-five or whatever you were, decide to dedicate that kind of time?

I knew that I wanted to write.

You didn't like it but you wanted to do it?

I wanted to be able to do to other people what other people's books did to me. I wanted to be able to create that. And knowing that I couldn't do it wasn't as much of a problem as you would think, because I felt like it was something that I could learn to do for the rest of my life.

It's not as if I were twenty-five and decided I wanted to be a professional basketball player, where I would be pretty much closing in on the end of my career. With writing, I could do this, I could do it until I died, till I go crazy. You know?

I even thought about it—I said, Well, if I can't use my hands, I can learn how to dictate. I can use these things. And you know, they have the voice-activated software now. I'm set.

You have an illustration business, and you write. I don't think I've interviewed anyone that did that combination of things.

Writing and drawing?

Yes. And I wonder, do they—

Complement each other? Yes. They really do, surprisingly, in two different ways. Because one of the reasons that I wanted to be a writer—and it doesn't sound as high-minded as it might—is to be able to live the kind of life that I wanted to live. Which is not a nine-to-five environment in an office, and not to be working for somebody else. It's to be able to work according to my own schedule, to be self-employed. I mean, a writer is the ultimate self-employed person. Nobody cares about you. They don't care if you write another word, because if you don't write, somebody else will. There's not going to be any dearth of books around here, as you well know. So I wanted to be able to live a certain kind of life, and that is to be at home when I wanted to be at home. Away when I wanted to be away. I knew I was not gonna be a painter. I could go down the list of things that I can't do. But I felt like I could learn to do what is done in a book. So that's what I tried to do. And the drawing—I was never artistic in that respect growing up, either. Never drew, ever. I never could. I mean I tried, but it didn't come out the way I wanted it to.

It takes a different part of your brain to draw than it does to write. You don't use the same critical functions to draw. You don't have to think as hard. And at the same time, it provides food, gives me the ability to do what I want to do, which is to be at home. Writing has not been making me enough money to support myself, but the drawings have.

That's something.

It is. I was just drawing pictures for the kids. They would come down for breakfast in the morning, and I would draw them a little note. Each of them had a character—Lillian had a dog—which would be doing things every day. I would write, "Good morning, Lillian. Hope you have a nice day." Abby had a rat. And we would dress up the characters in clothes and stuff, and out of these drawings Karen thought we could do a business.

And it was true.

It was true. That's how it started happening. Just from that. That's when I started drawing. And now I just love that. We do greeting cards and T-shirts.

It's almost unbelievable that you would go from being a child who did not draw or write, to being an adult who supports himself drawing and writing.

It's hard to believe, really. I did play music when I was a kid. I thought about becoming a professional banjo player, actually.

And then you thought about your old age and you thought, You know, I'll starve.

Fingers wouldn't have been able to keep up.

SIGRID NUNEZ

interviewed by Linda B. Swanson-Davies

Before high school, were you noticed for your writing ability?

Not really. I hadn't really done much when I was a little kid. I wrote some poems and so on. But almost as soon as I got into high school, I began to be very much encouraged by my teachers, you know, with work on the newspaper and such, and I began to form the idea that writing would be what I wanted to do, so I began to practice. I knew early on that it would be a real long study, that it would take a long time to learn how to do it well, even to satisfy myself. Fairly early on, I got this print of a Sassetta painting called *Marriage of St. Francis and Poverty*. I figured if you want to be a writer, you'd better marry poverty. So Francis has been over my desk almost my whole adult life. He's been my inspiration.

Is there a particular setting in which you feel most at ease?

Yes, I feel most at ease when I'm alone in my room. Absolutely.

Any particular room?

My home. My home is my room. I have a one-room apartment.

There is a part in the book [*A Feather on the Breath of God*] where the narrator talks about getting into ballet, and she says, "When I was in class and doing my tendus, no matter how difficult or how bad I was at it, I was fully present." She has a sense that during that time—of course, she turns out to be wrong—she was doing what she should be doing. And then she realizes she really wasn't cut out to do this, anyway. But with me, with the writing, I do feel that I'm doing what I should be doing.

And you have enough feedback to know that the world thinks so, too.

Yes, and so I feel like I have a job.

....

THE SOLACE OF WRITING

Chang-rae Lee, interviewed by Sarah Anne Johnson

I know that you worked on Wall Street right out of college. How did you get started writing, and what did you do to develop your craft?

I worked at that job for a year, and all throughout that year I was starting to write in earnest, trying to write a novel. I found that it was too hard to work and write, and that's when I decided to quit my job after a year to focus on writing. I was living in New York then and my mother was diagnosed with terminal cancer, and it was a good time not to have a steady job, if not necessarily a good time to be writing. I wrote as much as I could. I did part-time jobs to support myself, and my parents helped me out with the apartment where I was living. And I spent a lot of time with my mother going back and forth between New York and Syracuse, where she lived. When I wasn't with my mother, I worked hard, seven or eight hours, but without any real direction. I was working, but had no real clue as to what I was doing, though I did work hard at it. I feel now that that time was not wasted, because I learned something about the endurance and stamina it takes to write a novel.

Was this *Native Speaker*?

No, it was a novel that I couldn't publish. It was an escapist novel. I was trying a lot of things, a lot of voices. I was exploring. It had a certain kind of very intellectualized energy. But it wasn't a happy time for me, though I did get a kind of solace from the writing.

....

DOING THE HEAVY LIFTING
Roy Parvin, interviewed by Linda B. Swanson-Davies

There's something very magical that happens when you use your body. I get a lot of ideas when I'm bike riding. Not only is my mind off the task of writing, but I'm doing something very physical with my body in a very different way. There's nothing like exhaustion, the joy of exhaustion, after a very physical day of work. I don't really do any adult athletic pursuits besides hiking and bike riding. I do lift weights, because I think I like the feeling of pushing against something heavy.

Which is why you're a writer.

....

Allen Morris Jones: Before I started writing full-time on *Last Year's River*, I would write catch-as-catch-can. I try to write every day. When I'm really cooking, when the gears are all turning and the cylinders are all firing, I try to write about fifteen hundred words a day. It's not often that I actually hit that, though.

as interviewed by David Abrams

UNTIL DROPS OF BLOOD FALL

Amy Bloom, interviewed by Sarah Anne Johnson

⟹⟾

What would you say to a writer working on her first stories or a novel?

There's no turning back. It's good news and bad news. The good news is that if this is what you really want to do, you will do it. The bad news is that however much you may want to do this, nothing more may come of it than the writing itself, so you better really prize that process, because maybe other people will read it and maybe only your writing group will read it. It's very difficult for people to do. There's that great line from Red Smith: "There's nothing to writing. You just sit at the typewriter until drops of blood fall." There's nothing to it but to do it. If you must write, you will. If you're lucky, maybe it'll turn out that you don't have to write. Maybe you could just garden, or do ceramics, or something else.

....

THE JOY OF A GOOD NIGHT'S SLEEP

Patricia Henley, interviewed by Andrew Scott

⟹⟾

What do you like least about being a writer?

That's hard to answer. What I like least happens as a result of what I like the most. I love the feel of obsession. Totally submerged in a project. That often means I don't sleep well, get up at 2 A.M. to write, nap when other people are socializing, fear for myself and others when driving, and neglect my so-called real life. All that obsession has its downside, and I find I can't go on too long like that. A good night's sleep is something I treasure.

ELIZABETH COX

interviewed by Sarah Anne Johnson

What would you say to new writers? What advice would you give?

To pay attention! To look at the world around you as though every moment matters, because it does. To forget the wish to publish and just write. Are you going to write the next book whether or not it will be published? The pleasure of writing is so different from the pleasure of publishing—which can't hold a candle to it. And another thing—read, read, read. Read everything—all the sciences, philosophy, history, poetry, folktales, plays. Read and study the thing that strikes your curiosity. Now, as a teacher, I have a story for you, an old story about a teacher who took his students out to see the night sky, and as he pointed upward he said, "Now I want you to look closely at my finger." The students got the point. Pay attention and be willing to be amazed with the day. God, what a way to live!

....

DELIGHTING IN THE CHATTER

Mark Salzman
interviewed by Linda B. Swanson-Davies

I think of myself as a person who actually does experience silence regularly. I work by myself, all day, every day. I don't have an active social life. I have a few friends that I see a couple times a month. Jessica goes off to work, and I'm by myself in the house.

So you actually are one of those people with silence in their lives?

Yes, although I fill the silence with thinking, whereas the contemplatives, like the Zen Buddhists, try to silence that chatter. I don't make an effort to silence that chatter. I delight in my chatter. I live by my chatter. I'm not an internally silent person, but external silence is a part of every day—long hours where there's no noise. I never listen to the radio or music or anything. I like pure silence. When I went to the MacDowell Colony to write the last of this book, there were some people there who found it kind of disturbing, being in a cabin, having no noise, but for me, it wasn't drastic. It's refreshing. I need that every day. If I don't have several hours of just no sound at all, I feel scattered.

THE PRICE YOU MUST PAY
Carol Roh-Spaulding
interviewed by Linda B. Swanson-Davies

I have sometimes felt resistance to being a writer. I just want to lead a normal life and watch cable television. It's worth it in some ways, but if you had a choice, you'd certainly take an easier life. There's a lot attached to having the kind of sensitivity and awareness that writers need to have—and I don't mean to glorify it or romanticize it, but—

It's pricey.

It is.

ALICE MATTISON
interviewed by Barbara Brooks

Almost ten years passed between *Animals* and *Great Wits*, your first short-story collection, which came out in 1988, and then you published three novels and two story collections in the next eleven years. It seems as though your writing life suddenly opened up.

Oh, yes. It took me a while to write stories and revise them until they were worth printing, but that wasn't the only reason for the delay. Having young kids probably enabled me to write because it gave me an excuse not to have a full-time job, but it also interrupted me. I had three kids, and by the 1990s, they were teenagers or out of the house, and that made a big difference.

When did you begin writing seriously?

My oldest son was born in 1970, and when he was a year old I was pretty unhappy. We were living in the woods in California, it was dark—our house was under redwood trees—and I was depressed a lot of the time. My husband had a time-consuming job, and I had quit teaching to have the baby. I didn't know anything about babysitters or anything like that, so I just took care of him. It wasn't easy for either me or the baby. And then it suddenly dawned on me that I could get a sitter. I could call up the local junior college and hire somebody—and I did. A young woman would come two afternoons a week and I would go down into the basement while she took care of Jacob. We were miles from anyplace, so there wasn't anywhere else to go. I thought I'd read a book, or do laundry, or I'd write. I'd been writing all my life, but not seriously since college. I started writing, and all I did was write. I was absolutely newly excited about writing and being a writer. That was when I became serious about it. It was 1972. There's a poem about this in my first book, *Animals*. It's called "The Facts."

RICHARD RUSSO
interviewed by Robert Birnbaum

I can write on the road, but I can't draft a novel on the road. I could revise a novel on the road. I can write screen work, essays, I can write introductions. Nonfiction is easy to write on the road, on rare occasions when I do that. I can do all those kinds of things, but there is something different about drafting a novel that requires me to work at the same time each day. I need to work in the morning, every morning, six or seven days a week. I need that kind of routine to slip back into. I need to pick up right where I left off. I hate to miss a day. I need reliable blocks of time.

Margot Livesey: I'm a morning person. As I've got older, I've tried to learn to be more flexible. I used to have so many things in place. Up to a certain point it became prohibitive. If it was quiet and if the phone didn't ring, then maybe I could write a sentence. I try to be less rigid as I get older.

as interviewed by Ellen Kanner

APPRECIATING THE APPRENTICESHIP
Mark Winegardner, interviewed by Robert Birnbaum

⇒◇⇐

The difference with writing is that it is the only one of the arts where people don't appreciate the apprenticeship. They know they can't just become a ballerina, that it takes incredible years of study. Or they can't just become a classical composer or be a great jazz musician. Everyone has this idea that maybe on the weekends, you could write a novel. As completely insulting as this is to writers, it's also flattering, and it's given a certain kind of credence because every four years, someone writes a novel that way. Unlikely, but it happens.

. . . .

THE TWO-WRITER HOUSEHOLD
Antonya Nelson, interviewed by Susan McInnis

⇒◇⇐

You and Robert Boswell are both writers, raising two children and carrying teaching responsibilities. How does that work out for you?

We've worked things out pretty well. I think the most important thing we did was to hire a housekeeper so the house will be as clean as I require, and Robert doesn't have to worry about my being angry. We never argue about anything, really, except housekeeping, so once it's been identified and dealt with, it ceases to be a problem, thankfully.

Do you find there's time enough to write and teach and nurture a household and be nurtured by all of it?

It works out as long as I have a good idea for a story. Everything's fine then, because I can make time to write. If I'm not inspired to write—if I'm not in the middle of something—I think everybody's pretty unhappy. For that reason I tend to make myself work. And somehow it works out. Once there's a good idea it's almost as if nothing can get in the way of it. The presence or absence of good ideas really makes or breaks my mood.

So the engine is well oiled when there's work, but when there's not, the gears grind you?

In a way. I start assigning blame. You know, "I can't come up with a good idea because I have too many papers to grade." It's not true, of course. It's absolutely not true. It's merely a matter of having to be inspired.

Is there a "best of both worlds" situation for you?

If there is, it's probably being inspired and being on a deadline, knowing that a publisher wants what I'm writing. There's a comfort in it because I have something to write and someone wants to publish it, and because someone wants it there's pressure to get it done.

....

Daniel Wallace: You can do so much, you can be so revolutionary in your art in ways that you can't really be in your life because you have so many important things that would be upset. You've got to be careful. You've got a family. You've got a business. I mean, goodness, you know, you can't be too wild.

as interviewed by Linda B. Swanson-Davies

LYNN FREED
interviewed by Sarah Anne Johnson

When you're in the throes of a novel, what is your writing schedule like?

I'm the last one who should be talking of writing habits. I'm haphazard. I write, but I also teach. I have friends I love to see. And I have a passion for travel. All of which is to say that I write in furious surges, and then I take a month, or months, off. When I'm in the middle of a novel, however, I write all the time. When I'm inching in, starting up, I'm best in the afternoons. Mornings, I pretend to write. I write letters and e-mail, I fiddle with what I've written the day before. But the real time for writing, for me, is the late afternoon and evening. This is not the best way to run one's life if there's anyone else in it. But there it is. I have nothing but envy for those who wake up, don't even clean their teeth, and settle into the writing. Not me, not at all. I'm hopeless.

....

THE NECESSARY CREATIVE DISTANCE
Lorrie Moore, interviewed by Jim Schumock

You've written that many writers feel like disenfranchised guests in the world. Do you feel this remove yourself?

I don't know. To some extent, a writer is not in the midst of things, not belonging to the world with every fiber of his or her body, but that helps one observe. It also helps you see and take a certain interest in life as well. What writers are doing is observing the world and finding in it what can be put together in combination with their own imagination to make something that's different, that's not already in the world. Writers are busy with the process of creating new worlds that refer to the existing one in some way. And that's a kind of scary and mad project, and for writers to go through their lives like that day to day creates some kind of distance or guesthood.

AMY BLOOM

interviewed by Sarah Anne Johnson

I know that your original career was in psychotherapy. How did you go from psychotherapy to writing?

It doesn't seem to me that I went from one to the other. I was on my way to becoming a psychoanalyst, and having talked to the guy who was going to be my training analyst, a very nice guy named Sam Ritvoe, I came home and started making notes for a mystery. By the time I got home, I had about fifteen pages sketched out in my head, and I started writing. I wrote the mystery over the course of the next two years, and while I was writing the mystery, short stories started showing up.

Whatever happened to that mystery novel?

I sold it to HarperCollins, and then I bought it back. I didn't think it was good enough.

Are there aspects of your experience as a psychotherapist that contribute to your writing?

Being a good listener certainly helps if what you want to do is write about people. Learning how to pay attention to how people think and feel and talk. I think I could've done that in another profession as well, but it helps to have that experience and training.

I have a very good memory, which helps also. I was really trained as an old-fashioned social worker. I used to have to do what was called process recording, which was to write the entire verbal and nonverbal parts of an interview from beginning to end without a tape recorder. And I had to turn in dozens of those on a weekly basis. So that was good practice.

Probably just being exposed to peoples' lives in that intimate way gives you the opportunity to see things that it might be difficult to see otherwise. Not that you couldn't see them if you were willing, but it's easier when you're invited into peoples' lives. So I'm grateful to those parts.

....

Lynn Freed: I was in the "no future" hell and felt I should secure a means of income so that I could live and write. So I took the LSAT and got into law school. And then I panicked and withdrew. Sometimes one needs to drive oneself into a situation so horrible that one is forced to make a bold choice. I chose to write, and, more or less, to struggle.

as interviewed by Sarah Anne Johnson

THE SLOW EVOLUTION

Pam Durban, interviewed by Cheryl Reid

You wrote that when you were in college, it never occurred to you that "writing was something people—girls—did." How and when did that change?

It changed over time, and I think it changed more as I began to be dissatisfied with what I was doing. I was always doing some kind of writing, either working for a newspaper or doing interviews in Cabbagetown, an old factory town in Atlanta. But I knew that wasn't what I wanted to do. I knew that there was something out there, something of my own. Something more than reporting on what other people did, even transcribing other people's stories. It was a slow evolution, rather than a revelation.

....

TO EACH HIS OWN
by Melanie Bishop

Some people work best late nights, others early mornings, some work crazy hours and then take several days off, while others respond best to a more balanced approach. I doubt any two writers maintain identical routines, and many writers I know don't have a reliable routine, as in one that never changes. After ten years of college teaching, I am currently on a year-long sabbatical from my job. My goal is to finish a book manuscript this year. Initially,

I was frightened by how much time I had before me. A couple of days into the actual writing, I managed to let that fear silence me. There is always something else to do, some distraction to keep you from the misery that surrounds some of us when it comes to our craft. It took me a couple of months of floundering around with a new scheme every week before I found what really works best for me. And I would not go so far as to say I'm now wedded to this system. It could very well change, but it's working for now. Instead of rolling over and going back to sleep, I try to get up the first time I wake, often four or five A.M., always pre-six.

I make a cup of coffee, feed the cats, and go into the room where I work. I find this such a rich time of day. With the blinds open, I get to watch the sky go from dark to pinkish blue. No one else in the house is awake, and the silence has a different quality to it. Dawn is, symbolically, a beginning, a good time for creative energy. I find two hours of this early morning time to be more valuable to me than four hours of time later in the day. Later, I'm already distracted by other things, and have already expended much of my daily quota of energy on miscellaneous tasks. At that point, it sometimes feels impossible to get the jumpstart I require. But in the early morning, pre-dawn time, I'm just right there. No having to travel or arrive. Straight from a dream state to the paper and pen, by way of a strong cup of coffee.

A close writer friend of mine could not conceive of the routine that works for me. He likes to write late nights, after the rest of the world has gone to bed. He might read or watch some television after dinner, and then begin writing at eleven or midnight and go to three or four A.M. This is his most productive time. Everyone is different. Find what works for you and don't be rushed about it, and know that your own routine may change, just to keep things interesting.

....

A DIFFERENCE OF STYLE

Siri Hustvedt

interviewed by Jennifer Levasseur and Kevin Rabalais

⟹⬧⟸

Your poem "Squares" begins, "He was making a paragraph on a yellow page." You seem to have a strong interest in the physical act of creating written language.

I think that it's because I find written language strange. It is odd that we can look down at those little signs and understand them. Reading and writing are peculiar activities, and yet when I write, there is an odd confluence of the physical and mental. I often need the physical act of typing to bring something out. It is not enough to just think. The words seem to come through my fingers. I prefer typing to writing by hand because I need the distance of print. My husband, Paul Auster, likes the words to leak out of his body mediated only by a pen. He needs to write by hand first. It seems to me that my handwriting obfuscates the text. These are differences of work and style, but I think they are deep and related to style itself.

Do you keep yourself on a certain schedule?

I work five days a week from about 9 A.M. to 2:30 or 3 P.M. I find, unless I'm revising or near the end of a book, I can't work many more hours because my head dries up.

The narrator of Graham Greene's *The End of the Affair*, who is a novelist, talks about unconsciously writing whatever book he is working on at all times of the day.

You are always writing a book, even when you're not at your desk. I write at night in my head, which is very pleasant. I begin to compose the next paragraph before I fall asleep, or I hear the characters having conversations with each other. Sleep is good for books. Movement is also good. Sometimes when I'm stuck, I go to the bathroom, and the act of getting up and walking loosens the thought, and the words come to me when I'm away from the computer.

EXPECTING

Chris Offutt, interviewed by Rob Trucks

"Aunt Granny Lith," "Old of the Moon," and "Leaving One" are sort of stylistically different, and those were written when my wife [Rita] was pregnant. It was like a magical, mystical time. I had this pregnant wife and I couldn't believe it. It was wonderful. I was going in the woods all the time. She and I would go into the woods together and I was existing in this zone of magic and joy and terror. Those stories came out of that experience, particularly "Old of the Moon."

I wrote "Old of the Moon" during the time when she was due, and two weeks later when she had the baby. I wrote that story and revised it probably twelve to fifteen times. I revised it every single day of that two-week period waiting for her to go to the hospital. I mean, a drastic revision. Not just commas. Huge revisions. I have no idea what I threw away from that story. And that story is about my worst fear, the death of a baby. I wouldn't let Rita read it.

There's a lot of mysticism there. Those three stories all have that otherworldly quality.

Well, I think it's related to when Rita was pregnant; we were existing in another world. We really were. I was reading mythology. I was reading legends and lore and folk stories and borrowing from them, because I grew up hearing that sort of thing, and I was trying, in many ways, to create my own stories. But what you're talking about is really related to that time. I just can't describe the intensity of my feelings of being a part of an otherwordly experience, and it was really, you know, that my wife was pregnant, and it was amazing.

Did the process of the second child match the intensity of the first?

Oh yeah. When she was pregnant with the second child, we were living in a three-room cabin on the Iowa River, and I was completing the final draft of *The Same River Twice*, so I was writing about the first child while living the second child; and it was unbelievable, this little zone that I was in, of unreality, of otherworldliness. This three-room cabin had a porch on the back. Just poles to hold up the plastic, corrugated roof. I boxed it in and threw down a floor, and my landlord gave me a window, and I did all the work, built it in three days, and wrote in there. So I would write in there, go out, and there would be my wife who was pregnant, my little boy who was learning to walk, and the woods. It was just unbelievable. And I would go out and wander around these woods and go back into the house, and it was the happiest two years of my life.

ON THE MOVE

Daniel Mason, interviewed by Linda B. Swanson-Davies

When it comes to Mr. Drake and Dr. Carroll in *The Piano Tuner*—because they were both such vivid characters—I imagine that you would identify with both of them in different ways, and I wondered what ways those might be.

Anthony Carroll's the kind of person I would love to be. I would love to have that kind of energy. I'd love to be so far away from home for such a long time. I'd love to be able to disappear into the jungle and try to learn everything possible. Edgar [Drake] is more of who I am. He's easily distracted and he tends to be shy. He likes to just watch, mostly. I think that a writer just watches, and it's something that's frustrating about being a writer, because it gets in the way of actually doing things. You write about a dancer rather than actually dancing. That's been his whole life: He observes things rather than actually doing them.

In one of the interviews I read, you said you admired that Dr. Carroll was such a polymath. It seems to me that you're very much like that, that you have interests in many different areas, and I wonder if you would be willing to draw a little sketch of the areas of life that are really interesting or important to you.

Like a pie?

Like a pie, or just circles with the things that matter to you.

I don't even know how I could do that. I don't even know where I'd start, honestly.

How do you think of your life?

Since the book came out, there's been very little space for making my own decisions.

Oh, wow.

School demands most of my time, and then I have responsibilities for the book. I've been writing since *The Piano Tuner*, but very little because of all the time that I've taken out of school traveling for the book. This is the last trip that I'm going to do now, so I will be able to write again. When I'm not in school, it's split between writing and family and friends.

Your plan is to continue with medicine and with writing and probably continue to travel throughout your life?

Right.

You've known that forever.

I think so. I mean, it's strange in a way because I can't see a date when I'm going to settle down. But at a certain point, I'm going to sit down in one spot and stop, but I just don't know exactly when that's going to be.

Life is just beginning.

Right. I haven't been in one place for more than a month in the last—almost two years, I think.

You've never had your own home as an adult.

I rent apartments month to month. I can't even sign a year lease because I'm not in a spot for a year at a time. There's something unsettling about that. Fortunately, my parents live close to San Francisco, so I sort of have a base there where I keep all my books. I mean, it's mainly my books—where I put my books.

Home is where you put your books.

Where I put my books. My room is entirely books.

WRITER, KNOW THYSELF

David Malouf, interviewed by Kevin Rabalais

Does one book grow organically out of the one before it? While working on one book, are you already thinking about the next?

I'll often have what seems to me like a good idea and write a few scenes or sketch some dialogue, but somewhere along the way, interesting as the idea may be, I will see that there's not enough there to take me through a book. It's not going to be a novel. Or it may start developing a kind of tightness of plot that I recognize as being a good idea for a book, and even a good book, but for someone else. It's not one of my books. I wait then until an idea comes along that does seem to have enough blank spaces, enough complexity, to keep me curious.

You seem to be as interested in the arc of your body of work as in the arc of an individual book.

It's really about knowing what it is that you do. You must be able to recognize that there are other things that you could do, but basically they're not you. You could write those books, but it would be like producing imitations rather than real creations.

....

FLOAT LIKE A BUTTERFLY ...

Andre Dubus III, interviewed by John McNally

Is there anything about the training or the mindset of a boxer that's applicable to the fiction writer?

Let me first clarify that I never fought any sanctioned amateur bouts, though I did have an AAU number for the Golden Glove tournament down in Lowell, Massachusetts, and boxed off and on for years in gyms and boys' clubs. I had a good jab and a lot of stamina, but I hated getting punched in the face, and so would "stick and move" too much and not plant my feet and try and throw a more damaging combination.

I know other writers far better than I'll ever be—Hemingway, Mailer, etc.—have talked about boxing and writing. For me, the only real parallel has to do with stamina and precision. Most of my life, I've run long distances to clear my head and feel good, anywhere from eight to twelve miles. As all those who do endurance workouts know, it can hurt! So if you haven't boxed before, imagine running up the tenth long hill in the tenth mile of your even longer run, sweat burning your eyes, panting for air, all while somebody's hitting you in the head and trying to knock you down and out.

Writing fiction never approaches this degree of physical suffering, of course, though it can have its spiritual equivalent. The truth is, it is hard to work at something for years that nobody ever seems to take an interest in, all while stealing the time to do it, enduring most people's belief that it's just a hobby and nothing substantial will ever come of it, and never mind how difficult it is to do that thing in the first place. Yet you still have to keep finding the right word—the truest word—in that sentence and in that paragraph and in that page. And even if you do that, you may have to cut it all anyway because it doesn't work for other, sometimes mysterious, reasons.

What I'm trying to say, I think, is that it helps a boxer if he or she simply enjoys the inherent pain of boxing the same way it helps the writer if she likes, or can cheerfully tolerate, the inherent difficulty of trying to write well and alone, all while trying to be a normal person making a living and raising a family, too.

THE EMOTIONAL RISK OF POETRY
Philip Levine, interviewed by Jim Schumock

You've known a number of poets who have committed suicide. How have you weathered your own spiritual crises?

Well, not too well, but well enough that I'm still here at seventy. I have never really been powerfully tempted to kill myself. I guess partly because I didn't put myself on the planet. I have that sense that since I didn't put myself on the planet, I don't really have a right to take myself off. I have a terrific wife and I've got terrific kids who pull me through and I've got wonderful friends. We've all had down times and difficult times. Certainly my poetry reflects it. We have an expression in Yiddish, *Keine hora*. It means, "May the evil eye not be watching."

It's like knocking on wood. I shouldn't brag, I don't know what's down the line, I don't know next year. I may want to do a number with the oven, but I don't know. I recently read a biography of Randall Jarrell; it seems he was such an upbeat guy up until a point, and then he fell into a heavy depression. He may or may not have killed himself. His wife says he didn't, but there's evidence that he stepped in front of a moving car, a speeding car, and died that way. So who knows what kind of chemical imbalance suddenly seized him and drove him to that? I don't know. I think one of the things that makes it risky to be a poet is you can't close off your emotions. They've got to constantly be there. You've got to be with them or you've got no source for your writing. So a good deal of what's wounded you in your life remains vital and alive because, in a curious way, you need it for your writing. Berryman once said that the best thing that could happen to a poet is that he suffers some trauma that will almost kill him, but not quite. Well, I think that's a romanticized version. When I look at our greatest poet, Whitman, I don't sense that he suffered a trauma that almost killed him. There's great joy in his writing. There's a vision of men and women at peace in this country and the great richness that we share. I know there's a Sylvia Plath in my generation, but there's also a W. S. Merwin and Galway Kinnell and an Adrienne Rich. You can see, here's a woman who's determined to fight for what she thinks is justice. She couldn't be more different than Plath, and they're both terrific poets.

CAROL ROH-SPAULDING

interviewed by Linda B. Swanson-Davies

How has having your own child affected your writing?

Well, I was a single mom on the tenure track, and his life depended on my keeping my job. I couldn't stop and write a novel. I continued to write and publish, but I had to really focus on getting tenure. And you have this short period of time to do everything you can for your child—you know, the first four or five years are so important. I'm not saying that I did that brilliantly; I'm sure he's been compromised by the fact that I was a stressed-out parent. I did my best, and he's still very young. It's just a non-negotiable area, you know; I made the choice to have him. My career is not as highpowered as it would be had I not had him. There's still time.

What are your goals now as a writer?

To write book after book after book. Well, story after story, sentence after sentence. Let's put it this way: I've had plans for two, three books out in as many years, and I get very impatient wanting to get to them, but I dreamed that I was going to live to a hundred and two, so I may have some time.

YOUR FIRST NOVEL

Elizabeth McCracken
interviewed by Sarah Anne Johnson

What would you say to someone working on a first novel?

If you think, "Is this a novel? How do I know that I'm writing a novel? How do I know it's not just one damn page after another?"—that's how it is. Most of my advice has to do with preparing yourself for depression and heartbreak in the actual writing of the book. You must be prepared to break your own heart.

....

FINDING WHAT'S RIGHT FOR YOU
by Melanie Bishop

I have written as many as sixteen hours a day, several days in succession, when I've been up against a deadline and had no choice. During other periods I considered myself to be writing "full-time," I have had days where I wrote not at all, or one hour or two. Two is actually quite common for me. Two is, I believe, the number of hours Flannery O'Connor says (in *The Habit of Being*) was her daily limit.

More important than number of hours is the quality of the time spent. I've forced myself to sit and stare at the page for as many as six hours at a time, not allowing myself breaks other than to go to the bathroom or get something to eat. No matter how long I sat there that particular day, nothing was going to come of it. Not one word appeared on that page, and I was miserable. Described it to another writer friend of mine as "feeling like a kid in detention." I doodled, I made lists, I brushed my cat, I did everything but. Much more productive than this, I've found, is a less stringent interpretation of "writing full-time." While I got nothing out of those six forced hours, on a different day, I actually got six fresh pages out of one painless hour, after which I felt like stopping, and did.

I know of writers who put in the nine-to-five work day, five days a week, treating it like any other job. And I know of writers who are parents who have no choice but to work when their kids are in daycare or with the nanny, however many hours that adds up to. It's a situation each writer needs to work out individually. I recommend trying different approaches and seeing what feels right. I also recommend starting out with modest goals, timewise. If you say, "I'm just going to write for the next hour," it's completely unintimidating, so you're likely to have no trouble reaching that reasonable goal. And if that hour goes well, you will likely write on into the next hour or the next, without even planning to. Always remember that writing, as a pursuit, involves much more than just the time spent at the computer or with pen in hand. There's all the thinking and gestation. Be lenient with yourself. There will always be those crunch days when you've pushed some deadline to the limit and have to punch in for a full day or an all-nighter. Allow yourself a more relaxed and accommodating routine the rest of the time. While some are fine with eight hours a day of actual writing, others swear by one hour or two. By experimenting, you'll find what's right for you.

COMPASSION, COMMITMENT, AND FAITH

Lee Martin, interviewed by Linda B. Swanson-Davies

I really want to ask you about something, and I hope it's not an imposition. I know that as a kid you were "saved," but I have no idea what your spiritual perspective is now. As a teenager, I was also "saved," trying to escape my own troubles, and I really understand the desire to start fresh, to leave things behind. I wonder why we don't allow ourselves or each other to make real changes without God or magic or something. It would be so much more humane if we allowed people to earnestly turn a page. It seems to be why we have to turn to something supernatural—because it's so hard to do otherwise. Surely lots of people wish they could push something behind them and go forward constructively, and I wish we allowed ourselves and each other to do that.

Yeah, and so it's either, you know, it's a twelve-step program or it's God or it's something outside the self. I kind of feel bad about saying the twelve-step program, because of course there are many people who need that sort of structure.

Neither of us means to take away from those things.

No, not at all. Here's the interesting thing that you started me thinking about. If we are talking about individuals not being able to walk through that door without something external, then would we put the act of writing in that same category? I often think that the most spiritual thing that I do is this. You know, when I sit down every morning to try to do this work, I think it really does require many of the same things that are required of a more traditional religious faith.

Right, because there is faith involved.

Very much so; there is faith involved. There's compassion for other human beings, there's the commitment to trying to accept and—

And see that something good will happen.

Right, right. So I think there are a lot of things that are very spiritual about writing.

....

THOM JONES

interviewed by Jim Schumock

I've been told that an interview you saw with fellow Iowa Writers' Workshop attendee Tracy Kidder stimulated you to begin publishing your work. Is that true?

Well, yes. I had arranged my life so I could work out—swimming, boxing, lifting weights, running marathons—and I remember I was working as a janitor. I had just won a trip around the world by writing a little ad jingle—I had been an ad writer. I got back, and I remember we were in a transition house—it was really sort of a dump—waiting to buy a house. And I came home from the graveyard shift and cracked a six-pack of Rainier Ale, and I remember drinking a few. I was sitting there, in my janitor's shirt, which was sort of like a bowling shirt (it shone in the dark), and there was Tracy, an old friend from Iowa, talking to Tom Brokaw.

And I thought, "Ooh, what have I been doing? I have sort of let my life get out of control here. I'd like to write again."

But I didn't at that time; I got drunk and continued to work and just think about it, and finally, when I bought a computer just after my daughter was born, I started writing.

Most first novelists are about forty years old. It takes a long time to figure things out and produce. Hemingway wrote *The Sun Also Rises*, I think, when he was twenty-six or twenty-five, and Carson McCullers wrote the *The Heart Is a Lonely Hunter* when she was twenty-five, but that kind of thing is pretty rare. Swiss writer Robert Walser, one of Kafka's literary fathers, ultimately committed himself to an asylum and didn't write for the last thirty years of his life, saying, "I have not come here to write; I have come here to be mad." Do you ever feel like throwing in the towel and just going mad?

I think that a lot of times a writer will be in a frame of mind … I mean, to have this exquisite perceptual sensitivity, you pay a very big price. And most fiction writers I know have seen the dark night of the soul, so that when you come back from that, you may be able to tell your tale, or you may be too shaken to do it. You may be able to hang on and tell your stories for a year or two or three, or for the rest of your life, or you just might go over the edge into the abyss. I think there are a lot of gifted artists out there who experience this and can never really get it down, because it's happening so fast, and they might be just a shade over the edge—or not a shade—in terms of degrees and velocity of it and the pressure of it.

Sometimes it would be nice, I think, just to be a normal person—optimistic, easy going, and trusting, and not too obsessed with this business that I'm obsessed with—life and people, the world, and God, and so forth.

....

ELIZABETH McCRACKEN
interviewed by Sarah Anne Johnson

What's your schedule like when you're writing?

I'm so bad. When I write, I write hard, frequently in Provincetown. It's a point of superstition that a huge percentage of all three of my books have been written in 6 Fishbourne Upper at the Work Center. That's the apartment I had both years when I was a fellow, and I've rented that apartment for a total of five months over the last few years. I've written much of this book in that apartment. I certainly do plenty of work away from Provincetown. It's not like I write two months out of the year, but I don't write every day. I don't write even close to every day. When I do, I write awful stuff. I know it's important for some people, but for me, it's not a useful exercise at all. Which isn't to say that I don't have to make myself write. I really do. I vow I'm going to be good, then I turn on the TV and waste time, and I hate doing that. If I'm reading a book, I'm much more likely to write. I write the best at night. My concentration is better then. I sometimes write in the afternoon. The only time I write in the mornings is when I'm in Provincetown and I'm really in writing mode. I go to sleep and I wake up in the morning and go right to work.

AN ACT OF SURVIVAL
Alice Mattison, interviewed by Barbara Brooks

A writer engaged in a novel is a happy person, because once you figure out what you are doing—once you have characters and they start taking on flesh and saying things you don't expect them to say—it is a lovely thing to go on and write the book.

In part, I think I wrote *The Wedding of the Two-Headed Woman* because in my own life I was dealing with my parents' extreme old age, which has been depressing and difficult. One thing that is not in the book is the extreme old age of anybody. I kept being interrupted by my parents' needs, and I felt that I was not honoring the work. One day, I made up my mind that I was going to work every day on that book, no matter what happened. From then on, it kind of became addictive. I couldn't stop. I wrote when my father was in the hospital, and when he died. I felt a little brutal doing that, but I also felt it was my survival. It was making me happy.

. . . .

DAY JOBS AND DAIQUIRIS
Jonathan Raban, interviewed by Michael Upchurch

So much of the time, you can feel like you're not really working at all. You spend whole days reading, making notes, cogitating, taking a bath. Days and days and days can go by, and you try to persuade yourself feebly that you're working. Sometimes it works, and sometimes you get very neurotic indeed. Sometimes you feel like you're the only human being in the whole world whose existence is totally unjustified—you ought to be going out and teaching school, doing something arduous and useful.

I think this feeling of being a sponger and a wastrel—which is the natural affliction of the professional writer—is far more easy to feel in places where other people are continuously on holiday, like the West Indies or Florida, than it is in good, solid nine-to-five-ish sort of places like Seattle, where, on the whole, the example of the people around you who have proper jobs to do is reassuring. I never understand how those people do it, who move out to the West Indies or the south of France. They must feel so odd. I feel odd enough as it is. To be just surrounded by tourists drinking daiquiris—crazy!

ELIZABETH COX

interviewed by Sarah Anne Johnson

When did you know you were a writer?

I don't think that I've ever thought of myself as a "Writer." I had done so many other things before writing fiction. I was married, I had two children, and I taught special education for six years, so it just hadn't occurred to me to write until I was in my early thirties. By that time, I was already somebody in the world: a teacher, a mother, a wife. My brothers published books of poetry, and I thought to myself, I can do that. I wrote poetry first, published some poems, and returned to school to get my MFA in poetry. While there, I tried my hand at some short stories. Writing stories felt more natural to me. I felt as though I had moved into a slot. I didn't think of myself as a "Writer," I was just writing.

....

WHATEVER IT TAKES
Nomi Eve, interviewed by Linda B. Swanson-Davies

⟫◦⟪

When I got to MacDowell, which was a wonderful place for me, I told people—and this was only a year and a half ago—I told people that I needed ten more years to write this book, and I'd already been writing for four years. A few months ago, I spoke to a painter from MacDowell, Mark Wethli, a wonderful painter, and he said, "So, Nomi, how's the writing going?" And I said, "Two, three more years," and he said, "Nomi, you've made great strides! At MacDowell, you said a decade." But the time doesn't matter. Whatever it takes.

....

LIVING MULTIPLE NARRATIVES
Margaret Atwood
interviewed by Linda B. Swanson-Davies

⟫◦⟪

In an earlier interview, you'd said that each person has a story, a personal narrative that is constantly replayed and revised. Would you be willing to name a couple of significant aspects of your own personal narrative at this time?

The thing about novelists is that they more or less duck the issue of their personal narratives while constructing narratives for other people. In a way, the personal narrative of the writer is not really a personal narrative; it is connected with all of the narratives of these other people. In other words: What was I doing in 1992? Was I living my personal narrative, or was I living the personal narratives of the three characters I was involved in? You can't really separate them. When I think about what I was doing at the time, well, some of the time I was having lunch and going for walks, but at the same time, all of the time, I was engaged with these other people. The writer lives multiple narratives, and that's what makes the writer different from the person who is not a writer, who is usually just working on one story—namely, their own.

KATHLEEN TYAU

interviewed by Linda B. Swanson-Davies

More than anything, writing takes so much stamina. Stamina is the main thing, because you've got to get through all your little hissy fits. When you're writing a book, you have a very long period where you have no book. A very long period. And you have to live with that.

I've wanted to be a writer since age nine, but I was told I had to learn to put food on the table. I started the statistical business in order to write. So I'd have money and time. The business was a full-time job, but it was one that I could start at noon. So I started at noon. I wrote from four o'clock in the morning until eleven. I've done this since 1989.

This is the first year I've ever had just to write, and the results have been … mixed. I don't get up now until about 5:30. It's bad.

I feel like I should still be getting up at that time I've really gotten accustomed to, and have come to rely on for its craziness. It's a time when whatever it is you dreamt about is right there.

....

MAKING THE BIG (APPLE) MOVE
Amy Hempel
interviewed by Debra Levy and Carol Turner

⟹◆⟸

Do you think a writer should be in New York?

I don't see how it could hurt anybody, certainly early on. You know, put your face in front of people and go to a million readings. As to whether it's essential, certainly not. For a lot of people I know, almost everyone I know, it's easier to write somewhere other than New York, because New York is about publishing, not writing.

....

SHATTERING THE BEAUTIFUL DREAM
Ann Patchett, interviewed by Sarah Anne Johnson

⟹◆⟸

Elizabeth McCracken told me that you often conceive of a novel, turn it around in your head and consider your idea from all angles for months and months, then sit down and simply write the book. Is that true?

Yes, except, take the word "simply" out of that sentence. I just wrote one of those Writer on Writing columns for *The New York Times*, and I'm writing about the fact that I have this beautiful book in my head for such a long time, and I'm so happy dreaming about it, and I get all settled and it's so lovely. Then comes the moment when I have to take it out of the air and put it onto paper, which is the process of killing it, beating all of the life and the beauty out of it. It's incredibly depressing for me to start writing a novel, because it's going from this fantastic realm of imagination to the reality of words. It's as if you had a pen pal that you were in love with, and then one day you had to get married and start living together. From everything being your perfect and beautiful dream, to having to go through the physical aspects of the day with somebody. It's very hard. Not as hard as having a real job, of course.

SIGRID NUNEZ

interviewed by Linda B. Swanson-Davies

[Regarding old age,] I guess I feel that most of the changes would be physical. In other words, I would feel weaker, slower, but I don't think I would really be all that different.

If I'm a writer and life is going to go on like this, unlike other people's, my life is not going to change that much. I'm not going to have children or grandchildren. So basically the way my life is now is the way I see my life in the future. I hope I'll be writing and producing books and so on. I'll always be reading and listening to music. I'll never live in a very large space; it's just not something I would do. I'll always be in a similar room—I can see that. It is who I am. I'm doing what I should be doing …

Writing is a job like anything else. The books have to follow each other. You have to be writing all the time. You have to do your job and you have to do it well.

Margaret Atwood: I thought that I would always have to have a day job and write in the evening. I did that for a long time, and I'm just as glad not to have to do it, particularly with a family. If you have a day job, a family, and you try to write, that's really about one more thing than you can manage. In Canada at that time, it was not really possible for anyone to make a living writing. I would say the possibility now is about the same as it is in the States, namely ten percent, but it is a possibility.

as interviewed by Linda B. Swanson-Davies

CAROLYN KIZER

interviewed by Jim Schumock

When Richard Hugo was asked what made poets different from other people, he said, "Poets think about death all the time!"

Yes, he did say that.

Do you?

Oh, yes. But as I get older, it bothers me far less. I remember, I think I was in my late twenties—I had had three children in three years and I was kind of tired. I was not happily married. I said to my mother, "Mama, at what age did you feel oldest?" She thought about it for a while and she said, "Twenty-eight." I think that's a great truth. When you get to be really old, you reach a kind of accommodation, and you don't think about it nearly as much. I think when we're young and when we're writing, one of the ways we fend off the notion of our mortality is with putting words down on a piece of paper.

What about alcohol? That's a way to fend off mortality. For your generation, it was really a major catalyst.

Of course, Dick Hugo and James Wright were alcoholics. But look at the previous batch. Lowell and so on. They were not only alcoholics, they were all crazy. I think all poets, with the exception of William Stafford, tend to drink. I remember the first time I was at a conference where several of us were giving readings and someone asked Bill if he'd like a preliminary drink and he said, "Oh, I never drink before a reading." We all just sort of looked at him. Yes, we do drink. That's very true.

Why?

Oh, I think it takes the edge off things a bit. I think most poets are rather shy. We can come on awfully strong, but it doesn't mean a whole lot. We're all rather reticent. We're very vulnerable. A couple of drinks makes us a little more socially comfortable.

THE NEED TO BE SELF-PROTECTIVE
Askold Melnyczuk, interviewed by William Pierce

I don't think any person has the right to do their work at someone else's expense. The claims some studied bohemians made about their need to be ruthless and selfish to pursue their art were, as often as not, the hash and the absinthe talking.

On the other hand, we as writers need to be a little, not to say ruthless, but self-protective. Life is rich and endlessly fascinating, and we could let ourselves get yanked into its dance and never stop until it was too late to write the little volumes that were our only real mission here. Horace had it right: Art is long and life is short. If you can arrange it and have the discipline and the temperament for it, you can devote yourself 24/7 to the study of your art and expect to be rewarded by a lifetime of exhilaration and discovery. This may make it hard to be attentive to a spouse or a child—very often this dawns on artists a little after the fact, and they suffer the rest of their lives trying to reconcile the conflicting demands on their time.

WRITING AS IDENTITY

Sigrid Nunez, interviewed by Linda B. Swanson-Davies

It's impossible for me to imagine a life without writing. It's what I do and who I am. I live by myself; I've never been married; I don't have children; I don't even have a hobby, really. Every job that I've ever had was a job that I had in order to keep myself writing. I mean, they were not careers; they were money jobs to support my habit of writing.

It's hard to imagine what I would be if I weren't a writer. It's a little bit like that section in the book [*A Feather on the Breath of God*] about how difficult it would be to imagine Christa not being German. It was so much a part of her, how she saw herself and presented herself to the world, that if you tried to separate her from that and think of her without her Germanness, you couldn't see her anymore. There's no Christa there. I feel that way about myself as a writer. If you take away that part of my identity, I don't really know what's there.

....

MAKING ENDS MEET

Nomi Eve, interviewed by Linda B. Swanson-Davies

Now I'm at a point where I've been writing a little amount of time a day, from half an hour to two or three hours, and producing tons of stuff, good stuff. Other times, I need a month to write a hundred pages no one will ever see. Of sitting there every hour of the day, doing it. And then the next month, I can write easily again. It just demands different time from me. Sometimes I'm incredibly productive in half an hour. Other times, I really need all day to get a paragraph.

Do you think that's related to the material?

Very related to the material. Very related to the material.

How do you make a living?

Well, I've had crazy years. They're getting less crazy. But for two years, I wrote a lot of book reviews and made a good amount of money—not enough to support an apartment in New York, but a good amount. Then I stopped book reviews and I went to Israel, and I didn't do anything but write for a while. I had saved a little bit of money and my grandmother gave me a little money, and I just sat and wrote. For the last six months or so, I've been back in the States, living in Boston with my wonderful fiancé, Aleister, a scientist, a post-doc at Harvard. And I recently got a job teaching English as a second language, and that's what I do in the morning from 9:00 to 12:30, and then I write. I've also taught Hebrew school. Every season is different. I never make a ton of money, but the past month I made as much as my scientist sweetheart teaching various things.

I think this English-as-a-second-language thing is going to be good for me. I enjoy the teaching, and schedule-wise, it's terrific. I can tell them month by month if I want to work, because the courses are a month long and they pay pretty decently. I wouldn't be able to have kids and support a family on what I make right now, but we're doing okay. We're not saving anything, but we're doing okay.

....

BALANCING BABIES AND BOOKS
Mary McGarry Morris
interviewed by Linda B. Swanson-Davies

⟹⬥⟸

When the children were young, I could never go into a room and shut the door to write. I wrote with them in the room, or nearby—or outside in the yard, but that never lasted for too long, because I'd just keep running to the window to check on them. There really wasn't any "hiding away" so that I could write. I mostly wrote when they were asleep, but of course by that time, I was usually too tired to write for very long.

I can remember sitting at the kitchen table writing, with one leg crossed to cradle the baby, and its bottle would be propped, and the whole thing would work as long as my right hand was free to hold the pen. A lot of what I wrote in those years was about my frustration at not being able to write. Raising children is a messy, intensely passionate affair that can be distracting and very draining for a writer. I used to wish I had more time, two more hands, more energy and patience, a room of my own, an office, an island far, far away from the runny noses and diapers, the arguments, and the sticky floors, but I never, ever wished that I didn't have children. I needed them the way I needed to write. It was a convoluted and prolific dilemma.

KEVIN CANTY

interviewed by Linda B. Swanson-Davies

Instead of saying, "I want to be a writer," and then sitting around wishing I were a writer, I've been really trying to throw myself into it, giving it as much energy as I could. It's meant that I don't get to spend as much time with my family as I'd like to; it's meant that the hours in the week are sometimes very constrained. Right now, I'm teaching, and trying to write a novel, and doing this traveling around on business, and trying to have a family life. It ends up being more hours than there really are in the week.

It's really taken me a long time to get around to writing. I'm forty-one years old, and this is my first collection of short stories [*A Stranger in This World*]. I don't think I could have gotten to it much earlier, but I'm really looking forward to having the time to write. I've made my life in the expectation I'm going to have the time to write a novel. To me it's a challenge and a wonderful project. I feel like there's a lot left undone.

I'm sitting here as a writer with a book out. I have a job. If I hadn't been in Portland with a dream of doing that eight or nine years ago—I sound like Michael Jackson or something—but without that dream, that fantasy, the imaginary life that was not the life I was living, I wouldn't be where I am now.

HOW PARENTHOOD DEEPENS WRITING
Andre Dubus III, interviewed by John McNally

When you first began writing, you were a single guy. Now you're married and have three kids. In what ways has having a family impacted your writing?

Yes, now I'm blessed with a family. And I do see it as just that—a blessing. I had no idea all those sweet old ladies were right all along, that when you meet the one you're going to marry, you just know it, and if you're fortunate enough to have kids, you'll feel more love in you than you ever thought possible.

To answer your question, when I was single, my sole enduring thought from day to day was my writing. Now it is, and will forever be, my children. How to nurture them, keep them safe and healthy, send them out into the world as strong, loving, responsible people. This is not to say I no longer think of my writing daily. I do! In fact, because of the deep spiritual changes parenthood opens up in you—a greater capacity for love, vulnerability, fear of loss, acceptance of your place in the mortal coil, etc.—it has got to ultimately deepen the writing, too. And yes, the truth is there are more demands on my time than there were when I was still single, which makes time at the desk a bit lean sometimes, but so what! In no time at all, I'll be sitting on the couch in an empty house wondering why my children aren't calling me from their adult lives I'm no longer really part of; if I miss an occasional writing session to be with them, that's good!

KEEPING THE CHANNEL OPEN
Robert Olen Butler, interviewed by Heather Iarusso

Do you tell your students to write every day?

Having to go to the depth of your own unconscious to create a work of art is very scary and demanding, and it has an interesting characteristic to it. That is that if you have not been writing, it's a terrible and excruciating process to force your way down as deep as you must go to write well. But once you get there and you go back the next day and the next day and the next, it is still challenging and daunting, but it's not nearly as difficult. The channel stays open for a while.

But if you tell yourself you're going to write on the weekends or this week but not the next or during the summer, it's literally impossible. I think you cannot be an artist in fiction doing that. For me, if I stop writing for three or four days, when I go back to the work, it is as if I have never written before in my life. The way in to that very difficult place seals itself up and erases all traces of itself.

Stephen Dixon: I know what should be at the top of a to-do list; it's always the same: take care of my family, write, work, keep going, try to stay healthy so you can do the other things. There isn't much else that means anything. I read a lot, but that's not a must-do or a to-do, it's simply a do-do.

as interviewed by Linda B. Swanson-Davies

ANDRE DUBUS III
interviewed by John McNally

Your birthday is September 11th. Where were you and what were you doing when you first learned of the attacks?

On that terrible day, I had just made my morning coffee and was heading up to my attic office when I overheard my wife on the phone with her sister, who'd just told her to turn on the news, that a plane had crashed into the World Trade Center. We turned it on, and, like so many people, saw the second plane crash into the second tower. I ended up staying in front of the TV for most of that day, interrupted by my calling friends and colleagues in New York to make sure they were safe. They all were, thank God. A few people called me as well, because I'd been flying quite a bit in and out of Logan Airport all year. In fact, I'd flown in on United the night before and was scheduled to fly out again on United a couple days later. I didn't write that day, and when my family came over to celebrate my birthday it was, as it should've been, a very low-key and quiet gathering, and if I could, I would've skipped it altogether.

I know what other writers mean when they say they felt as if their own "tinkering with a short story" was trivial in the light of all that, but I was spared that feeling by an editor at the *Toronto Globe and Mail* who wanted me to write a piece about the attack for that weekend's paper. Man, that was a tough one to write! I was still so full of rage and hurt and shock and grief, like everybody else. How in the world would I write anything with any clarity or insight at all? That's what I think Truman Capote was onto when he said, "A writer must write as cool and detached as a surgeon." Somehow I wrote and submitted the essay, then got back to work on the novel I've been wrestling with for years. While I hated most of what I was seeing on the desk in front of me—a normal feeling—it didn't feel trivial to be working on it. If the attacks of 9/11 have taught us anything at all, it's that life is horrifically short and precarious, sacred and fragile, and we should live as fully, deeply, and richly as we possibly can. Other than trying to be as good a father and husband as I can be, I can't think of a better way to live than to try and create something worth reading for someone you'll probably never even meet.

SWINGING ON THE PENDULUM

Thom Jones, interviewed by Jim Schumock

When I write, I go into a manic state. When I write in the first voice, I become the character, like a method actor. And I get so excited when I'm working on something that I can't wait to get back to the computer and polish it. I'll rewrite maybe thirty times, and then I know pretty much when a piece is done, and then I'll have to go through a new incubation. I sort of crash, and about three weeks later, I'm charged up enough again to write another one; so I was doing one a month or a chapter a month. That seems to be my rhythm now, and it's working out nicely.

THE OBSESSIVE QUALITY

Tim O'Brien, interviewed by Jim Schumock

I've written now for twenty-some years, and, like smoking, writing is a kind of obsession for me, and not always a good one. That is, I put in nine-hour days. I work on birthdays, Christmas, Halloween—in part, because I love it so much, and I'm passionate about writing, but also there's an obsessive quality to it, a habitual quality to it. Like reaching for a first cup of coffee, I reach for a cigarette, and then reach for the typewriter. I need to break away for a while, find the world again, get out of those white walls, out into the world.

A VERY AMIABLE COMPANION

William Styron, interviewed by Jim Schumock

I've read that you used to spend your evenings drinking and imagining your characters and the scenes for the next day.

That aspect has probably been exaggerated, either by myself or by people who have asked me questions about that drinking habit, to the extent that this visionary experience that I would have certainly didn't happen regularly. It happened intermittently.

I do remember that alcohol was a very amiable companion. I described it as a kind of senior partner of my intellect, and one which I found very valuable. Since that period, when I was using alcohol as an adjunct to the imagination, and now having stopped that kind of drinking, I have not found that I have missed anything. My imagination is functioning just as well.

IN THE WRITING FRENZY

Kevin Canty, interviewed by Linda B. Swanson-Davies

I've always thought that writing was something I could do and something that I wanted to do. But on the other hand, from the time that I took that workshop with Joyce Thompson to the time that this book [*A Stranger in This World*] was published was eight or nine years of pretty steady, flogging work. I tried to get up in the morning and put in three or four hours a day, Monday through Friday. James Joyce wrote *Dubliners* in about a year when he was twenty-six or twenty-seven, but he was a genius.

I usually do it sometime after the first cup of coffee in the morning. That's because I lock myself in a room and sit there and try to write, and restlessness just goes with the territory. I have to have a swivel chair. I talk to myself when I write. I tried to write at my office at the University of Florida, and it was awful because I'd get all coffeed up and get into a writing frenzy, and I'd roam the hallways, cornering people and yelling at them. I'd get off into my own world and it took a while to switch back. Restlessness is a habit of mine.

THE BOOK IS THE THING

Paul Theroux, interviewed by Michael Upchurch

The monotony of staying in one place is the best thing for writing a novel. Having regular habits, a kind of security, but especially no big surprises, no shocks—for me, I'm talking about. Just to be in a room plugging away. That's the best thing for you. Personal appearances, prizes—those are all disruptions. You need encouragement; you need good things to happen to you, cheerful people around you. But I have never been able to work well except in a very monotonous, predictable atmosphere, with placid, even-tempered people. I can't be around excitable people.

I always loved writing in the winter when it was dark. "Writing weather," I used to think. "Writing light." It was dark, with just a pool of artificial light. Everyone indoors. I was indoors, working on something good. And there was a completeness to it and a monotony to it that I needed.

Every good thing that has happened to me has been a surprise. It's never been something I expected or demanded. It was always a bonus of writing. Publishing books early on and getting advances for only one or two thousand dollars—it didn't matter to me. Of course I would have wanted more. But that didn't discourage me. It didn't make me say, as it does some people, "I'm not going to sweat my guts out for a pittance."

I was perfectly willing to sweat my guts out for a pittance because I had the book. I always felt that the book was the thing, that if a book was any good, it had a long and fruitful life. So

I wasn't looking for a killing early on. I honestly don't think it would have changed anything.

I wouldn't have had as interesting a life, though. That's for sure.

....

PEACE AND SUSTAINABILITY
Thisbe Nissen, interviewed by Linda B. Swanson-Davies

In another twenty years, what ability or quality, either professional or personal, do you hope you will have discovered, acquired, or refined?

Whether it's the answer to that question or not, the first word that comes to my mind, and maybe it's because of the state of things right now, is—okay, two—two words—peace and sustainability. I am trying to live sustainably, and writing is a sustainable life for me. It's tied in with teaching and listening to people, and hearing and sharing stories. A writing life is also a life that makes sense to me, because it can involve vegetable gardening, and it can involve a community of people who are engaged in projects and processes together. Then I start to sound like the flaky hippy I really am. I want to keep going, and I want to keep going well, and I want to keep going in a way that I'm proud of, and that I can look on and say, I have tried to live my life well.

CHAPTER

13

APPROACHES TO WRITING

Dorothy Grace Howland, ca. 1937

Katherine Vaz: My father has painted every single day of his life—he once covered his father's car tarp with his rendition of the Last Judgment—and it is this quiet, steady, joyful focus that infuses my habits as a writer. So often, people think of "discipline" as a cold, steely business, instead of a habit of calmly wading in and agreeing to get carried out to a deeper place.

....

ALLOWING IT TO BE WRITTEN
Thomas E. Kennedy
interviewed by Linda B. Swanson-Davies

━━━◆◆◆━━━

It took me, I guess, from the time I was thirty-one or -two until I was about thirty-eight—and that was fairly intensive work—before I was able to write a story that was publishable. It was from that point, that story, that I found the way that I could write, found out how to reach the material and how to shape it into fiction.

Of course I have to ask you: What is it that you found out? How did you get to that place?

It was a strange process. I had been working very hard at it, but the problem, my problem, was—and I think maybe a lot of aspiring writers have this problem—I couldn't get free of my mind. I couldn't learn how to write with my whole being. That was the key for me. Then, one day, I had torn a tendon in my leg and had a cast on, and I was home alone for three weeks. I sat around looking for people to talk to. My wife was at work and the kids were off in daycare. It was a hot summer, and I went hobbling out, and some man across the street walking past waved at me. I waved back, and he looked and he came back and he said, "Excuse me, I'm sorry I waved. I thought you were someone else, but I can see now you're much smaller than the person I thought you were."

We got to talking, and he turned out to be a retired general. He started telling fantastic stories about how he witnessed the detonation of the hydrogen bomb years before, and he told it in the strangest way. He mentioned the fact that suddenly, when the bomb went off, it got so unbearably hot. He said it was very uncomfortably hot because he had all this heavy protective gear on. I realized the man was senile, but there was some strange truth in what he was saying, which I couldn't pinpoint. I went inside and started to write the story "The Sins of Generals," which is in *Unreal City*. That was the first time that I reached that place where I found what, for me, were truths which went beyond simple conscious comprehension. That was a strange experience. A lot of it is literally included in the story.

I mentioned earlier that one of the things that was hardest for me to learn was to try not to understand everything; you can't understand everything. Life is a mystery. There's a mystery in fiction as well. I asked Robert Coover once whether he at some point fully understood his stories, and at what point that was, and his answer was very enlightening. He said that his best fictions were not those that he wrote so much as those that he allowed to be written—that he allowed free movement to whatever it is in us that combines all of these elements into a story, that he just catered to that spirit and gave his skills to that spirit, and allowed the thing to be written.

THE PATH YOU WALK

Richard Bausch

interviewed by Jennifer Levasseur and Kevin Rabalais

You've kept up such an amazing endurance—eight novels, three collections of stories. Do you see yourself at any point concentrating on one genre?

I hope it will always be both. I'd like to write twenty novels and books of stories. I don't know if I'll wind up doing it, but I'd like to.

I don't think of writing as hauling things up out of myself, like drilling oil out of a well. I think of it as a path I walk. In fact, I'm convinced that's the secret. If you think of yourself as containing the material, then everything becomes limited by what you can contain. I mean, you can empty a well. But if it's a path you're taking—hell, you can go anywhere, right? So when I sit down to write, I'm not thinking about pulling stuff out of myself. I'm thinking about going somewhere, walking around, and seeing what I find. And there's never a time when I sit down and it isn't there. You just walk the path. There is a tremendous amount of work you can get done doing that. There is no part of that that's not fun. I never worry about whether or not it's good. I don't care, right then. I'm walking the path. I know that if I can bring enough attention to it, and be honest and open to it and not cheat it, it'll be fine. Whether it is the best I've ever done is not anything for me to worry about.

ALICE MATTISON

interviewed by Barbara Brooks

Was it difficult to write the scene in *The Book Borrower* in which the characters finally address the coincidence?

It was a hard scene to write. That book was written on a computer, but I had to write that particular scene on a typewriter, and I had to write it in a different room. Sometimes I think the things that we write are located in the air above us. But sometimes, for some reason, there's a column of air somewhere else that we have to get under in order to receive a piece of writing, and in that case, the column of air was in my bedroom. So I had to go in there, and I had to bring the typewriter with me on a rolling table and write the scene in there. It was hard. I did have to break through something to do it.

....

WHAT'S GOING TO HAPPEN NEXT?

Daniel Wallace

interviewed by Linda B. Swanson-Davies

It sounds like writing *Big Fish* was a somewhat unstructured process.

I've never plotted anything before. Actually, I've tried to plot, and it does exactly what you say it does. It saps the life right out of it. Why do it? I enjoy writing because I like to find out what's gonna happen next. It's the same thing that happens in my whole life—I mean, I have relationships with other people because I'm interested in what's gonna happen next. If you brought me a book of my life that said, Well, you're going to fall in love with somebody and you will do this and then this, and you gave me the plot of the whole thing, why go ahead and do it? Even if you're going to be happy. I don't see any reason to go through with it. The mystery is part of what makes it interesting for me, and if it's not interesting for me, I can't imagine how it's going to be interesting for you.

WRITING AS IF YOU'RE READING

Elizabeth Cox, interviewed by Sarah Anne Johnson

In "Saved," Josie Wire wants to save Beckett by offering him the Bible, but it's only when she offers herself that Beckett is truly saved, in that he abandons his original intention, and, instead, he is confronted with his own unwillingness to violate her. This is an unexpected turn of events. How did you arrive at this?

I did not know this is what would happen. I didn't know anything going into that scene. I love the position of ignorance. I love to approach a story or a scene as though I'm reading it instead of writing it. That's the fun for me—not knowing where it's going. I didn't know what Beckett was going to do until he did it. At the time, I was merely watching them. He could've done anything. I was afraid he was going to hurt her; but I also knew he was not evil. I also didn't know he would tell her his real name, or what his real name was, until he said it. When I'm working in this way of discovery, I feel most located in my imagination.

PAUL THEROUX
interviewed by Michael Upchurch

When you started [The Mosquito Coast], did you know Allie would be silenced by vultures plucking out his tongue? Or was that one of the imaginative discoveries?

That was one of the discoveries. I knew he was going to die, and I knew at what point in the book he was going to die. I just wasn't quite sure how it was going to happen—whether he was going to die from a bullet, whether it was going to be an accident, or whether his kids were going to kill him. Then, thinking about it, when I got nearer to it, worked up to it, I saw that that wasn't going to happen. They can't do it. They should do it—but if they do it, they're going to be marked by it. That was an interesting technical problem.

....

WALKING WITH A FLASHLIGHT
David Long, interviewed by Linda B. Swanson-Davies

I discover the story as I go. Very few of the stories do I know ahead of time. In *Blue Spruce*, for instance, there are maybe three pieces where I had the whole story in my mind the instant I thought it up. There's a story called "The Vote," which is like a day I actually spent, and so I knew the plot line. But stories like "Attraction," or "Blue Spruce," or "The New World," any of the longer stories …"Lightening," no. "Perro Semihundido" was the hardest story to write because I just simply didn't know what I was doing. These stories take six weeks to three months to draft out sometimes, and then longer to revise. Often, I'll let them sit for a while. What I'm finding writing the novel is it's like walking through the woods with a little flashlight—you just hope it doesn't conk out on you; you're smacking it against your leg; you can see just beyond your shoes, you know?

In "Perro Semihundido"—"The Half-Submerged Dog"—I knew that Faith had to go to Seattle and find her brother, and I knew that something about finding her brother would be shocking to her, and that that somehow would have an impact on her decision of whether she wanted to stay with Rick or not. But I didn't know any of it beyond that. I just knew this barest outline.

....

THE COMPOST OF THE IMAGINATION
Robert Olen Butler
interviewed by Linda B. Swanson-Davies

Graham Greene once said, and I'm paraphrasing because I can't remember the quote, that all good novelists have bad memories. He says what you remember comes out as journalism. What you forget goes into the compost of the imagination. You know, there are writers in the world who are quite wonderful; in person, they tell wonderful anecdotes, one after another, and you can sit all night and listen to them talk. They're brilliant people, and you wonder why they never wrote even better books than they have. And I think the answer is that they've never forgotten anything. Their literal memories are so strong—they are terrific anecdotists, but their unconscious has never been fully stocked with the deeper essences of all the stories that they carry around with them.

SANDRA CISNEROS
interviewed by Robert Birnbaum

Tell me what it's like to spend such a long time on one project.

On writing *Caramelo*? For me, it didn't seem like it was that long. It just seemed like I had put my head down for a few seconds, and then when I looked up, nine years had passed. I think everyone around me was more impatient and more exasperated than I was. I was just working, and I work very slowly, so sometimes I lose touch with reality because I am so absorbed in another world. I think that people had to actually call me and say the towers had fallen. Or this and that is going on in the world—I really was in another world. Often times when I wanted to be social everyone was asleep. I was in my own world; when they wanted to be social, I had to apologize and avoid people. I think it's changed my life and my whole way of socializing—the way I was before this book and the way I am now. It's almost as if there are two different people. I was the kind of person that was very social and liked to be with an entourage and have lots of parties and have people around me. And now I find I am much more satisfied seeing people one on one. I avoid crowds, and I get really plagued by people, as if they are bees or something. I am talking about my friends. I can only handle them one at a time.

Can you connect that to anything in particular?

I think some of that is the intensity of the experience of writing this book. I feel as if I traveled and became someone else.

I asked you the question about the length of time that it's taken you to write this book. Your answer was very specific and individual, which leads me to think that we are given to generalizing this process of creating or writing something, and in doing that, we lose some understanding of it. When you describe it, it seems very natural. You put your head down, and then it was over.

Right. I was making something completely new, too. I wasn't writing *The House on Mango Street*. If I was writing that, I could have gotten that done in a couple of years. I didn't want to do something I had done before. I really wanted to expand and push myself and do something that I didn't have a model for. I didn't even know how to make what I wanted. I just knew that I could see it in my mind's eye for a flash of a second, and then I was in the dark. So I was mainly in the dark, experimenting with this book.

There is a place in the book where the main character and narrator says, "Art can keep you from dying." You've alluded to being in the dark on this book for long periods. What if you had been unable to figure it out—that is, how to write it or finish it? What might have happened then?

I felt like throwing the book away several times. But I don't think I would have. Every book takes you to the terror, that terrible place of possible failure. That seems to be a pattern for me when I work on things that are pushing me to my limits. When I wrote the story "Eyes of Zapata," which I thought was my best story in the collection—which hardly anyone ever mentions in the *Woman Hollering Creek* book—that took me to the same process of writing little bits and pieces in the dark and stumbling about and not knowing who's speaking, or what am I going to do with this? I feel it's important, but I don't know where I am going with this, and then finally, at the end, all the pieces fitting together as if I had planned it from the outset. And I had, but in a very subliminal way. In this book, it was the same. Except for nine months, it was nine years.

....

FEELING YOUR WAY THROUGH THE TUNNEL

Dan Chaon, interviewed by Misha Angrist

[Frank] O'Connor wrote at length about his method of composition. Specifically, he talked about reducing the story to four lines or less and committing it to paper in skeletal form, adding layers with each revision. Do you ever work that way?

I'm not sure what you mean. Do you mean starting out by reducing the premise to a shorthand or a formula?

It could be expressed that way. He actually talked about his students using algebraic terms to condense their premises to their most elemental forms. "X marries Y. Y dies. X visits Y's parents in Ireland but does not mention that Y is dead." In part, I think this was his way of avoiding descriptive distractions: "It was a steamy night, a new moon glowed against the black sky." He was a strong believer in putting all of that stuff into much later drafts, if at all.

Right. Actually, all of that descriptive stuff was very characteristic of many stories from O'Connor's era. I mean, when you go back and read certain stories by, say, Kay Boyle or Truman Capote or even Eudora Welty, there can be so much scene-setting that it's sometimes hard to pay attention—it can be hard to get in there.

Obviously, the sensibility has changed radically since then. During O'Connor's time [1940s–1960s], what many people considered to be a "well-made" story almost had to begin with a fair amount of description.

The implication is that the writer must know the ending before he or she starts. How often is that true for you?

Almost never. When I don't know the premise, then it's pretty safe to say I don't know the ending—or even much else sometimes. For example, when I sat down to write "Passengers, Remain Calm," I started out with that image of the snake with a girl in his mouth. From there, I "discovered" the little kid walking around the fair with his uncle, and then found my way to the rest of it. I had no idea what the story was about when I started it; I didn't know that the uncle and the kid were even in the story until they suddenly appeared. As I began to ponder why they were there together, background information began to come to me and the details filled in bit by bit. So, in that case, I discovered the premise last; it was as though it was built backwards. Sometimes as you write, you're feeling your way through the tunnel and the light begins to turn on as you go along.

It can be easier with those stories where I know the premise going in, but even then, not always. With "Big Me," I had the premise [young boy spies on a man in the neighborhood whom he perceives to be an older version of himself] and had written the first four pages in one night. I thought, "Oh, this is great—this is going to be fun." Then I spent something like four years trying to figure out how to finish it.

So when you had that germ of an idea and those first four pages, you didn't know that the kid was going to confront his older self at the end?

No. I didn't know what was going to happen, and that was part of the problem. I think there was a version of it where the kid's mother and the guy were having an affair—I tried all kinds of bizarre things before I finally had the kid go in there and just talk to the guy. And even then, I had no idea what the guy was going to say. So knowing the premise doesn't always make things go smoother for me.

MATTHEW SHARPE
interviewed by Sherry Ellis

Do you think it's important to have a disciplined plan as a writer—for example, writing every day, having intentions and goals and reaching them?

Oh yes. Otherwise, I'd die. I think the more you show up at the computer or the writing pad, the more likely it is you will discover the inspiration. There's a nice metaphor, which I am going to mangle, from Mary Oliver, the poet, where she talks about this wild part of yourself that doesn't want to be tamed, but if you show up at the same place and time every day, and you offer it your rigor, it will trust you more, and it may be more likely to show up, too.

WRITING ADVICE from Andre Dubus III

Trust your imagination; don't try and figure out your stories ahead of time, because that's walking the high-wire with a big net under you. We were all born with the ability to imagine and dream endlessly, terrifyingly, gorgeously, wildly, etc. Our job, it seems to me, is to work mercilessly on finding the truest language to bring out whatever it is that needs to be brought out. Which is one thing a good writing class or program can do! And, much like having children, the writer doesn't even get to choose what comes out, or how. So get in your daily sessions—if all you have is twenty minutes, then take it anyway; you're at least getting blood through the umbilical cord to that growing fetus. Don't think about the work or talk to anybody about it in any specific way; do other things in your life that make you feel good, because if you rely on writing to do that, it will disappoint you, especially if you're going deeply enough. And only quit writing if you find you can do that and still be you!

as interviewed by John McNally

RICHARD BAUSCH

interviewed by Jennifer Levasseur and Kevin Rabalais

When Bishop dies early in the novel [In the Night Season], that throws away all the reader's foundations. Because of this, the reader is never allowed to get comfortable. The intensity of the racism and the unexpected elements of the story make it quite suspenseful.

It's ironic because the death of Bishop is not a race crime. "We're equal-opportunity criminals," one of the killers says. The scariest character in the novel for me is the recreational killer, the one who shoots the cows. In the scene where he kneels down and unzips his pants in front of the boy, I didn't know what he was going to do. It scared the hell out of me. I didn't even think about what he might do. What he does is bad enough, but it wasn't what I was afraid he was going to do. And I didn't know, while I was writing, what he was going to do.

When you write a book like that, where plot is pretty heavy, you have to be aware of what you're doing a little more; it can't be arbitrary. But still a whole lot is stuff that you're dreaming up, and you don't know what's going to happen, how it's going to work out. I had no idea how the book was going to end, or if the boy and his mother were going to make it. It took me three days to figure out whether the boy lives. And when he did live, it wasn't resonant enough. I thought about the sheriff. I went away from it for a while and wrote a couple of stories. When I went back, I realized the sheriff had to have lost a child early, and then it could count. So I had to go through and re-earn the whole thing. I had to make every scene between him and the wife be about the lost child. And the only way to do that was to make it be the anniversary of the child's death so it's really weighing on his mind. It took about two months of going through and redoing everything just to make that one moment resonate as it should. I like to tell students about that experience because, as a writer, you have to be willing to take great pain to make it work, or to make it work better, anyway. It probably would have worked okay if it weren't for that, but it wouldn't have worked for me. It needed more.

FAR BEYOND CRAFT

Lynn Freed, interviewed by Sarah Anne Johnson

In reading through your novels, starting with *Heart Change*, *Home Ground*, then moving on through *The Bungalow* and *The Mirror*, one can see the development of your craft. You've often referred to *Heart Change* as a "teething novel." How would you describe the others in terms of what you struggled with or sought to develop by way of craft?

I never think of craft. I try not to teach it, either. I don't believe that craft creates the writer. Practice does. When I say "teething novel," I mean that there are lapses of ear in there. There are riffs that go on too long. And also quite a bit of what I refer to, thanks to Natalia Ginzburg, as "singing"—prose that takes off into song. With the later novels, I fell more comfortably into my own voice. And my timing was more precise, more crisp. But the real thing that makes a novel live is something far beyond craft—it's something that is not codifiable. It is the life that comes with the novel, as the novel is being written. All the craft in the world cannot hide a novel that doesn't want to be written. I've written both types, and I won't say which is which.

WORK GENERATES WORK

David Long, interviewed by Linda B. Swanson-Davies

I think I have a lot of patience for drudgery. I think it was John Gregory Dunne who said that writing a novel is like laying pipe, just laying a lot of pipe. If you can't make yourself sit still for that, then you can't do it. You can't rely on inspiration. I don't even believe in inspiration. I just believe in working. Work generates work. What frustrates me horribly is not knowing what I'm going to do next. And so you force something to happen. A lot of days, you know that by the end of the day you'll have some words on paper, and they'll be scenes and incidents and exchanges that you don't have any knowledge of yet. It just comes out of no place. So you're forced to rely on that process of things coming out of no place, and that part's nerve wracking. Some people would say that you have to love the possibility of it. Well, that's a little flaky for me.

I can look at days I've spent in the process of working on this novel and I can see there's stuff I like, and that I didn't have any knowledge of ten minutes before I wrote it. That's what I mean by "Work generates work." You can't sit around thinking. You have to sit around working.

Thomas E. Kennedy: When I was starting out, I took what undergraduate courses were available to me. My first help was the advice of a college professor to keep a journal in order to loosen up my style. I was seventeen, and four years of keeping a journal more or less every-day—sometimes just a couple of sentences, sometimes many pages, sometimes with gaps of weeks or even months—did indeed get me in the habit of writing, and writing freely. To learn to write freely is important.

....

LETTING THE IMAGINATION UNFURL
Stephen Dixon, interviewed by Jim Schumock

—————

Is there a point when you're writing that it seems as if the writing is coming out of your fingertips?

The first draft. The first draft is like a reel that comes out of my head. Very often, I don't know where it comes from. In fact, when I sit down to write a story, it's usually the day after I have finished a story or finished a novel. So I sit down feeling like I'm a bum. I'm not working at anything, and my life is a waste. I'm only happy when I'm writing, so I must sit down and write. I sit down the next day. I say, "Well, what are you going to write about?" I don't know. The best thing is to just let the imagination unfurl. I write the first thing that comes into my head. Maybe there's a line that's been circulating in my mind since I finished the last story or novel. I put that line down on the page. Immediately, magic occurs. Characters develop, and I have to chase them all over the page until I'm finished. Sometimes, I'm finished without even knowing it. Suddenly, there's a last line and I've finished the story. It might even be a great last line. I don't know where it came from, but I'm not going to question it. I have never questioned my creative process. It has always worked for me. I've never had a block. Something always comes. If something comes that I've done before, I just scrap it and start something else.

MARY YUKARI WATERS
interviewed by Sherry Ellis

What has been the hardest thing for you to learn about writing?

Without a doubt, the hardest thing is disciplining myself to write every day. I'm ashamed to say I've never gotten the knack of it. It depresses me terribly. It's like being on a diet every single day of your life, in the sense that I'm constantly falling off the wagon. There are periods when I'm so distracted by work or giving readings, etc., that I don't write for days, even weeks. I also find it hard to write when my house is a mess, which is the case much of the time. I do get on a good cycle occasionally, and I try to get my good writing done then, before the cycle peters out. I'm starting to wonder if some people just work better in cycles, rather than in a linear, write-every-day-without-fail approach.

When I'm not writing, I'm not consciously thinking about it. I'll immerse myself fully in cooking, or watching TV, or whatever else I happen to be doing. I'm a great believer in not pushing or straining when it comes to creativity, which is probably just an excuse for laziness. But I do think there's some validity to it. Looking back, I think that my best writing has been the kind that just seemed to float up to the surface of my mind on its own schedule, when it was formed and ready.

BE OPEN TO THE CREATIVE SPARK
Paul Theroux, interviewed by Michael Upchurch

The Mosquito Coast was very carefully planned out. All of them were. But if you plan a book too much, then the element of discovery and surprise, which all writing should offer, doesn't occur. So it's wrong to have it so heavily plotted that you're not open to the serendipity of the creative spark, where something just occurs to you. You begin writing, and your characters are speaking, and then they seem to take on a life of their own. That should happen in all books. But I've never really started a book without knowing where I was going.

Most of my time behind the keyboard, I'm in an almost half-dream state, and I do not remember writing most sentences.

POUNDING OUT THE FIRST DRAFT
by Merrill Feitell

I have the most fun with writing after I already have a first draft in place. Getting that first draft done can be murder. I get really unsure of what I'm up to, and I'll look for just about any excuse to get up from the chair. I'll take telemarketing calls. I'll snack between snacks.

But I generally try to stick with it, because there's nothing so satisfying as getting that first draft done. Once I have that, I can at least get a picture of what I'm really up to. I can start to see the general shape of the thing as it moves from beginning to end. It's kind of like having a map at that point, maybe a lousy map, but at least I can get a sense of the route and I can start having fun planning the side trips and figuring out who to visit, making some jokes, and enjoying the scenery as I go.

....

MAPPING THE WAY
by Melanie Bishop

Many novelists say that if they know what's about to happen or how the book will end, they are no longer having any fun with the work. Part of the thrill for them is discovery, being surprised as they go along by characters' words and actions, by certain turns of the plot. The book manuscript I happen to be working on is based in autobiography and pretty much wedded to actual events as they occurred.

I have found using notes and an outline extremely helpful. At the beginning, I just randomly jotted down every single thing I could remember about the event I was trying to render. These scrawled notes filled about twenty pages, and were in no particular order, i.e., they did not resemble an outline in any way. Later, about a third of the way through the first draft, I went back through these notes and crossed off everything I'd already dealt with. The notes not crossed off got divided into I, II, and III, sections of the book, as it had now presented itself to me in three main parts. As I approached the next section of the book, it helped to see that every scene that needed to be included had a II next to it.

But it still seemed such a mess, a haphazardly put-together list. So I made what I called a scene list, with every scene numbered. This first, this next, this followed by this, and so on. It became a sort of informal outline. Years before, when I'd participated in a screenwriting fellowship, I'd utilized an outline for the first time. Screenplays are such a different beast, and it was so difficult to keep scenes in my head, in the order I thought they needed to happen, so I made a scene outline, and it gave me a map every day to work from. This outline I made for the second part of my book has made approaching the work each day much easier. I can look at the list and see that I wrote scene numbers 13 and 14 yesterday, so I go to number 15, and it might say something as skeletal as "ice machine," but I know what it refers to and can conjure it up. So I write that and cross it out and go on to number 16, and so on.

It's hard to explain how much this system has saved me. It's a plan, it's a reliable map, it's always revisable; it tells you each day, "Begin here." And it allows you to fully focus on the scene at hand without trying to keep, in a different part of your brain, everything that has to follow.

ALLEN MORRIS JONES
interviewed by David Abrams

For me, the hardest part to read in *Last Year's River* was the forest-fire scene and the death of Henry's horse. A close second would have to be the childbirth scene. Both of these were emotionally wrenching and seemed to be written with intense passion. What, for you, was the hardest part of the book to write?

Compared to some other parts of the book, these scenes were relatively easy to write—or if not easy, at least enjoyable. I rewrote them a number of times, wanting to get them just right, but I always knew that they were working well. I always knew that they were going to be important moments in the book. And when you're writing well, when you're hitting on all cylinders, it's enjoyable, even when you're writing grisly stuff. The scenes in the book that tend to read less well—the Christmas party scene at Wapiti School, for instance, which I rewrote and rewrote but never seemed to get absolutely right—were much, much harder. They were the scenes that I needed to include in the interests of story, but they weren't necessarily being written out of any real passion.

When you come up with a scene of real drama—a horse dying or a child being born in a cabin or a man dancing with a corpse in a cave—it feels like an opportunity. A chance to strut your stuff. I knew that the scene with the horse was coming for a long time before I wrote it, and I remember looking forward to the writing. Not seeing the horse die, of course, but having the opportunity to describe the horse dying—if that makes sense.

And the two short scenes immediately after the death of the horse. When they're studying each other's faces. That might be my favorite moment in the book.

SUE MILLER

interviewed by Sarah Anne Johnson

So the work you do ahead of time is taking notes, and thinking about the interactions and personalities of the characters?

Yes. Sometimes they're very specific—dialogue, let's say—because it expresses the crux of a situation, and at other times they're more general description. But they don't cover everything. For instance, the scene in which Mack and Nina destroy Randall's room [in *Family Pictures*]. Mack essentially seduces her into this as a way of mourning Randall, but also, in this scene, Nina's taking sides against her parents and stepping over toward Mack's vision of what's going on in the family. I had notes that took me that far, but the chapter is long and much more happens around that event than I'd planned out. I knew that scene was coming up, but I didn't know how it would happen, only that they would peel the wallpaper and that it would be a defining moment in Nina's life, in her allegiance with Mack.

THE MOMENTS THAT TOUCH US

Carolyn Chute, interviewed by Barbara Stevens

How do ideas come to you? Is it a character? Do you get captivated by an idea, a scene, a personal experience?

When I work, I sort of go into a very quiet, almost meditative state, not dreamy, but kind of. So probably no ideas are involved. It almost feels sometimes like you're psychic, like you're pulling in something that already exists. It feels like that.

I feel that the best fiction that comes from us comes from our subconscious. It comes from associations, and it comes from moments in your life that were highly dramatic. I think that's what we tend to work on all the time, these little highly dramatic moments that really touch us.

SURRENDERING TO THE STORY

Roy Parvin, interviewed by Linda B. Swanson-Davies

How do you do your work? Computer?

I do. I do a lot of stuff. I'm an avid note taker. I get a lot of ideas just riding the bike. Once you leave the writing table, you suddenly get flooded, especially if you're doing something physical. I have a typical fifteen-mile loop I'll do every day. Some days it takes me an hour and some days it takes me like three or four hours, because I'm stopping every hundred yards to write things down.

It's not the best workout in the world. I'm not going to get the aerobic exercise I should. But I typically get a lot of good material out of that. Some of what you do as a writer is fooling yourself into writing the story. A lot of my note taking is giving me the courage to sit down at the writing table.

Props, to move from.

Right. But one cannot control the process. You need these props, as you said, to navigate your way through. I think ultimately what happens in every story that I really love is that I finally surrender myself to the story and say, Okay, I've written enough—I don't know what I'm talking about here. Let me regroup. And usually that means about five to ten days of not writing at all and just moping and brooding about the story. Usually something comes at that point and I'm reusing a lot of things from the earliest versions of the story. From all the other ghosts of the revisions that have crashed and burned.

They've all been hanging around in the back of your head.

It feels that way. It feels like all of a sudden I've created this world, like I'm a scientist who is trying to create life for just a little bit in these molecules. And usually the molecules have a spark in them, and then they—

They take over.

Yeah. And then they crash. But I remember—oh, there's a spark there, and then something happens that unlocks the story, often a very, very tiny thing.

CONNECTING LANGUAGE AND PERCEPTION

Chris Offutt, interviewed by Rob Trucks

I was also starting to write in journals in college. The journal was an arena of combat for me, and the combat was between acting and theater and painting, all my creative frustrations. I didn't know what to do. Also, relationships with girls went into the journal. Everything was going in there, and all of a sudden I was finished with college and I didn't know what to do, and that's when I sort of began traveling and having what turned out to be over fifty jobs, all part-time. I've never worked full-time, except in college when I worked for the maintenance department during the summers.

What happened between leaving Kentucky and meeting Rita is I had all of these jobs, and I didn't write anything but journal entries. I would write twenty-page journal entries in a spiral-bound notebook, three times a day: in the morning, then I would write at lunch, and in the evening. I would carry it around with me all the time. I didn't have a car. I lived without a car or a phone for almost ten years. I had a bicycle and a backpack, and I would just get around that way and live in really tiny, cheap rooms, and write. When I first got some money, I bought a typewriter in Salem, Massachusetts. I was writing my journal entries to an astonishingly obsessive degree. And I really didn't know why I was doing it. I was just doing it. What it did was it developed the skill of putting my emotions and thoughts in very close contact to language, particularly how I perceived the world.

In *The Same River* you write, "If riding a bicycle through a snowstorm sounded like good material for the journal, I borrowed a bike in a blizzard. The actual ride didn't matter. What I did was try to observe myself as carefully as possible, while simultaneously imagining myself writing everything down later."

Right. I'm still doing that.

WAITING FOR INSPIRATION
Dan Chaon, interviewed by Misha Angrist

Tell me about your work habits. Do you have a set time every day when you write?

I do, but I don't always get a lot done during that time, at least in terms of getting words on paper. Much of the work is going on in the back of my mind during that period.

There is a kind of "waiting for inspiration" aspect to it, too. I can work for months and not get a lot done, and then suddenly everything will come together fairly quickly with all of the pieces I've been working on.

Do you work on multiple stories at any one time?

Always. Very often I'll have maybe five or six things going at once. I'll move though each one of them and see where I can get. If I can't get anything, then I'll start something new.

What about for the novel you're working on now?

I've been using a similar method: I'll work on multiple chapters at the same time and start a new chapter if I get bogged down. The problem has been that my editor wants to see what I've got, and most of what I've got is chapters that are only partially done.

Have you also tried a chronological approach?

Yeah. I wrote a draft straight through and found that it wasn't really working. In part, that was my fault, I suppose, because I didn't really understand how the novel works—the pacing of it.

NEVER KNOWING, BUT TRUSTING
Tim O'Brien, interviewed by Jim Schumock

What interests me as a human being is when someone sits down beside me in a bar, or a restaurant over dinner, and says, "I gotta tell you what happened to me today. You're not going to believe this …" And it's those words—"You're not going to believe this"—which give me the expectation of something extraordinary, which stories are. That's why we tell a story, because it's out of the ordinary. I've become more of an emotional person since I began writing. I'm trusting more in my instincts as a human as opposed to my instincts as a man doing analysis or intellection. I love stories. And now I'm starting to trust more in story, not knowing what happened to my character—where did she go? And not even knowing some of the secrets inside John, or whether he had something to do with his wife's disappearance. Never knowing, and yet trusting in story to be sufficient. And that's a good feeling for a writer. No moral, no point to it sometimes, just story, story, story.

Story is its own meaning, self-contained. What's the point of *Huckleberry Finn*, for example? Don't leave home? What's the point of *Moby Dick*? Don't get obsessed with whales? Novels and stories don't have single points; they are what they are. And *In the Lake of the Woods* is what it is. It's a love story about a woman's vanishing. And a story about love gone bad. And betrayal and secrecy. It just is what it is, and stories ultimately are that.

....

ROBERT OLEN BUTLER
interviewed by Heather Iarusso

If a work has been conceived not from the dream space, not from the unconscious, but from the mind, if this is, in fact, a willful elaboration of an idea, the proof of that will be in the text; the only thing to really do with a work that has come from the wrong place is to put it aside and never look at it again. It is a serious mistake, and I'm afraid too many workshops fall into this. They rush downstream from the basic problem and begin working at the level of technique and craft, and this scene and that scene, and this line and that metaphor, and so forth. The writer continues to edit and refine and re-edit, and all that editing and re-editing is going on even more so from the rational faculty, and the writer is actually getting farther and farther away from the breakthrough that he needs in order to really create a work of art.

So I think it's misleading and destructive to go into technique and craft when, in fact, the problem with the piece has to do with the fundamentals of artistic process. In which case you put that aside and go on and look at a different place in your self. There are causes and symptoms mixed up here. But the fundamental cause is that you are going to the wrong place inside you to create a work of art.

DREAMING IT UP AS YOU GO

Richard Bausch

interviewed by Jennifer Levasseur and Kevin Rabalais

The novel I've just begun is called *Hello to the Cannibals*, and it's about friendship, contemporary friendship as we normally understand it, and the kind of friendship that takes place across time and the grave. This friendship—a spiritual relation, call it—between two women separated by a century: my made-up character, Lily Austin, who is graduating from college at the end of this century, and a real historical person, the British explorer Mary Kingsley, who died in 1900. I don't know very much about how it's all going to work out yet, but I will. I'll find it out by writing about it.

I dream it up as I go. I don't really know much about it when I start, and I am usually surprised by where it goes. In fact, if it doesn't surprise me, I'm suspicious of it. I'm writing a story now about some guys playing golf. Two of them have been in touch over the years, and a third one has come in who they used to play baseball with, but they haven't seen him in twenty years. He claims he was in an alcoholic haze all that time. I don't know what it's really about yet, but I'm working on it a bit every day.

Chris Offutt: With *Kentucky Straight*, I hadn't written about Kentucky for years. I knew that I would one day. I didn't have the courage. It took me a long time to get the courage up, and then ultimately I got the courage out of desperation. Most of the acts in my life have been motivated by desperation. And the things that ultimately have paid off for me have been acts of despair. People have often said to me, "Oh boy, you're so courageous. You are so brave." But I'm not. I'm a desperate coward who takes action.

as interviewed by Rob Trucks

MORE THAN CREATIVITY

Robert Olen Butler
interviewed by Linda B. Swanson-Davies

When you are communicating with your characters or your characters are communicating with you, or whatever it is that's going on, do you feel like there's any chance that you are drawing upon something more than creativity?

Yeah, I think there's quite a good chance. Many times during the writing, I feel like I'm channeling something as opposed to inventing it. Without getting too mystical about the process, it would not surprise me at all if there's some connection between the process of artistic creation and some other aspect of human beings that may well have an existence or a reality beyond the apparent ones.

KEVIN CANTY

interviewed by Linda B. Swanson-Davies

I feel as if I've been talking about myself and these stories [*A Stranger in This World*] for a week. In some ways, it all runs together and I feel as though I've been one big nerve ending. But I'm happy to talk about approaches to writing and about where it comes from, because it's one of the things that has taken me a long time to learn, and I wish I could save somebody else the time that I spent learning for myself. Not so much my idea of the self or my idea of where writing comes from or my idea of what kind of characters are instrumental—that's all just personal. But the idea that it takes a long time and it's a learned thing as opposed to something that you were born with. It's something that I find myself going back to again and again. When I talk about where my writing comes from and all the rest of it, to some extent it is bullshit, because what I'm doing when I'm writing is so unconscious—it's so much before the conscious level. I'm playing the English professor, after the fact. I'm not doing that kind of analysis when I'm writing my writing.

COMBINATIONS OF INTELLIGENCE

Barbara Scot, interviewed by Linda B. Swanson-Davies

When Jean [my agent] took *Prairie Reunion* back to New York, we had four bids on it, major bids. It was an incredible thrill. Especially to an unemployed school teacher; I haven't firmly identified myself as a writer yet.

I had this amazing discussion with one woman who had bid on the book who said, "You know, not to use Presbyterian terms, but this book seems to have a strange kind of predestination, and I think that you will choose where you should be [which publisher should take *Prairie Reunion*]; you will choose the right one." It was very interesting. And I felt that all along: that this story is more than my own. I don't want to use a word like channeling, but I think that at certain times it's almost as if combinations of intelligence come together for you. I'm dealing in a sense with my mother's mind, with that community mind, and partly with the land itself. My role was almost translator and combiner, and I had to be very careful and respectful of everything that I was dealing with.

STAYING IN THE ROOM
Ron Carlson, interviewed by Susan McInnis

Is that a pleasure for you in writing, to sit down and let yourself go wherever the writing takes you?

Well, pleasure's an interesting word, and an odd fit for what's happening when I'm writing, but I'll take it anyway. The answer is yes. I'll go into a story and about the fourth or fifth day, as I'm working on it, it starts to dawn on me, and then, yes, then pleasure breaks. It breaks when I start thinking, "Oh, whoa, I want to read this story."

When I start a story, I don't exactly know what it will be like when I'm done with it. But I know that I'm going to get it. When you're a writer, you spend days in the room without knowing what you've got, but you're still willing to keep reeling it in and following it. You're willing to be true to it. It may mean you have to write thirty pages to get fifteen. The big secret to such writing is the ability to stay in the room. The writer is the person who stays in the room.

That feels like it might come from the Baba Ram Das school of writing. "Be here now."

People have accused me of it. They say, "You're talking Zen here." And I just say, "Zen this: The secret is to stay in the room." Who can do it? Nobody. It's hard.

All the good writing I've done—and this is the truest thing I'll say to you today—all the good writing I've done in the last ten years has been done in the first twenty minutes after the first time I wanted to leave the room. I've learned to stay there and keep writing.

I think, "Oh, I'll just go get some coffee." Well, I love coffee, but I don't really want any coffee at that moment. What's happened is that I've confronted a little problem that's got me kind of rattled. I can't identify it. I don't even know I'm rattled. I just don't want to go on. A threshold's come up between me and the page, and I want to get out of there. I have a Mr. Coffee in the kitchen and, when I get to it, I find I also have a Mr. Refrigerator. There's Mr. Kitchen Table, Mr. Newspaper, Mr. Big Long Couch, Mr. World Outside the Window, and honest to God, my career as a writer is over and I'm dead in the water.

So I've learned to stay there. I don't really want any coffee. What I want to do is avoid this problem. So what I do is say, "Why don't you just stay here another minute, Ron." And, before

I know it, it's an hour later and, man, I've solved it! I've gotten through to a point where I'm breathing again. I'm breathing. I'm over the threshold and the problem, and I've managed to get myself down the road.

Then—and I suppose this is good news—I've learned that the cup of coffee I fix afterward is really good. Staying in the chair improves the quality of that beverage.

The bottom line is, I'm very careful with myself. I pay attention. I take care of myself. And I tolerate the discomfort of ambiguity, of not knowing where I'm going. When things aren't going well, I just counsel myself to hang on a little longer. Not too long. Just a few minutes. Just long enough to get through the rattled energy and over that stress threshold back into the writing.

And I know, when I start a story, that I'm going to get it, which comes from having written over a hundred stories. It's harder for someone who's writing her third. The biggest difference between us is that I'm willing to tolerate the unknown.

Flannery O'Connor said the writer should be the person who is most surprised by her story. If the writer isn't more surprised than the reader, then the story isn't any good. That's an astounding thing to say, but it's true.

SEEING EVERY SENTENCE
Kevin Canty, interviewed by Linda B. Swanson-Davies

When I was an undergraduate, when I was twenty or twenty-one, I was trying to write. I could move the words around on a page, but I had nothing to say. I haven't read that many writers under thirty who I thought really had it together. I think it is unusual.

It seems the pattern is that people tend to come to writing later in life than is so in a lot of other disciplines. I think that really has to do with the ability to sit there. One thing I know is that when I was twenty, I thought that to write a story you'd be standing on the roof and lightning would strike you and the story would come to you, and you would write it down and then you'd go out and have a beer with your friends. It's a damn shame it doesn't work. It really is. It would be a nicer way to live. My whole experience with being a writer has been that it's the patience to sit there in your chair and wait for the words to come, wait for the ideas to arrive, to slow down long enough to really see every sentence, every paragraph. I just couldn't sit still that long when I was younger.

The one thing I can say that is not bullshit is that you do have to learn to write in a way that you would learn to play the violin. Everybody seems to think that you should be able to turn on the faucet one day and out will come the novel. I think for most people it's just practice, practice, practice, that sense of just learning your instrument until—when you have an idea on the violin, you don't have to translate it into violin-speak anymore—the language is your own. It's not something you can think your way into, or outsmart. You've just got to do it.

CONTRIBUTOR BIOGRAPHIES

Born in New York and raised until age ten in the Dominican Republic, **Julia Alvarez** (1950–) is a writer-in-residence at Middlebury College in Vermont. Her most recent novel is *Saving the World*. The novel *How the García Girls Lost Their Accents* was a *New York Times Book Review* Notable Book, and *In the Time of the Butterflies* was made into a movie. She also has published poetry and books for young readers. juliaalvarez.com

Margaret Atwood (1939–) is an internationally recognized novelist, poet, and short-story writer. Her most recent story collection is *The Tent*; among her novels are *Surfacing*, *The Handmaid's Tale*, and *The Blind Assassin*. Her poetry collection *The Circle Game* won the Governor General's Award, Canada's highest literary honor.

Russell Banks (1940–) is the author of many novels, two of which, *Continental Drift* and *Cloudsplitter*, were finalists for the Pulitzer Prize. Two novels, *Affliction* and *The Sweet Hereafter*, were adapted into feature films. *The Angel on the Roof* is a collection of thirty years of his short fiction.

Andrea Barrett (1954–) is the author of five novels, most recently *The Voyage of the Narwhal*, and two collections of short fiction, *Ship Fever*, which received the National Book Award, and *Servants of the Map*, a finalist for the Pulitzer Prize. A MacArthur Fellow, she's also been a fellow at the Center for Scholars and Writers at the New York Public Library, and has received Guggenheim and NEA Fellowships. She lives in western Massachusetts and teaches at Williams College and Warren Wilson College.

Richard Bausch's (1945–) novels include *Hello to the Cannibals*; *Good Evening Mr. & Mrs. America, and All the Ships at Sea*; *Rebel Powers*; *Violence*; and *The Last Good Time. The Selected Stories of Richard Bausch* was published in 1996. He is the recipient of the Lila Wallace–*Reader's Digest* Writers' Award and the Award in Literature from the American Academy of Arts and Letters. He lives in rural Virginia.

© Michael Hough

Charles Baxter's (1947–) work includes four novels, most recently *Saul and Patsy* and *The Feast of Love*, which was a National Book Award finalist and is being made into a motion picture; four story collections, most recently *Believers*; a book of poetry, *Imaginary Paintings*; and two books of essays about writing, *Burning Down the House* and *Beyond Plot*, which will come out in 2007. His stories have appeared in *The New Yorker*, *The Atlantic*, *Glimmer Train Stories*, and *Harper's*, among other journals and magazines. His fiction has been widely anthologized and translated into ten languages. He is the Edelstein-Keller Professor of Creative Writing at the University of Minnesota.

Louis Begley (1933–) is a writer and retired lawyer. His novel *Wartime Lies* won the PEN/Hemingway Award and other awards; *About Schmidt* was a National Book Critics Circle Award finalist and was made into a feature film. His latest novel, *Matters of Honor*, will be published in 2007.

Melanie Bishop (1956–) teaches writing and literature at Prescott College in Prescott, Arizona, where she is also founder and editor of the literary magazine *Alligator Juniper*. She received an MFA from the University of Arizona. She's published fiction and nonfiction in *Glimmer Train Stories*, *Georgetown Review*, *Greensboro Review*, *Florida Review*, *Valley Guide*, *Hospice Magazine*, *Puerto del Sol*, *Family Circle*, and *UnderWire*, and has received the Chesterfield Screenwriting Fellowship sponsored by Steven Spielberg. She is currently at work on a memoir and a screenplay.

© Sigrid Estrada

Amy Bloom (1953–) is the author of a novel, *Love Invents Us*, and two collections of stories: *Come to Me*, nominated for a National Book Award, and *A Blind Man Can See How Much I Love You*, nominated for the National Book Critics Circle Award. Her stories have appeared in *Best American Short Stories*, *Prize Stories: The O. Henry Awards*, and numerous anthologies. Her book *Normal: Transsexual CEOs, Crossdressing Cops, and Hermaphrodites with Attitude* is an exploration of the varieties of gender. Her new novel, *Away*, will come out in 2007. A practicing psychotherapist, she lives in Connecticut and teaches at Yale University.

Sir Robert Olen Butler (1945–) has published ten novels, most recently *Fair Warning* and *Mr. Spaceman*; three volumes of short stories, including *Had a Good Time* and *A Good Scent from a Strange Mountain*, which won the 1993 Pulitzer Prize for Fiction; and *From Where You Dream: The Process of Writing Fiction*, edited by Janet Burroway. Butler, whose work has been widely published and won numerous awards, teaches creative writing at Florida State University in Tallahassee, where he lives with his wife, novelist Elizabeth Dewberry.

© John Foley/Opale

Kevin Canty (1954–) is the author of the novels *Into the Great Wide Open*, *Nine Below Zero*, and *Winslow in Love*, as well as the short story collections *Honeymoon* and *A Stranger in This World*. His work has been published in *The New Yorker*, *Esquire*, *GQ*, *Details*, *Story*, *The New York Times Magazine*, and *Glimmer Train Stories*. He lives in Missoula, Montana.

The latest of Australian-born **Peter Carey**'s (1943–) novels is *Theft: A Love Story*. Two of his novels have been awarded the Booker Prize: *True History of the Kelly Gang* and *Oscar and Lucinda*, which was made into a film. His *Collected Stories* appeared in 1994. He lives in New York City.

Ron Carlson (1947–) is the author of seven books of fiction, including *At the Jim Bridger* and *The Hotel Eden*, a *New York Times* Notable Book and *Los Angeles Times* Best Book of the Year. In 2003, Norton published *A Kind of Flying: Selected Stories*. He is a professor of English at Arizona State University.

Born in New Delhi, **Vikram Chandra** (1961–) teaches at the University of California in Berkeley. Both his novel *Red Earth and Pouring Rain* and his story collection *Love and Longing in Bombay* received the Commonwealth Writers' Prize. His latest novel, *Sacred Games*, was published in 2007.

© Melanie Abrams

Dan Chaon (1964–) has published two story collections, *Fitting Ends* and *Among the Missing*, a finalist for the National Book Award. His novel *You Remind Me of Me* was published in 2004. His fiction has appeared in numerous journals and anthologies, and won both Pushcart and O. Henry awards. He teaches at Oberlin College in Ohio.

Carolyn Chute's (1947–) novel *The Beans of Egypt, Maine* was adapted for a motion picture in 1994. Her subsequent books include *Letourneau's Used Auto Parts*, *Merry Men*, and *Snow Man*. She lives in Parsonsfield, Maine.

© Ruben Guzman

Sandra Cisneros's (1954–) novel *The House on Mango Street* won the American Book Award from the Before Columbus Foundation. Her other books include a novel, *Caramelo*, a story collection, *Woman Hollering Creek*, and several books of poetry. She lives in San Antonio, Texas.

George Makana Clark's (1957–) story "The Center of the World" was included in *The O. Henry Prize Stories 2006*. The collection *The Small Bees' Honey* appeared in 1997. His short stories, plays, and poetry have appeared in *Chelsea, The Georgia Review, Glimmer Train Stories, Massachusetts Review, The Southern Review, Transition Magazine, Zoetrope: All-Story,* and elsewhere. He has just completed his first novel, *The Raw Man.*

© Rikki Clark

Elizabeth Cox's (1942–) most recent book is the novel *The Slow Moon.* Her other books are the novels *Night Talk, The Ragged Way People Fall Out of Love,* and *Familiar Ground,* and the story collection *Bargains in the Real World.* Her poetry has been widely published, most recently in *The Southern Review* and *The Atlantic Monthly.* She is an instructor at the Bennington Graduate Writing Seminars and teaches at Wofford College in South Carolina. She lives in Spartanburg, South Carolina.

© Jill Krementz

Haitian-born **Edwidge Danticat** (1969–) grew up in that nation's capital, Port-au-Prince, and moved to Brooklyn when she was twelve years old. Her most recent book is *The Dew Breaker,* which was preceded by the story collection *Krik? Krak!* and the novels *The Farming of Bones* and *Breath, Eyes, Memory.* She has published two young-adult novels, *Anacaona: Golden Flower* and *Behind the Mountains,* as well as a travel narrative, *After the Dance: A Walk Through Carnival in Jacmel.* She also is the editor of *The Butterfly's Way: Voices from the Haitian Dyaspora in the United States* and *The Beacon Best of 2000: Great Writing by Men and Women of All Colors and Cultures.* Her writings have been anthologized and translated into many languages and won numerous honors.

Toi Derricotte's (1941–) books of poetry include *Tender*, which won the 1998 Paterson Poetry Prize, *Captivity*, *Natural Birth*, and *The Empress of the Death House*. *The Black Notebooks*, a literary memoir, was published in 1997 and won the Anisfield-Wolf Book Award for Nonfiction. She teaches at the University of Pittsburgh.

Chitra Banerjee Divakaruni (1956–) is an Indian-born author and poet whose work has been published in more than fifty magazines, including *The Atlantic Monthly* and *The New Yorker*. Her latest novel is *Queen of Dreams*. Her other novels are *The Vine of Desire*, *Sister of My Heart*, and *The Mistress of Spices*. Her collections of stories are *The Unknown Errors of Our Lives* and *Arranged Marriage*. She teaches at the University of Houston and divides her time between Houston and northern California.

Stephen Dixon (1936–) is the author of thirteen novels, most recently *End of I.* and *Phone Rings*. His novels *Interstate* and *Frog* were both finalists for the National Book Award. Dixon has written more than 450 short stories, which have appeared in *Harper's*, *Glimmer Train Stories*, *Playboy*, *Esquire*, *The Paris Review*, *Triquarterly*, and *Boulevard*. He has received many awards, including the O. Henry Award, two NEA Fellowships, and the Pushcart Prize. He is a professor of fiction at Johns Hopkins University.

Siobhan Dowd is deputy editor of *PEN International*, a twice-yearly global magazine. She has published a novel for teens, *A Swift Pure Cry*, as well as short stories, columns, and articles. She edited *This Prison Where I Live: The PEN Anthology of Imprisoned Writers* and contributes a regular column on persecuted writers to *Glimmer Train Stories*. While living in New York, she was named one of the "top 100 Irish Americans" by *Irish America* magazine and AerLingus, for her global anti-censorship work. Her next novel, *Solace*, is forthcoming in 2007. She lives in Oxford, England. siobhandowd.co.uk

Andre Dubus (1936–1999) served five years in the Marine Corps before becoming a full-time writer of short stories. His last story collection was *Dancing After Hours*, preceded by *Selected Stories*, *The Last Worthless Evening*, and others. In 1998, he published a volume of essays, *Meditations from a Moveable Chair*. Dubus received the PEN/Malamud Award, the Rea Award for excellence in short fiction, the Jean Stein Award from the American Academy of Arts and Letters, and *The Boston Globe*'s Lawrence L. Winship Award.

The second novel by **Andre Dubus III** (1959–), *House of Sand and Fog*, was a finalist for the 1999 National Book Award and was made into a movie. His other books are *The Cage Keeper and Other Stories*, and his first novel, *Bluesman*. He is the son of Andre Dubus, and he teaches at the University of Massachusetts at Lowell.

Pam Durban (1947–) is the author of two novels, *So Far Back* and *The Laughing Place*, as well as a collection of short fiction, *All Set About with Fever Trees*. Her stories have been anthologized in *The Best American Short Stories of the Century*, *The Best American Short Stories 1997*, and *New Stories from the South: The Year's Best*. She teaches at the University of North Carolina at Chapel Hill.

Stuart Dybek (1942–) is the author of three collections of short fiction, *I Sailed with Magellan*, *The Coast of Chicago*, and *Childhood and Other Neighborhoods*, as well as a volume of poetry, *Brass Knuckles*. A professor of English at Western Michigan University, he lives in Kalamazoo.

© Marion Ettlinger

Nomi Eve (1968–) has an MFA in fiction writing from Brown University and has worked as a freelance book reviewer for *The Village Voice* and *New York Newsday*. *The Family Orchard*, her first novel, was based on her own family's history. Her stories have appeared in *The Village Voice Literary Supplement*, *Glimmer Train Stories*, and *The International Quarterly*. She lives outside Philadelphia.

Merrill Feitell's (1971–) first book, *Here Beneath Low-Flying Planes*, won the Iowa Short Fiction Award. Her stories have been published in many places, including *Glimmer Train Stories* and *Best New American Voices*, and have been short-listed in *The O. Henry Prize Stories* and *Best American Short Stories*. She lives in Brooklyn.

Maria Flook (1952–) is the author of the novels *LUX*, *Open Water*, and *Family Night* (which received a PEN/Hemingway Foundation Special Citation and was a *New York Times* Notable Book), and the nonfiction books *Invisible Eden* and *My Sister Life: The Story of My Sister's Dis-*
© Nancy Crampton
appearance. She has also published a collection of short stories and two books of poems. She teaches in Boston, where she is a writer-in-residence at Emerson College. mariaflook.com

Lynn Freed's (1945–) latest book is *Reading, Writing, and Leaving Home: Life on the Page*. She has published five novels, most recently *House of Women* and *The Mirror*, and a collection of short stories, *The Curse of the Appropriate Man*. Her work has been published in *Harper's*, *The New Yorker*, and *The Atlantic Monthly*, among others, and is widely anthologized and translated. She is the recipient of the inaugural Katherine Anne Porter Prize in Fiction from the American Academy of Arts and Letters. lynnfreed.com

Ernest Gaines (1933–) has published eight books of fiction, including *Catherine Carmier, Bloodline, The Autobiography of Miss Jane Pittman, In My Father's House*, and *A Gathering of Old Men*. *A Lesson Before Dying*, his most recent novel, won the 1993 National Book Critics Circle Award. *Mozart and Leadbelly: Stories and Essays* appeared in 2005. He has been awarded a MacArthur Foundation grant for writings of "rare historical resonance."

Henry Louis Gates Jr. (1950–) has published numerous books of criticism and commentary, including *America Behind the Color Line, The Signifying Monkey*, and *Colored People*, a memoir. He served as the chair of the department of African and African American Studies at Harvard from 1991–2006 and is now the W. E. B. Du Bois Professor of the Humanities and the Director of the W. E. B. Du Bois Institute for African and African American Research at Harvard.

Mary Gordon (1949–) is the author of the novels *Pearl, Spending, The Company of Women, The Other Side*, and *Final Payments*; a collection of novellas entitled *The Rest of Life*; two books of essays; and a biography of Joan of Arc. She has also written a memoir, *The Shadow Man*. Winner of the Lila Wallace–*Reader's*

Digest Writers' Award, a Guggenheim Fellowship, and the 1997 O. Henry Award for best short story, Gordon teaches at Barnard College and lives in New York City.

Jim Grimsley (1955–) is the author of five novels: *Boulevard*; *Winter Birds*, a finalist for the PEN/Hemingway Award; *Dream Boy*; *My Drowning*, a Lila Wallace–*Reader's Digest* Writers' Award winner; and *Kirith Kirin*. He lives in Atlanta and teaches at Emory University.

Patricia Hampl (1946–) has published two memoirs, *A Romantic Education* and *Virgin Time*. She has contributed stories to *American Poetry Review*, *The New Yorker*, *The Paris Review*, and *Iowa Review*. She also is the author of two volumes of poetry and an essay collection, *I Could Tell You Stories*. She teaches at the University of Minnesota and lives in St. Paul.

Kent Haruf's (1943–) honors include a Whiting Writers' Award and a special citation from the PEN/Hemingway Foundation. His latest novel is *Eventide*; a previous novel, *Plainsong*, won the Mountains and Plains Booksellers Association Regional Book Award and was a finalist for the National Book Award, the *Los Angeles Times* Book Prize, and *The New Yorker* Book Award. He lives in his native Colorado.

After publishing four collections of stories, **Amy Hempel** (1951–) published her complete *Collected Stories* in 2006. She has a keen interest in guide dogs for the blind, and this theme found its way into her 2005 collection, *The Dog of the Marriage*. She teaches and lectures in libraries, hospitals, and universities including Bennington and Columbia, while remaining involved in writing workshops such as Bread Loaf.

© Mary Ruth Cowgill

Patricia Henley's (1947–) forthcoming novel is entitled *Home Plate*. Her first novel, *Hummingbird House*, was a finalist for the 1999 National Book Award and *The New Yorker* Book Award. She has also written two books of poetry and three story collections: *Friday Night at Silver Star*, which won the 1985 Montana Arts Council First Book Award; *The Secret of Cartwheels*; and *Worship of the Common Heart: New and Selected Stories*. Henley has taught in Purdue University's MFA program for nineteen years and also teaches in the low-residency MFA program at the University of Nebraska at Omaha. patriciahenley.com

Siri Hustvedt's (1955–) latest novel, *What I Loved*, was nominated for the Prix Femina Étranger. She has published two other novels, *The Blindfold* and *The Enchantment of Lily Dahl*, as well as collections of essays, most recently *A Plea for Eros*. She lives in Brooklyn.

War Trash, the most recent novel by **Ha Jin** (1956–), was a Pulitzer Prize finalist and winner of the PEN/Faulker Award; his novel *Waiting* won the National Book Award. He was born in Liaoning Province in China and began publishing in English in 1990. His most recent story collection is *The Bridegroom*.

© Jerry Bauer

Allen Morris Jones (1970–) co-edited *The Big Sky Reader* and is the former editor of *The Big Sky Journal*. He has published a novel, *Last Year's River*, and a book about hunting, *A Quiet Place of Violence*. He has lived and worked in Montana most of his life.

Thom Jones (1945–) is the author of three story collections: *Sonny Liston Was a Friend of Mine*, *Cold Snap*, and *The Pugilist at Rest*, a National Book Award finalist. His short fiction has appeared in *The New Yorker*, *Playboy*, *Esquire*, *GQ*, and *Harper's*.

© Alice Guldbrandsen

Thomas E. Kennedy's (1944–) most recent books include the story collection *Cast Upon the Day* and the novels of The Copenhagen Quartet, four novels about his adopted city: *Kerrigan's Copenhagen, A Love Story*; *Bluett's Blue Hours*; *Greene's Summer*; and *Danish Fall*. Also recently published are *The Literary Traveler*, a book of travel pieces co-authored with Walter Cummins, and a collection of essays on the craft of fiction, *Realism & Other Illusions*. His stories, poems, essays, and translations from Danish appear regularly in the U.S. and Europe. A resident of Denmark, he teaches in the low-residency MFA program at Fairleigh Dickinson University. thomasekennedy.com and copenhagenquartet.com

Jamaica Kincaid (1949–) is the author of several works of fiction, including *Annie John*, *The Autobiography of My Mother*, *Lucy*, and *At the Bottom of the River*. The most recent of her nonfiction books is *Among Flowers: A Walk in the Himalaya*.

Maina wa Kinyatti (1944–) is director of the Mau Mau Research Center in New York. He spent more than six years in prison for his research, and after his release in 1988, he won the PEN/Barbara Goldsmith Freedom to Write Award. Among his works are a collection of Mau Mau poetry and songs, *Thunder from the Mountains*, and *Kenya's Freedom Struggle: The Dedan Kimathi Papers*.

Carolyn Kizer's (1925–) volumes of poetry include *Yin*, which won a Pulitzer Prize, *Mermaids in the Basement*, *The Nearness of You*, and *Harping On: Poems 1985-1995*. In 2000, she released *Cool, Calm & Collected: Poems 1960–2000*. She has also published a collection of essays, *Proses: On Poems and Poets* (1993), and edited *100 Great Poems by Women*.

Doug Lawson's (1968–) work has appeared in numerous publications, including *The Mississippi Review*, *Sycamore Review*, and *Glimmer Train Stories*. His collection of short fiction, *A Patrimony of Fishes*, appeared in 1997. He has received the Transatlantic Review Award, a fiction fellowship from the Virginia Commission for the Arts, a Henry Hoyns fellowship from the University of Virginia, and an honorable mention from the O. Henry Awards anthology. He is editor of *The Blue Moon Review*, the oldest online-only literary quarterly, which he founded and has published since 1994.

Chang-rae Lee (1965–) is the author of the novels *Aloft*, *A Gesture Life*, and *Native Speaker*, which won the PEN/Hemingway Award for first fiction and other honors. Selected by *The New Yorker* as one of the twenty best writers under forty, he teaches writing at Princeton University.

Doris Lessing (1919–) is one of the most celebrated writers of the twentieth century. Her most recent books include the novels *Ben, In the World* and *Walking in the Shade*. A Companion of Honour and a Companion of Literature, she was awarded the David Cohen British Literature Prize in 2001. She lives in North London.

Philip Levine (1928–) worked at a succession of industrial jobs before settling in Fresno, California, where he taught at the university until his retirement. He has received many awards for his books of poems, including the National Book Award in 1991 for *What Work Is*, and the Pulitzer Prize in 1995 for *The Simple Truth*. His nonfiction works include *So Ask: Essays, Conversations, and Interviews*.

Banishing Verona is the most recent novel by **Margot Livesey** (1953–). Her stories were collected in *Learning by Heart*, and her other novels include *Eva Moves the Furniture*, *The Missing World*, *Criminals*, and *Homework*. Born in Scotland, she currently lives in the Boston area, where she is a writer-in-residence at Emerson College.

David Long's (1948–) short stories appear in *The New Yorker*, *GQ*, *Story*, and many anthologies, including *The O. Henry Prize Stories*. His third collection of stories, *Blue Spruce* (1997), was given the Lowenthal Award from the American Academy of Arts and Letters. His novels are *The Falling Boy*, *The Daughters of Simon Lamoreaux*, and, most recently, *The Inhabited World*. He has written a book on writing, *Dangerous Sentences*, and is at work on a new novel. davidlonglit.com

Beverly Lowry (1938–) is the author of six novels, including *The Track of Two Desires* and *Breaking Gentle*. She has published two nonfiction titles: *Her Dream of Dreams*, about Madame C.J. Walker, and *Crossed Over*, about her friendship with Karla Faye Tucker. She directs the creative-nonfiction program at George Mason University and lives in Washington, D.C.

Novelist and poet **David Malouf** (1934–) was born in Brisbane, Australia, and has lived in England and Italy. *Johnno*, his first novel, is considered an Australian classic. He is the author of five other novels, including *The Conversations at Curlow Creek* and *An Imaginary Life*, as well as several books of poetry and two novellas, *Child's Play* and *The Bread of Time to Come*.

© Jane Bown

Lee Martin's (1955–) most recent book, *The Bright Forever*, was a finalist for the 2006 Pulitzer Prize in Fiction. In 2003, he published *Turning Bones*, part of the American Lives series from the University of Nebraska Press. He is also the author of *Quakertown*, *From Our House*, and *The Least You Need to Know*. He directs the MFA program in creative writing at Ohio State University.

The latest novel by **Valerie Martin** (1948–) is *Property*. Other novels include *Mary Reilly*, *The Great Divorce*, and *Italian Fever*. Her most recent nonfiction title is *Salvation*, a reconsideration of St. Francis's life. A native of New Orleans, she now lives in upstate New York.

Daniel Mason (1976–) published his novel **The Piano Tuner** while attending medical school. His story "A Registry of My Passage Upon Earth" was published in *Harper's*, and his second novel, *A Far Country*, is due in 2007.

Alice Mattison teaches fiction in the Bennington Writing Seminars. The most recent of her story collections are *In Case We're Separated* and *Men Giving Money, Women Yelling*. Her novels are *The Wedding of the Two-Headed Woman*, *The Book Borrower*, and *Hilda and Pearl*.

© Paul Beckman

Elizabeth McCracken (1966–), author of the novels *Niagara Falls All Over Again* and *The Giant's House*, was honored as one of *Granta*'s Best American Novelists Under 40. She also is the author of *Here's Your Hat, What's Your Hurry*, a short-story collection.

Thomas McGuane (1939–) has lived in Sweet Grass County, Montana, for more than thirty years. He is the author of nine novels, including *The Bushwacked Piano*, *Ninety-two in the Shade*, and *The Cadence of Grass*, and a collection of stories, *To Skin a Cat*, as well as two collections of essays, *Some Horses* and *The Longest Silence: A Life in Fishing*.

John McNally (1965–) is the author of two novels, *America's Report Card* and *The Book of Ralph*; and a story collection, *Troublemakers*. He also has edited four fiction anthologies. A finalist for the National Magazine Award for Fiction, he teaches at Wake Forest University in Winston-Salem, North Carolina.

Askold Melnyczuk (1954–) is the founder of the literary magazine *AGNI* and the director of creative writing at University of Massachusetts Boston. He has published two novels, *Ambassador of the Dead* and *What Is Told*. He has published poems, stories, translations, and reviews in *Partisan Review*, *The Nation*, *Ploughshares*, and *Poetry*.

© Debi Milligan

Most recently, best-selling novelist **Sue Miller** (1943–) has written *Lost in the Forest*. Among her other novels are *The Good Mother*, *For Love*, *While I Was Gone*, and *Family Pictures*. She has published a memoir, *The Story of My Father*. The title story of her collection *Inventing the Abbotts* was made into a movie, for which she co-wrote the screenplay.

Lorrie Moore (1957–) is known for her short stories, published in the collections *Birds of America*, *Like Life*, and *Self-Help*, as well her her novels, *Who Will Run the Frog Hospital?* and *Anagrams*. Her stories have been included in *The Best American Short Stories of the Century* and the *O. Henry* and *Best American Short Stories* anthologies. She teaches at the University of Wisconsin—Madison.

Mary McGarry Morris (1943–) is the author of *Vanished*, which was a finalist for the National Book Award and the PEN/Faulkner Award; *A Dangerous Woman*, which was chosen by *TIME* magazine as one of the five best novels of 1991; *Songs in Ordinary Time*, an Oprah's Book Club selection; and three other novels. She lives in Andover, Massachusetts.

Jordanian-born **Abdelrahman Munif** (1933–2004), in his Cities of Salt trilogy of novels, chose as his subject the effects of Western oil interests on traditional Arab societies in the last century. His books, widely read in the Middle East, have been banned in Saudi Arabia.

Antonya Nelson's (1961–) latest offering is *Some Fun*, a story collection. Previous collections are *The Expendables*, *Female Trouble*, *Family Terrorists*, and *In the Land of Men*. She has published three novels, most recently *Living to Tell*. In addition to writing, Nelson teaches, dividing her time between New Mexico State University and the University of Houston.

Thisbe Nissen (1972–) is the author of two novels, *Osprey Island* and *The Good People of New York*, and a story collection, *Out of the Girls' Room and Into the Night*. She also co-authored *The Ex-Boy-*

© Sandra L. Dyas

friend Cookbook. Her work has appeared in *Story*, *Seventeen*, *Vogue*, *Glamour*, *StoryQuarterly*, and *The Virginia Quarterly Review*, among others. A native New Yorker and a graduate of Oberlin College and the Iowa Writers' Workshop, where she was a Teaching-Writing Fellow and a James Michener Fellow, she lives, teaches, gardens, and collages in Iowa City.

Sigrid Nunez (1951–) has published five novels, including *A Feather on the Breath of God*, *For Rouenna*, and, most recently, *The Last of Her Kind*. Her work has also been included in several anthologies, including two Pushcart Prize volumes. Among her other awards are a Whiting Writers' Award, the Rome Prize in Literature, a Berlin Prize Fellowship, and a fellowship from the New York Foundation for the Arts. sigridnunez.com

Tim O'Brien (1946–) received the National Book Award for Fiction for *Going After Cacciato*. His novel *The Things They Carried*, which reflected his tour of duty in Vietnam, was excerpted for *The Best American Short Stories of the Century*. *In the Lake of the Woods* was named best novel of 1994 by *TIME* magazine. His most recent novel is *July, July*.

Chris Offutt (1958–) is author of the story collections *Kentucky Straight* and *Out of the Woods*, the novel *The Good Brother*, and the memoirs *The Same River Twice* and *No Heroes*. He lives in Iowa City. He recently made his comics-writing debut with "Another Man's Escape" in an issue  of *Michael Chabon Presents: The Amazing Adventures of the Escapist.*

The title story of **Roy Parvin**'s (1957–) collection *In the Snow Forest* originally appeared in *Glimmer Train Stories*. A previous collection is entitled *The Loneliest Road in America*, and his essays have appeared in *Northern Lights*. He's won the Katherine Anne Porter Prize, and his fiction has been recommended for a Pushcart Prize. He lives in the woods of northern California.

© Tony Baker

Ann Patchett (1963–) is the author of *Bel Canto*, which won the PEN/Faulkner Award. Her other novels are *The Magician's Assistant*, *Taft*, and *The Patron Saint of Liars*. Her memoir, *Truth and Beauty: A Friendship*, appeared in 2004.

Susan Perabo (1969–), a professor of English at Dickinson College, has published a story collection, *Who I Was Supposed to Be*, and a novel, *The Broken Places*. Her stories have appeared in *Glimmer Train Stories*, *The Sun*, *The Missouri Review*, *Story*, *TriQuarterly*, and in the anthologies *Best American Short Stories* and *New Stories from the South*.

Jayne Anne Phillips (1952–) is the author of three novels, *Machine Dreams*, *Shelter*, and *MotherKind*, and two books of widely anthologized short stories, *Black Tickets* and *Fast Lanes*. Excerpts of her forthcoming novel, *Termite*, have appeared in *Granta*, *The Southern Review*, *Ploughshares*, and on NarrativeMagazine.com.

Melissa Pritchard (1948–) is a professor at Arizona State University. She is the author of two story collections, *The Instinct for Bliss* and *Spirit Seizures*, and two novels, *Phoenix* and *Selene of the Spirits*. Pritchard has been awarded a Pushcart Prize and has been included in *The O. Henry Prize Stories*. She lives in Tempe, Arizona.

Annie Proulx's (1935–) *The Shipping News* won the Pulitzer Prize for Fiction, the National Book Award for Fiction, and the *Irish Times* International Fiction Prize. She is the author of two other novels—*Postcards*, winner of the PEN/ Faulkner Award, and *Accordion Crimes*—and two
© Isolde Olhbaum

collections of short stories, *Heart Songs* and *Close Range*. *The Shipping News* and her story "Brokeback Mountain" have been made into movies. She lives in Wyoming and Newfoundland.

© Michael Doucett

Jonathan Raban (1942–) is the author of *Waxwings*, *Soft City*, *Arabia*, *Foreign Land*, *Old Glory*, *For Love and Money*, *Hunting Mister Heartbreak*, *Bad Land*, *Passage to Juneau*, and, most recently, *Surveillance*; he also has edited *The Oxford Book of the Sea*. Raban has received the National Book Critics Circle Award (for *Bad Land*), the Heinemann Award for Literature, the Thomas Cook Travel Book Award, the Pacific Northwest Booksellers Association Book Award, the Washington State Governor's Award, and the PEN West Creative Nonfiction Award, among others. He lives in Seattle.

Frederick Reiken (1966–) has published two novels, *The Lost Legends of New Jersey* and *The Odd Sea*, which was chosen by *Booklist* as one of the twenty Best First Novels of the Year and won the Hackney Literary Award. He lives in Boston and teaches at Emerson College.

Alberto Ríos (1952–) was born in Nogales, Arizona, on the Mexican border, the son of a Guatemalan father and an English mother. His short-story collections include *The Iguana Killer*, which won the Western States Book Award, and, most recently, *The Curtain of Trees*. His memoir is *Capriatada: A Nogales Memoir*. He has won the Walt Whitman Award from the Academy of American Poets and the Pushcart Prize. He is a professor of English at Arizona State University.

Carol Roh-Spaulding's (1962–) fiction and poetry have appeared in numerous journals and anthologies. She is the author of the chapbook "The Brides of Valencia," which won the A. E. Longman Prize for Long Fiction, and is completing *Navelencia*, a thematic collection of stories based on her mixed-race Asian-American background. Her fiction has won several awards, including the Heathcote Award from the National Society of Arts and Letters, a Cohen Award for best story of the year in *Ploughshares*, and a Pushcart Prize.

Richard Russo (1949–) lives in coastal Maine. He has written five novels: *Mohawk*, *The Risk Pool*, *Nobody's Fool*, *Straight Man*, and *Empire Falls*, the Pulitzer Prize-winner that he adapted for a television miniseries. His collection of short stories is entitled *The Whore's Child*.

Mark Salzman (1959–) taught English in Hunan Province, China, and drew upon his experiences there to write the memoir *Iron and Silk*, which was made into a film. He has published another memoir, *Lost in Place*, and three novels: *Lying Awake*, *The Soloist*, and *The*

© Emily Mott

Laughing Sutra. True Notebooks is an account of his work teaching writing to juvenile delinquents. He is the happy father of two girls, Ava and Esme.

© Lawrence Manning/
Corbis

Lynne Sharon Schwartz's (1939–) most recent story collection is *Referred Pain* (2004); her poetry collection *In Solitary* appeared in 2003. Among her other works of fiction are the novels *Disturbances in the Field*, *Leaving Brooklyn*, *Rough Strife*, and *In the Family Way: An Urban Comedy*. Her works of nonfiction include *Ruined by Reading* and *Face to Face: A Reader in the World*. She has received awards from the Guggenheim Foundation, the NEA, and the New York Foundation for the Arts.

Barbara Scot (1942–) is a former high-school teacher who now lives in a houseboat moored near Portland, Oregon. Her first book was *The Violet Shyness of Their Eyes: Notes from Nepal*; her second, *Prairie Reunion*, was a *New York Times* Notable Book for 1995. Most recently she published a memoir, *The Stations of Still Creek*.

Bob Shacochis (1951–) is a writer-in-residence at Florida State University. His first collection of stories, *Easy in the Islands*, won the National Book Award for First Work of Fiction, and his second collection, *The Next New World*, was awarded the Prix de Rome from the American Academy of Arts and Letters. He has published a novel, *Swimming in the Volcano*, and the nonfiction works *Domesticity: A Gastronomic Interpretation of Love* and *The Immaculate Invasion*.

Matthew Sharpe (1962–) is the author of the novels *The Sleeping Father* and *Nothing Is Terrible*, as well as the story collection *Stories from the Tube*. He is the writer-in-residence at Bronx Academy of Letters, a writing-themed public high school. His stories and articles have appeared in *Harper's*, *Zoetrope*, *BOMB*, *American Letters & Commentary*, *Southwest Review*, and *Teachers & Writers* magazine.

Susan Richards Shreve (1939–) has published twelve novels (most recently, *A Student of Living Things* and *Plum & Jaggers*) and twenty-six books for children, and has co-edited five anthologies. An original board member of the PEN/Faulkner Foundation in Washington, D.C., she served as its president from 1985 to 1990. She is a professor at George Mason University.

Robert Stone (1937–) is the author of the memoir *Prime Green* and seven novels, among them *Bay of Souls*, *Damascus Gate*, *Outerbridge Reach*, and *Dog Soldiers*, which won a National Book Award for Fiction. His story collection, *Bear and His Daughter*, was a finalist for the Pulitzer Prize. He wrote the screenplays for the films *WUSA* and *Who'll Stop the Rain*, both based on his books.

William Styron (1925–2006) published his first novel, *Lie Down in Darkness*, in 1951. He is best known for two controversial novels: the Pulitzer Prize-winning *The Confessions of Nat Turner* and *Sophie's Choice*, which was made into an Oscar-winning film. *Darkness Visible* is a memoir; his other works include a play, *In the Clap Shack*, and a collection of his nonfiction pieces, *This Quiet Dust*.

Karen Swenson (1936–) is the author of several books, including *An Attic of Ideals*, *East-West*, *A Sense of Direction*, and *The*

Landlady in Bangkok, which won a National Poetry Series prize. She has been nominated for the Pushcart Prize three times, and her work has appeared in *The New Yorker, The Nation, The Paris Review, American Poetry Review*, and other periodicals.

Paul Theroux's (1941–) novels include *The Family Arsenal, Millroy the Magician, My Secret History, My Other Life*, and *Kowloon Tong*. His travel books include *Riding the Iron Rooster, The Great Railway Bazaar, The Old Patagonian Express*, and *Fresh Air Fiend*. His novels *The Mosquito Coast* and *Dr. Slaughter* have both been made into films. He divides his time between Cape Cod and the Hawaiian Islands, where he is a professional beekeeper.

Joyce Thompson (1948–) is the author of five novels, including *Bones, Merry-Go-Round*, and *Conscience Place*, and the story collection *East Is West of Here*. She has been a writing teacher and an editor. She lives in Oakland, California.

Patrick Tierney (1957–1996) was known for reciting poetry on the streets of Dublin. He published several chapbooks and an autobiography, *The Moon on My Back*.

Kathleen Tyau is the author of two novels that draw upon her Hawaiian-Chinese heritage: *A Little Too Much Is Enough* and *Makai*. A winner of the Pacific Northwest Booksellers Association Book Award, her work has appeared in many journals, including *American Short Fiction, Story, Glimmer Train Stories, Bellingham Review, ZYZZYVA*, and *Boulevard*; and has been anthologized in *Intersecting Circles, Growing Up Local, Fishing for Chickens, Writers' Journal*, and *The Stories That Shape Us*.

Katherine Vaz (1955–) is the author of two novels, *Saudade* and *Mariana*, which was selected as one of the Top 30 International Books of 1998 by the Library of Congress and has been printed in six languages. Her collection *Fado and Other Stories* won the Drue Heinz Literature Prize. She teaches fiction writing at Harvard and has published more than thirty short stories in literary magazines.

© Frank Stewart

A.J. Verdelle's (1960–) novel, *The Good Negress*, was awarded a PEN/Faulkner Finalist Award, an award from the American Academy of Arts and Letters, a Bunting Fellowship at Harvard University, and a Whiting Writers' Award. She also writes creative nonfiction, primarily essays on photography. She has taught writing at Princeton University and at the Fine Arts Work Center in Provincetown, Massachusetts.

Daniel Wallace (1959–) is the author of the novels *The Watermelon King*, *Ray in Reverse*, and *Big Fish*, which was made into a film directed by Tim Burton. His stories have been published widely in magazines and anthologies, including *The Yale Review*, *The Massachu-*

© Paol Alto

setts Review, *Shenandoah*, and *Glimmer Train Stories*, and his illustrated work has appeared in the *L.A. Times* and *Italian Vanity Fair*. He recently finished writing and illustrating a novel called *Oh Great Rosenfeld!* He lives in Chapel Hill, North Carolina. danielwallace.org

© Beth Herzhaft

Mary Yukari Waters (1965–) was born in Kyoto, Japan, and moved to the U.S. at the age of nine. She has published a story collection, *The Laws of Evening*, and her work has been included in *The Best American Short Stories*, *The Best Stories from a Quarter-Century of the Pushcart Prize*, and *Zoetrope: All-Story*. She is the recipient of an O. Henry Award and a Pushcart Prize.

Brad Watson is the author of a story collection, *Last Days of the Dog-Men*, and a novel, *The Heaven of Mercury*, which was a finalist for the National Book Award. His most recent story "Precious Bodies" appeared in the Amazon Shorts series. Now working on a collection of stories and a collection of novellas, he teaches at the University of Wyoming in Laramie.

Gary D. Wilson's (1944–) work has appeared in *Glimmer Train Stories*, *The Baltimore Review*, *The William and Mary Review*, *City Paper of Baltimore*, *Wisconsin Review*, *Kansas Quarterly*, and others. A *City Paper* story was anthologized in *Street Songs I: New Voices in Fiction* from Longstreet Press. Another was included in *Anyone Is Possible*, a fiction anthology from Valentine Press. His novel, *Sing, Ronnie Blue*, is due for publication in 2007. He teaches fiction writing at the University of Chicago Graham School of General Studies.

Mark Winegardner (1961–) published two novels, *Crooked River Burning* and *The Veracruz Blues*, and a story collection, *That's True of Everything*, before he wrote the best-seller *The Godfather Returns*. Another sequel, *The Godfather's Revenge*, appeared in 2006. His stories have been published in *The Best American Short Stories*,

American Short Fiction, and other periodicals. He teaches and directs the creative-writing program at Florida State University in Tallahassee, Florida.

Tobias Wolff (1945–) is the author of several story collections and two memoirs: *This Boy's Life* (which was made into a movie in 1993) and *In Pharoah's Army*, a finalist for the National Book Award. His novel *The Barracks Thief* won the 1985 PEN/Faulkner Award for Fiction.

Monica Wood (1953–) is the author of three novels, *Any Bitter Thing*, *My Only Story*, and *Secret Language*; and a book of linked stories, *Ernie's Ark*. She is also the author of three books for writers: *The Pocket Muse*, *Pocket Muse II: Endless Inspiration*, and *Description*. Her short stories

© Dan Abbot

have been read on Public Radio International, awarded a Pushcart Prize, and published in numerous magazines and anthologies. Born and raised in the mill town of Mexico, Maine, she now lives in Portland, Oregon. monicawood.com

Robert Wrigley (1951–) teaches at the University of Idaho in Moscow. His most recent book of poetry is *Lives of the Animals*. A former Guggenheim and NEA Fellow, his collection *Reign of Snakes* won the Kingsley Tufts Poetry Award.

INTERVIEWER BIOGRAPHIES

David Abrams interviewed Allen Morris Jones.
David Abrams's stories, essays, and reviews have appeared in *Esquire*, *The Readerville Journal*, *The Missouri Review*, *Greensboro Review*, *The North Dakota Review*, *Fish Stories*, and other literary quarterlies. He regularly contributes book reviews to the *San Francisco Chronicle*, *January Magazine*, and *The Long Island Press*. Abrams lives with his wife and three children in Richmond Hill, Georgia, where he is currently at work on a novel about the Iraq War.

Misha Angrist interviewed Dan Chaon.
Misha Angrist's fiction has appeared in *The Michigan Quarterly Review*, the *Best New American Voices* anthology, *Elysian Fields Quarterly*, and elsewhere. He works as a science editor in Durham, North Carolina.

Kevin Bacon interviewed Peter Carey with Bill Davis.

Janet Benton interviewed Valerie Martin.
Janet Benton, who works as a writer and editor, has an MFA in fiction writing from the University of Massachusetts, Amherst. Along with teaching a fiction workshop, she has taught courses in creative writing, editing, grammar, and composition at several universities, and works with authors on work in progress, including *The Mozart Effect* and *Ticket to Ride: Inside the Beatles' 1964 Tour*

That Changed the World. She has received three fiction fellowships and two awards and is currently at work on a historical novel set in nineteenth-century Philadelphia.

Robert Birnbaum interviewed Charles Baxter, Louis Begley, Sandra Cisneros, Colum McCann, Richard Russo, Brad Watson, Mark Winegardner.
Robert Birnbaum is editor-at-large of the literary and cultural website IdentityTheory.com, where he has published hundreds of interviews.

Barbara Brooks interviewed Alice Mattison.
Barbara Brooks's fiction and interviews have appeared in *Glimmer Train Stories, Writer's Digest, The Writer's Chronicle, Inkwell, The Ledge, Jabberwock Review,* and elsewhere. She lives in Cazenovia, New York.

Mike Chasar interviewed Julia Alvarez with Constance Pierce.
Mike Chasar's poems have been published in *Poetry, Alaska Quarterly Review, Antioch Review,* and *The Black Warrior Review.* He is guest editing (with Dee Morris and Heidi Bean) an issue of *The Iowa Journal of Cultural Studies* with the special theme "Poetries," and is writing about American poetry and literary culture at the University of Iowa.

Bill Davis interviewed Peter Carey with Kevin Bacon.

Sherry Ellis interviewed Matthew Sharpe and Mary Yukari Waters.
Sherry Ellis is the editor of *Now Write!*, an anthology of fiction-writing exercises. She is at work on *Illuminating Fiction*, which is an anthology of author interviews, a novel tentatively called *The Goode Books*, and a second anthology of writing exercises. She

teaches writing in Concord, Massachusetts, and provides private coaching to writers.

Stephanie Gordon interviewed Beverly Lowry.
Stephanie Gordon received her PhD in creative writing and American literature from the University of Georgia in 2003. She currently teaches writing at Auburn University. Her work has been published in *The Writer's Chronicle*, *Studies in American Indian Literature*, *Southern Poetry Review*, *Studies in the Humanities*, *GSU Review*, and others.

Katherine Perry Harris interviewed Susan Richards Shreve.
Katherine Perry Harris holds an MFA in fiction from George Mason University. Her work has appeared in *So to Speak*, *The Writer's Chronicle*, and *The Writer*, among other publications. She is currently a communications coordinator for the University of Missouri.

Heather M. Iarusso interviewed Robert Olen Butler.
Heather M. Iarusso currently produces corporate training and marketing videos in Austin, Texas, and still makes time to write stories and screenplays. She earned an MFA in creative writing at McNeese State University, where she studied fiction writing with Robert Olen Butler.

Stewart David Ikeda interviewed Charles Baxter.
Stewart David Ikeda is the author of the novel *What the Scarecrow Said* and vice president of the publishing company IMDiversity, Inc. His work has been published in *Story*, *Ploughshares*, *Pacific Citizen*, *The Mineta Review*, *Glimmer Train Stories*, and the anthologies *Voices of the Xiled*, *Yellow Light*, and *Last Witnesses*. sdikeda.com

Sarah Anne Johnson interviewed Andrea Barrett, Amy Bloom, Elizabeth Cox, Edwidge Danticat, Chitra Banerjee Divakaruni,

Maria Flook, Lynn Freed, Ha Jin, Chang-rae Lee, Elizabeth Mc-Cracken, Sue Miller, Ann Patchett, Jayne Anne Phillips.

Sarah Anne Johnson is the editor of *Conversations with American Women Writers* and *The Art of the Author Interview*. She is program coordinator of the YMCA National Writer's Voice program.

Ellen Kanner interviewed Margot Livesey.

Ellen Kanner's fiction has appeared in the anthology *The Luxury of Tears* and in *Florida Living* magazine. She is contributing editor of *Pages* and *The Edgy Veggie*, and is a syndicated columnist featured in the *Miami Herald* and in five hundred newspapers weekly. She is a contributor to *Bon Appetit*, *Eating Well*, *Vegetarian Times*, and others.

Stephanie Kuehnert interviewed John McNally.

Stephanie Kuehnert's fiction has been published in *Hair Trigger*, *fó magazine*, and on inkstains.org. Her interviews and essays have appeared on *Virginia Quarterly Review*'s website and on freshyard.com. Her zine was featured in *Zine Scene* by Francesca Lia Block and Hillary Carlip. Stephanie received her MFA in creative writing from Columbia College Chicago. She has recently completed her first novel, *All Roads Lead to Rock 'n Roll*, and is working on a second novel.

Jennifer Levasseur interviewed Richard Bausch, Vikram Chandra, Andre Dubus, Stuart Dybek, Siri Hustvedt, with Kevin Rabalais.

Jennifer Levasseur and Kevin Rabalais, editors of *Novel Voices: 17 Award-Winning Novelists on How to Write, Edit, and Get Published*, have appeared in numerous international publications, including *Brick*, *Glimmer Train Stories*, *The Kenyon Review*, *Tin House*, *Missouri Review*, *World Literature Today*, and *Five Points*. Louisiana natives, they live in Melbourne, Australia.

Debra Levy interviewed Amy Hempel with Carol Turner.
Debra Levy's work has appeared in *Columbia*, *Alaska Quarterly Review*, *Glimmer Train Stories*, *Carolina Quarterly*, and elsewhere. She lives in Indiana.

Melissa Lowver interviewed William Styron.
Melissa Lowver is a marketing director for Ascent Media, which provides services to electronic-media content providers. She has written for trade magazines, including *Millimeter* and *Broadcast Engineering*.

Susan McInnis interviewed Ron Carlson, Toi Derricotte, Patricia Hampl, Antonya Nelson, Alberto Ríos, Karen Swenson.
Susan McInnis writes and teaches writing for the Center for Distance Education in Fairbanks, Alaska.

John McNally interviewed Andre Dubus III.
John McNally is the author of two novels, *America's Report Card* and *The Book of Ralph*; and a story collection, *Troublemakers*. He also has edited four fiction anthologies. A finalist for the National Magazine Award for Fiction, he teaches at Wake Forest University in Winston-Salem, North Carolina.

Nancy Middleton interviewed Lynne Sharon Schwartz and A.J. Verdelle.
Nancy Middleton's short stories, author interviews, and books reviews have appeared in *The South Carolina Review*, *Glimmer Train Stories*, *Belles Lettres*, and other literary magazines. A native of upstate New York, she now lives in Pennsylvania and is currently at work on her first novel.

Jim Nashold interviewed Kent Haruf.

Jim Nashold is co-author of the biography *The Death of Dylan Thomas*. He lives with his wife in Durham, North Carolina.

Constance Pierce interviewed Julia Alvarez with Mike Chasar. Constance Pierce recently retired from the English department at Miami University and now lives in St. Augustine, Florida. Her work includes a novel, *Hope Mills*, and a story collection, *When Things Get Back to Normal*.

William Pierce interviewed Askold Melnyczuk.
William Pierce is senior editor of *AGNI*. He is a past finalist for a *Glimmer Train* short-story award, and his fiction has appeared in *American Literary Review*, *The Cream City Review*, *The Dos Passos Review*, and elsewhere. His essay "Fabulously Real," first published in *AGNI* 59, received special mention in *Pushcart Prize XXX* (2006).

Kevin Rabalais interviewed Richard Bausch, Vikram Chandra, Andre Dubus, Stuart Dybek, Siri Hustvedt, with Jennifer Levasseur; and David Malouf.
Kevin Rabalais and Jennifer Levasseur, editors of *Novel Voices: 17 Award-Winning Novelists on How to Write, Edit, and Get Published*, have appeared in numerous international publications, including *Brick, Glimmer Train Stories, The Kenyon Review, Tin House, Missouri Review, World Literature Today*, and *Five Points*. Louisiana natives, they live in Melbourne, Australia.

Cheryl Reid interviewed Pam Durban.
Cheryl Reid completed her MFA in creative writing at Georgia State University in 2004. She is raising her children, Reid and Grant, and working to complete a novel, *My Banishment*, in Atlanta.

Jim Schumock interviewed Robert Olen Butler, Stephen Dixon, Henry Louis Gates, Jim Grimsley, Thom Jones, Carolyn Kizer, Philip Levine, Thomas McGuane, Lorrie Moore, Tim O'Brien, William Styron, Paul Theroux, Robert Stone, William J. Kennedy, Tobias Wolff, Robert Wrigley.

Jim Schumock is the main host of "Between the Covers," a weekly literary radio program on KBOO in Portland, Oregon. His book of interviews is *Story Story Story: Conversations with American Authors*. He is currently working on a novella, a memoir, and a second collection of interviews.

Andrew Scott interviewed Patricia Henley.

Andrew Scott lives in Indianapolis. His latest project is *Welcome to the Moon*, a screenplay based upon one of his short stories. He teaches at Ball State University.

Barbara Lucy Stevens interviewed Carolyn Chute.

Barbara Lucy Stevens is a writer and artist. She lives in Providence, Rhode Island, with her husband and four children.

Linda B. Swanson-Davies interviewed Margaret Atwood, Charles Baxter, Kevin Canty, George Makana Clark, Stephen Dixon, Siobhan Dowd, Nomi Eve, Thomas E. Kennedy, Jamaica Kincaid, Maina wa Kinyatti, David Long, Mary McGarry Morris, Thisbe Nissen, Sigrid Nunez, Roy Parvin, Carol Roh-Spaulding, Mark Salzman, Barbara J. Scot, Bob Shacochis, Joyce Thompson, Patrick Tierney, Kathleen Tyau, Daniel Wallace.

Linda B. Swanson-Davies is co-editor, with Susan Burmeister-Brown, of *Glimmer Train Stories* and *Writers Ask*.

Charlotte Templin interviewed Mary Gordon.

Charlotte Templin is Professor Emeritus of English at the University of Indianapolis. She is the author of *Feminism and the Politics of Literary Reputation* and editor of *Conversations with Erica Jong*. Her articles and interviews with contemporary women writers have appeared in *American Studies*, *The Missouri Review*, *The Boston Review*, and other publications.

Rob Trucks interviewed Russell Banks and Chris Offutt.
Rob Trucks is the author of five books, including *Cup of Coffee: The Very Short Careers of Eighteen Major League Pitchers* and *The Pleasure of Influence: Conversations with American Male Fiction Writers*, as well as countless essays, reviews, and features. His work has been published in *Spin*, *BookForum*, *No Depression*, *Philadelphia Weekly*, *Glimmer Train Stories*, *Black Warrior Review*, *New Orleans Review*, *The Distillery*, and *River City*. He lives in Long Island City, New York.

Carol Turner interviewed Amy Hempel with Debra Levy.
Carol Turner has a BA in English from Sonoma State University and an MFA in creative writing and literature from Bennington College. Her work has appeared in *Byline*, *Cottonwood Review*, *First Intensity*, *Flyway*, *Love's Shadow: Writings by Women* (anthology), *Many Mountains Moving*, *Owen Wister*, *The Portland Review*, *Primavera*, *Rag Mag*, *Strictly Fiction*, *Sulphur River Literary Review*, *Glimmer Train Stories*, and others. She also is the author of *Economics for the Impatient*.

Michael Upchurch interviewed Ernest Gaines, Doris Lessing, Abdelrahman Munif, Annie Proulx, Jonathan Raban, Paul Theroux. Novelist Michael Upchurch is the author of *Passive Intruder* and *The Flame Forest*, and his short fiction has appeared in *Christopher Street*, *Carolina Quarterly*, and *Glimmer Train Stories*. His reviews and essays have appeared in *The New York Times Book Review*, *American Scholar*, *The Washington Post*, *Chicago Tribune*, and other publications. Since 1998, he has been the book critic for *The Seattle Times*.

Eric Wasserman interviewed Frederick Reiken.
Eric Wasserman is the author of a collection of short stories, *The Temporary Life*. He is writing the screenplay adaptation for his book and is completing a novel set during the height of McCarthyism. He lives in Los Angeles, where he teaches at Santa Monica College, West L.A. College, and Compton College.
ericwasserman.com

Leslie A. Wootten interviewed Melissa Pritchard.
Leslie A. Wootten lives and writes on a farm in Casa Grande, Arizona. Her author interviews have appeared in *Bloomsbury Review*, *Glimmer Train Stories*, *Tin House*, and *World Literature Today*.

COPYRIGHT NOTICES

INDEX